SUSS

Desmond Seward was educated at Ampleforth and
Cambridge, and is the author of over twenty books
of history, biography and travel. (His latest is an
account of the impact of the Wars of the Roses on
five men and women.) He has lived in Sussex for
thirty years and takes a keen interest in its history,
architecture and wildlife.

Pimlico County History Guides
(General editor: Christopher Hibbert)

Already published:

Dorset by Richard Ollard
Suffolk by Miles Jebb

Forthcoming:

Bedfordshire by Simon Houfe
Norfolk by Tom Pocock
Somerset by Shirley Toulson

SUSSEX

DESMOND SEWARD
with a Foreword by Christopher Hibbert

A PIMLICO COUNTY HISTORY GUIDE

PIMLICO

An imprint of Random House
20 Vauxhall Bridge Road, London SW1V 2SA

Random House Australia (Pty) Ltd
20 Alfred Street, Milsons Point, Sydney
New South Wales 2061, Australia

Random House New Zealand Ltd
18 Poland Road, Glenfield
Auckland 10, New Zealand

Random House South Africa (Pty) Ltd
PO Box 337, Bergvlei, South Africa

Random House UK Ltd Reg. No. 954009

First published by Pimlico 1995

1 3 5 7 9 10 8 6 4 2

Papers used by Random House UK Limited are natural,
recyclable products made from wood grown in sustainable
forests. The manufacturing processes conform to the
environmental regulations of the country of origin

Typeset by Deltatype Ltd, Ellesmere Port, Cheshire
Printed and bound in Great Britain by
Mackays of Chatham plc, Chatham, Kent

ISBN 0-7126-5133-0

For Maxine Langford-Holt

Contents

Acknowledgements

I would like to thank Viscount Hampden for his help with the pages on Glynde Place, and Lord Egremont for his help with those on Petworth House. I owe a special debt to Mr Bob Copper, whose books and songs have been a lasting inspiration.

Among the very many friends who have given me information, advice or encouragement, or all three, I am particularly grateful to: Mr Con Ainsworth, the Revd. Gerald Coates, Peter Drummond-Murray of Mastrick (who read the proofs), the Revd. Mark Elvins, Mr and Mrs James Heagerty, Mr and Mrs Robin Hooper, Mr Michael Kadwell, Dr and Mrs Martin Knott, Mr Andrew Low, Susan, Viscountess Mountgarret, Mr Rick Novis, the Hon. Nigel and Mrs Parker, and Mr David Plumtree.

I must thank the staffs of the County Record Offices at Chichester and Lewes, and of the Libraries at Brighton and Hastings for unfailingly kind and courteous assistance.

I have benefited enormously from the constructive criticisms and many helpful suggestions of my almost unbelievably patient editor Mr Euan Cameron.

Foreword

For thirty years Desmond Seward has been exploring Sussex, walking across the Downs and into little known corners of the Weald, looking round the country's parish churches, visiting its great country houses; and in this enthralling book he communicates to us his affection for the area in which, born in France, he has chosen to live. His is not an affection as uncritical as that of so many of those other writers who have made Sussex their home. He quotes Rudyard Kipling who lived at Bateman's, a house of honey-coloured stone in Burwash which he bought in 1902 and which his widow bequeathed to the National Trust:

> I'm just in love with all these three,
> The Weald and the Marsh and the Down countrie;
> Nor I don't know which I love the most,
> The Weald or the Marsh or the white chalk coast.

Hilaire Belloc, who lived at King's Land, Shipley from 1906 until his death in 1953, loved Sussex in the same way; so did Henry James who, on returning to Lamb House, Rye after a visit to Florida, said how much he had missed his Sussex home and how, in the heart of the orange groves of his native America, he had 'yearned for the shade of the old Lamb House mulberry tree'; and so, too, did Leonard Woolf who, in 1912 settled with his wife, Virginia, at Asham in a green hollow beneath Itford Hill. 'This was the first time I had seen the South Downs as it were from the inside and felt the beauty of the gentle white curves of the fields beneath the great green curves of the hollows,' he wrote after he and Virginia had moved to Monks House, Rodmell where his wife was to drown herself in the river nearby. 'I have lived close to them ever since and have learnt that, in all seasons and circumstances, their physical loveliness and serenity can make one's happiness exquisite and assuage one's misery.'

Desmond Seward's happiness in Sussex is sometimes overcast by the encroachments of the modern world. He has his passions and his preferences and is eager to share them; but he is also refreshingly ready to condemn what he dislikes both in Sussex buildings and in Sussex people. The eleventh-century Saxon church at Worth, for example, is unequivocally 'the most beautiful thing in Sussex . . . one of the most glorious buildings in England'. West Firle is 'the least spoiled village in Sussex', its church so he tells us in a characteristic aside, containing 'a helpful Table of Affinity which explains that it is forbidden to marry one's grandfather'. He differs from received opinion and most architectural historians in finding the house which James Wyatt rebuilt for the Duke of Richmond at Goodwood 'very attractive, especially the side with the pillared portico, flanked by towers with green copper domes'. He takes issue with Ian Nairn over Hastings, finding the Old Town in late autumn 'one of the pleasantest places on the South Coast'. Yet Rye is not what it was: 'it can scarcely be described as "a little bit of the old world living pleasantly on, in ignorance of the new" as it was in Coventry Patmore's time'. 'If it has not been ruined architecturally, it appears to be visited by more tourists than any other town in Sussex except seaside resorts.' Desmond Seward has harsh things to say also of Brighton. To be sure, at its best Brighton can still be exhilarating, 'like a clean Naples in miniature'. 'It remains a town of stucco and bow windows; from the Palace Pier the cream coloured houses still run away into the west as in a pale Victorian watercolour.' Where there is redevelopment it is usually sympathetic nowadays, while almost every Regency building is safe from demolition. But much has been lost forever; high-rise flats and tall office blocks have replaced buildings that the Prince Regent and Mrs Fitzherbert knew; the old Bedford Hotel, where Dickens used to stay, has gone the way of the bathing machines and the fishermen; and Brighton has become a magnet it seems for down-and-outs, drug addicts and young dossers, many from the North since it is 'marginally better, perhaps, to be jobless in Brighton than in Runcorn or Sheffield'.

As for Virginia and Leonard Woolf and the Bloomsburyites who used to visit them at Rodmell – where 'old Sussex has been overlaid by the new' – Desmond Seward knows he would not have liked this 'mutual admiration society of bloodless men and anaemic women dabbling in art and literature, ineffably self-satisfied'.

In taking us for walks across the Downs and the Weald, he finds no cause for this acerbity. He delights in the colours and shapes of the Downs, the joyful feel of the summer air, the reedy ponds and fern-covered slopes of the Weald, the woods and forests which have made Sussex the second most heavily wooded county in England. He tells us of the trees we may expect to find, the butterflies and flowers and birds whose variety will surely persuade many of his readers – familiar as they may be with kestrels and woodpeckers, with hornbeam and Solomon's seal – to buy other books to guide them to the recognition of the holm-oaks and purple emperors, honey buzzards and birds' nest orchids, helleborine and Dartford warblers, duke of Burgundy fritillaries and viper's bugloss.

In Sussex's most lonely places Desmond Seward is uncomfortably aware of being watched by unseen eyes. For it is a county of ghosts and legends, of spirits rising from the neolithic long barrows, of the wraiths of hairy men whom H. V. Morton imagined grasping stone axes and driving sheep before them over the wide chalkland. Here lived the dragon like a giant lizard which was slain by St Leonard in the forest named after him; and the giant who munched a child for supper every night at Oxenbridge until the children of Sussex made him drunk with strong beer and then laid a huge wooden saw across his throat, see-sawing until they had cut his head off; and the witches who snatched the bones of the malefactor from the iron cage of the gibbet on Gibbet's Marsh to add to their cauldron's brew.

The Devil [Woden] is ubiquitous: he has given his name to Devil's Dyke and Devil's Grave, Devil's Ditch and Devil's Bog. At Chanctonbury Ring, so countless generations believed, if you ran round the trees seven times on a misty night the Devil would appear from between them and offer you a bowl of broth.

Numerous oddities, eccentrics and Sussex characters make brief appearances, like Blake and the Devil, in this book. There are nineteenth-century shepherds in blue smocks, carrying green umbrellas and gripping fossilised sea-urchins to ward off lightning, emerging from the holes in the ground, lined with dried fern and covered outside with furze bushes, which are their shelters; there are eighteenth-century wreckers looting ships they have caused to run aground on the coast; there is a whole chapterful of rogues engaged in smuggling, 'for centuries the country's main industry after agriculture', supplying luxuries at cheap prices for respectable families, with:

> Five and twenty ponies;
> Trotting through the dark —
> Brandy for the Parson,
> 'Baccy for the Clerk
> Laces for a lady, letters for a spy . . .

At Arundel the fifteenth Duke of Norfolk, shabby and unkempt, is accosted by a lady arriving at the railway station who gives him a penny for carrying her case to a cab, the first penny he has ever earned, so he politely informs her; and here is the learned Jacobean jurist, John Selden of Salvington, playing on his fiddle and making love to the Countess of Kent with the Earl's permission, as well as to one of 'my lady's weomen, a lusty, bouncing woman', in John Aubrey's words, 'who robbed him on his deathbed'. At Cowdray, Lord Montagu, a devout Papist, shoots his chaplain for presuming to begin the Sunday Mass without him and spends the rest of his life hiding in a priest's hole, visited occasionally by his wife who dons a white dress for the purpose, hoping to be mistaken for a ghost. At the Mint House, Pevensey, Andrew Borde, traveller and physician, loves Sussex but, like so many others, deplores its muddy, rutted roads which oblige one 'ancient Lady *and a Lady of very good Quality, I assure you*', to drive to church in a coach drawn by six oxen, 'the Way being so stiff and deep, that no horse could go on it'. At Petworth, the Duke of Somerset is so proud that he insists his children always stand in his presence, and on falling asleep one day and finding when he awakes that one of his daughters has sat down, he disinherits her on the spot. At Uppark, Sir Harry Fetherstonhaugh gets the seventeen-year-old blacksmith's daughter who becomes Lady Hamilton to dance naked on his dining-room table for the pleasure of his guests by one of whom she has a child of whose existence Nelson is never to learn. And at Aldworth House, Blackdown, drinking a bottle of port with his dinner and taking five baths a day, so pleased is he with the house's hot running water, Lord Tennyson looks across the Sussex countryside, so well described in Desmond Seward's entertaining and enlightening book:

> Green Sussex fading into blue
> With one grey glimpse of sea.

CHRISTOPHER HIBBERT

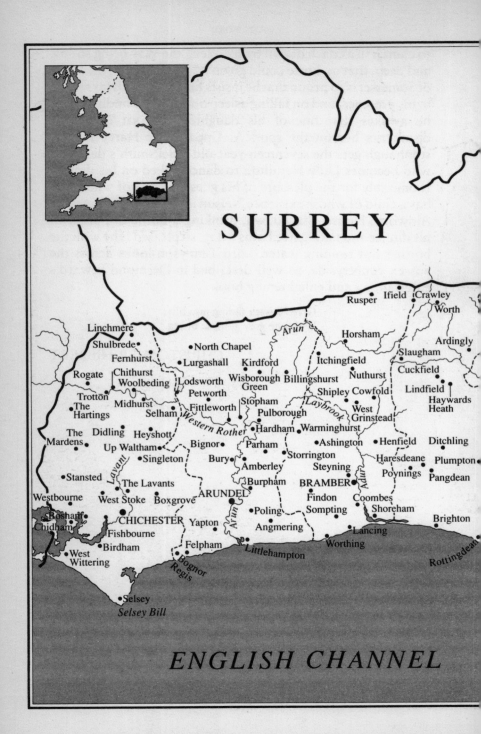

SURREY

Rusper • Ifield • Crawley
• Worth

Linchmere •
Shulbrede •
Fernhurst •
Rogate •
Chithurst
Woolbeding •
Trotton •
The •
Hartings
Midhurst •
Selham •

North Chapel •
Lurgashall •
Lodsworth •
Petworth •
Fittleworth •

Kirdford •
Wisborough
Green •
Stopham •
Pulborough

Arun

Horsham •

Itchingfield •
Billingshurst •
Shipley • Cowfold •
Laybrook
West
Grinstead •

Ardingly
• Slaugham
Nuthurst • Cuckfield
• Lindfield
Haywards
Heath

Western Rother

The • Didling
Mardens •
Up Waltham •
Singleton •

Heyshott •
Bignor •
Bury •

Hardham •
Parham •
Amberley •

Warminghurst •
Ashington •
Storrington •
Steyning •

Henfield • Ditchling
Haresdeane •
Poynings • Plumpton •
Pangdean

Adur

Stansted •
The Lavants •
West Stoke • Boxgrove •

ARUNDEL

Burpham •

BRAMBER •
Findon •
Sompting •
Coombes •
Shoreham •

Westbourne •
Bosham •
Chidham •

CHICHESTER •
Fishbourne •
Birdham •

Yapton •
Poling •
Angmering •

Arun

Littlehampton

Worthing • Lancing •

Brighton •

West
Wittering •

Felpham •

Bognor
Regis •

Rottingdean

• Selsey
Selsey Bill

ENGLISH CHANNEL

SUSSEX

KENT

Medway

Tees

East Grinstead

Hartfield Withyam Frant

Crowborough Wadhurst

Mayfield Ticehurst

Rother Bodiam

Northiam

Burwash Etchingham

Ous Uckfield Robertsbridge Ewhurst Iden

Uckfield Heathfield Rye

Framfield Brightling Mountfield

Warbleton Brede

Penhurst Battle Brede Winchelsea

Chiddingly Ashburnham

Ringmer Crowhurst

Glynde Herstmonceux

LEWES Firle Cuckmere Bexhill HASTINGS

Kingston Berwick

Rodmell

Alfriston PEVENSEY

Newhaven Jevington

Seaford West Dean

Friston Eastbourne

Beachy Head

- - - - - Rape boundaries

0 ——————————————— 10 miles

0 ——————————————— 16 kilometres

Introduction:
Does Sussex Still Exist?

And, in her secret heart,
The heathen kingdom Wilfrid found
Dreams, as she dwells, apart

Rudyard Kipling

'You be glad you are Sussex born', wrote Kipling, in *Rewards and Fairies*. I am neither Sussex born nor Sussex bred, but I have walked the Downs and explored the Weald for thirty years. No landscape is more soothing, more healing, especially in spring or early autumn; sometimes I feel that without it I would not be alive. Many people thank Sussex for their well-being. Some produce books about her, books which – in my opinion at least – are frequently too sentimental. But there is no denying the mysterious pull of Downs and Weald. Had I been asked if there was room for another book on the county (which of course there always is) I could only have replied that nothing would stop me from writing one.

Yet the question has to be asked, 'Does Sussex still exist?' Driving past that monstrous airport at Gatwick, through the relentless sprawl of Haywards Heath, into the unending outskirts of Brighton, along a coastline often ruined by development, it may well seem that the only possible answer is 'No.'

A century ago a Sussex ornithologist, William Borrer, complained of 'the whistle of the steam engine taking the place of that of the Wildfowl and the Wader'. 'The Downs too, once the peaceful haunt of the Bustard and the Lapwing, or disturbed only by the shepherd and his flock, are now to a great extent broken up by cultivation and harassed by the rattle of the steam plough.' As for the Weald, 'Where are the splendid stretches of heather, the sedgy bottoms? And where is the Black Game?'

Even so, despite all Borrer's concern, in Edwardian times a youthful Hilaire Belloc was still able to think that Sussex was the most beautiful landscape in the whole world:

> The great hills of the South Country
> They stand along the sea;
> And it's there walking in the high woods
> That I could wish to be

But by 1936, appalled by the new suburbs and the 'blind inhuman clatter' of motor cars, he was lamenting that 'the modern invasion will be the end of the Sussex we knew'.

Yet Belloc allowed himself a faint hope – 'the power which the county has shown itself possessed of for so many centuries to digest and absorb new comers will save it in patches'. And this is what has happened. Towns and villages have expanded, often horribly, sometimes irredeemably, but in most the centre remains, together with an ancient church and manor house. There are also those rare downland churches of vanished hamlets, which Gilbert White compared to dovecotes. Sometimes, going up on to the Downs is to leave late twentieth century suburbia for the rural England of the 1800s or indeed of much earlier. Admittedly there are far fewer sheep, to the detriment of the turf, while shepherds have vanished; since the Second World War large areas of downland have gone under the plough. But even if there may never be again so many sheep, the decline of intensive farming will see an end to ploughing; and as soon as the Downs are left fallow, despite the encroaching scrub such vulnerable plants as wild orchids or viper's bugloss return with heartening persistence, amid carpets of cowslip.

In Belloc's words:

The isolation of these summits is the more remarkable from the pressure of population which is growing so rapidly to the south of them, and which is beginning to engulf the Weald to their north. But no change has so far affected the character of these lonely stretches of grass. [He adds] Those who know the Downs best and have lived among them all their lives know how, in a whole day's walk, one may never meet a man's face.

It is still true, provided one chooses one's path with care.

As for the Weald, its centuries old pattern of farms, fields and copses survive despite encroachment, a pattern which had begun to take shape in the Bronze Age. In its own way it is no less mysterious than the Downs. Even nowadays it can only be known by long explorations on foot.

Twenty-eight miles from north to south, seventy-six miles wide, the boundaries of Sussex remain those of the diocese of Chichester, and therefore of the ancient kingdom of the South Saxons. Although divided into East and West Sussex, with two county towns (Lewes and Chichester), it keeps its single identity; Sussex is still Sussex. A framework is needed to explore it properly. The old division of the country into 'rapes' running from north to south is as good as any. Introduced by William the Conqueror, they were based strategically on the most obvious communication routes, so that roads still go along them.

Driving northward, in every rape save Hastings one is aware of geological symmetry. First the flat coastal plain; then chalk downland; then a narrow strip of greensand on the other side; and finally the Weald – clay, or clay mixed with sandstone. Sometimes the Weald is flat or marshland, sometimes it is deep valleys; in wooded areas the clay is covered by oak, the mixed clay and sandstone by silver birch. The coastal strip is the most densely populated, the downland the least, with a few isolated farms. The hamlets of flint and white stone at the foot of the Downs are very different from the wealden villages of timber-framed brick. The sheer variety of Sussex is extraordinary, a country which changes from east to west as well as from north to south, in both landscape and architecture.

There are other contrasts. On the one hand, roads choked by traffic (with blaring radios) and gentrified hamlets whose barns have been turned into expensive weekend 'cottages'. On the other, a wild and lonely land with an ancient and even sinister history. Behind the surburbia and the motorways the old, secret Sussex can still be found by those who try hard enough to find her, still beautiful and mysterious.

I

The South Saxons

On a Thursday morning, between 8.30 and 9.30 a.m., an astonished Sussex man (one source says he was a local thane, another a churl) watched a fleet of over 500 vessels land an army of 7,000 men and 2,500 horses. William of Normandy had come to claim the English crown.

It was 28 September 1066. The ships were beached in a line, their masts lowered. Scouting parties, each numbering a few dozen, saddled up and rode inland, burning and slaying. Others occupied Pevensey, firing houses and killing burgesses; they set up a pre-fabricated castle inside the old Roman fort – a simple wooden tower on a mound. Next day the Normans marched along the coast to Hastings, where they erected two more castles. Hoping to provoke King Harold, they began a campaign of systematic terror in East Sussex, destroying villages, driving off livestock. Meanwhile, the watcher galloped north to York to warn King Harold. The king, who had just defeated Harold Hardrada of Norway (the most famous warrior of the day, feared from the Baltic to the Black Sea) at once rode south with his housecarles at breakneck speed.

If the English had waited, gathering their full strength, luring the invaders inland and weakening them by ambushes, they would almost certainly have defeated the Normans. Even as it was, a veteran commander like Harold, with personal experience of their tactics – having fought in Normandy at their duke's side – had a very good chance of winning an immediate confrontation.

On the evening of Friday, 13 October, King Harold arrived at the 'hoar apple tree' on Caldebec Hill, seven miles from

Hastings, the rendez-vous where the shire levies were to meet. He had roughly the same number of men as William and hoped to take him by surprise the following morning. However, alerted by scouts, Duke William and his army rode out at dawn the next day to confront the English. Harold blocked the road to London. He had deployed his men on Senlac Hill, a low but steep ridge 135 metres deep and 730 metres long, its front guarded by boggy ground difficult for cavalry and its flanks by woods. Standing sideways with their long-handled axes, the Saxons formed a 'shield-wall'. The king commanded from a spot a little to the left of its centre, flying his banners of the Fighting Man and the Dragon of Wessex. Clearly he meant to wait for the Norman charge, break it and then counter-attack downhill.

William also commanded from the centre, where he had placed his Normans. His left consisted of Bretons, his right mainly of French mercenaries. His key troops were his mailed cavalry, armed with swords or javelins, while his infantry included a large proportion of archers. His strategy was simple enough: to break the shield-wall and drive the English off the ridge.

At 9 a.m. the Norman bowmen began shooting and then the knights charged. They were beaten off, the English, 'as if rooted in the soil', shouting 'Out! Out!' A second charge failed, making a Norman defeat more than likely. But the duke rallied his troops for a third attack, this time using his archers more effectively before the knights charged. A Norman broke through the shield-wall and hewed down King Harold. Then the English began to give ground and broke. The Normans camped on the battlefield. No one, not even Duke William, can have realised that they had conquered all England.

So many English fell that for centuries locals claimed the soil always turned red with blood after a heavy rainfall. Every fighting man in Sussex must have been there; the shire's thanes were decimated, survivors forfeiting their lands. The exact spot where Harold died is marked by the High Altar of Battle Abbey, built by King William.

*

Just over a century ago, in 1887, the *Encyclopaedia Britannica* claimed that Sussex 'is still one of the most thoroughly Saxon counties in England, and its inhabitants, speech, place-names, customs, &c., are almost entirely Saxon'. Yet there were men in Sussex long before the South Saxons. The first kept close to the coast and have left little trace. (In 1994 a fragment of bone came to light at Boxgrove from the skeleton of a man who lived half-a-million years ago, the oldest known in Europe.) About 6000BC 'hunter gatherers' began to penetrate inland; some of their hunting camps have been found in the Weald. The discovery and excavation of 'raised beaches' (notably at Boxgrove) have provided evidence of flint working in Palaeolithic times. As the Ice Age came to an end, oak, ash and thorn arrived. So did a small, dark haired people of Mediterranean origin, at some time before 3000BC. Semi-nomadic, they grew crops and kept livestock. They also practised cannibalism, perhaps ritual; the gnawed bones of children have been found at Whitehawk near Brighton. Settling on the Downs, they built tribal meeting places like the Trundle near Goodwood, and buried their chieftains in long barrows up to 200 feet in length. Their most prized commodity was the flint from which they made their tools and weapons. They mined the chalk for it, sinking shafts fifty feet deep and using antlers for picks. At Cissbury the skeleton of a girl flint-maker has been found, entombed when a galley fell on her.

About 2000BC men with bronze swords, spears and axes came across the Channel, named 'Beaker Folk' by Victorian archaeologists from their big drinking cups. They, too, settled on the Downs, supplied with bronze by itinerant smiths, living in round houses in isolated farms or hamlets, and burying their chiefs in barrows shaped like up-turned bowls. They dug sunken lanes or 'cross-dykes' across the Downs – concealed droveways along which they could drive their flocks out of sight of marauders. They also began to clear forest and scrub at the edge of the Weald by burning and then by pasturing goats.

*

Iron Age peoples started to arrive about 700BC, the first wave speaking a language which was the ancestor of Irish, the second a tongue akin to Welsh. Sharper axes enabled them to clear more forest and they smelted iron in the Weald, though the downland and the coastal plain were the most densely populated areas; the crest of the Downs was reserved for pasture, the lower slopes for farms. There was insufficient land to go round. Fierce inter-tribal warfare broke out in the third centuryBC and huge hill forts were built – Cissbury covered sixty acres.

A new people invaded West Sussex towards the middle of the first centuryBC, the Belgae from Belgium. They were ruled by nobles and druids, common folk being treated almost as slaves. They believed in transmigration of souls and knew much about astronomy. They also practised human sacrifice, immolating many men at a time in huge basket-work figures. John Masefield evokes them:

> Once the tribe did thus on the downs, on these downs
>   burning
> Men in the frame
> Crying to the gods of the downs till their brains were turning
> And the gods came

A sick noble would ask the druids to sacrifice a slave to ensure his recovery. Yet they were surprisingly sophisticated in other ways, importing Roman luxuries. The remains of amphorae of c.100BC for Falernian wine, discovered at a site near Pulborough, indicate that their chieftains knew all about the finest vintages of ancient Italy.

After the Romans had conquered Britain in 42AD they built a city at Chichester which they called Noviomagus, together with a palace at Fishbourne nearby for their client king Cogidubnus. (It was found in 1960, when a water-main was being dug.) After his death Sussex was ruled by a Roman official from the basilica at Chichester.

The Romans settled mainly in West Sussex, in the area favoured by their Iron Age predecessors, where over twenty villas have been discovered. There were few villas in East

8

Sussex but many iron foundries, while in the third century a large fort was built at Anderida (now Pevensey) as protection against Saxon raiders from the sea. There were two main roads through the great forest called '*Coit Andred*' by the British: Stane Street, running direct from Londinium to Noviomagus, and a second to Venta Belgarum (Winchester). There were lesser roads from the north to the mouth of the Adur and to Lewes through Ashdown Forest, together with a network of metalled tracks – one ran eastward from Lewes to join up with others in the east. A coastal road linked Noviomagus and Anderida.

After a breakdown of Roman rule in the fourth century, Noviomagus lost its trade and ceased to be a true town. The economic disasters which ruined it, followed by the final departure of Roman troops early in the next century caused famine and social collapse. Petty tyrants re-occupied the hill forts.

The *Anglo-Saxon Chronicle* tells a dramatic tale of conquest, which was accepted until very recently. In 477AD three Saxon warships landed at a place called Cymenesora, later thought to be Selsey Bill, bringing a king named Aelle and his three sons – Cynmen, Cyssa and Wlenca. Eight years later they fought the 'Welsh' near the bank of the 'Mearcredsburna' and in 491 they stormed Anderida, massacring every Briton whom they found inside. In the past, historians have pictured Aelle and his warband fighting their way steadily eastward towards Anderida. Yet it is much more likely that Aelle landed in the 450s, not at Selsey Bill, but between the Ouse and the Cuckmere, and that one of these rivers was the 'Mearcredsburna'. However, he undoubtedly established a 'Kingdom of the South Saxons'. He and his successors did not move into the deserted Noviomagus, living in the royal halls at Kingsham just outside the walls or at Kingham-by-Sea – both of which still await discovery.

Similarly, while the South Saxon nobles took over the great estates in the west, whose nuclei could be traced back through Roman times to the Bronze Age, they did not re-occupy the villas. The heavy Saxon ploughs could handle thick clay better than those of the Romano-British and began to clear the Weald. Nevertheless, during the sixth century the population of Sussex was probably no more than 40,000 while there were severe famines. 'It is said that frequently forty or fifty emaciated and starving people would go to a precipice, or to the sea-shore, where they would join hands and leap in, to die from the fall or drown' Bede tells us. This was ritual sacrifice, to propitiate Woden.

Cut off from the rest of England by forest, marsh and sea, this was the most backward of the Anglo-Saxon kingdoms, the last to stay pagan. The 'Apostle of Sussex' was St Wilfrid, Archbishop of York, whose ship ran aground off the coast while he was on his way home from France. Wreckers approached, a pagan priest screaming curses from a cliff. After a lucky sling-shot killed the priest, a pitched battle broke out; five of Wilfred's men were slain before the tide lifted the boat off the shoal. He returned in 680 and spent five years converting the natives, building a monastery at Selsey.

Although there was a King of the South Saxons as late as 774 and then dukes, Sussex was absorbed by Wessex in 823. Trade and town life revived, thatched huts appearing behind the crumbling walls of Chicester and inside the fort at Pevensey. A *witan*, or meeting of England's great men, was held at Lyminster (where a Saxon royal hall remains to be discovered). During his long struggle against the Danes, King Alfred – who had estates at West Dean and Steyning – established five fortified '*burhs*'; Chichester, Lewes, Hastings, Pevensey and Burpham. During the tenth century St Dunstan built wooden churches to replace those destroyed by the Vikings, but they went up in flames again when the Danes returned at the end of the century. They were rebuilt once more, in stone this time, during the comparatively peaceful reigns of Canute and Edward the Confessor. (A mound at Upper Barham on the edge of Angmering, excavated during the 1960s, was found to contain three Saxon churches built of stone.)

The Norman Conquest transformed 'Sudsexe'. King

William divided it into six 'rapes' – Chichester, Arundel, Bramber, Lewes, Pevensey and Hastings – each commanding a harbour or a river from a carefully sited castle. Nobody knows the origin of the term 'rape'. One guess is that it derives from an Icelandic measure, the *'hrapa'* but I myself think it comes from the Norman-French word *'rapiner'*, to plunder – there is some evidence that Sussex was systematically laid waste after the victory at Hastings, when the invaders were attempting to establish as broad a bridgehead as feasible. I also believe that the rape system, adopted in no other part of England, was inspired by military considerations. Sussex was the country nearest Normandy from where reinforcements could be rushed over the Channel in the event of a Saxon revolt. It was essential to make it a permanent bridgehead, held as strongly as possible. In every rape lesser castles and signal-towers, strategically sited, supported the main castle in holding down the native population.

Meanwhile cross-Channel traffic and trade increased enormously. The ports grew much bigger and the waterways were developed; ships went up the Adur under full sail as far as Bramber, while Steyning, Arundel and Lewes became thriving inland harbours. Norman and French settlers flocked in and soon the population, about 70,000 in 1066, began to rise sharply. French speaking lords replaced Saxons thanes at the manors, while French speaking merchants established themselves in the little towns. Romanesque churches, some of considerable magnificence, were built throughout the county. The taming of the Weald began in earnest, being completed by 1300, and the landscape of Sussex altered in appearance at a rate much faster than at any time until the twentieth century.

Then, in about 1300, a change in climate, with wetter, colder summers, caused repeated crop failure and famine, so that there was a marked decline in population and farmland had to be abandoned. The situation grew much worse when the Black Death struck in 1349, killing half the work-force. This was the end of the wealden clearances. Some villages disappeared altogether while others shrank to tiny hamlets.

Late medieval Sussex lived in terror of French raids. Large

or small, retaliatory or unprovoked, it is likely that far more of these took place than we realise. Privateer crews either landed on the sea-shore – sacking several coastal towns more than once – or else sailed up the rivers to attack inland villages, killing, raping, plundering and burning. The castles of Bodiam, Herstmonceux and Amberley, the barbican at Lewes, the gatehouses of Battle Abbey and Michelham Priory, the Ypres Tower at Rye and the town walls of Winchelsea were all built with such Frenchmen in mind. For most people, however, the tower of the local village church was the only refuge available, which is why so many Sussex church towers were always being rebuilt and strengthened during the fourteenth and fifteenth centuries. Some churches were even given a moat as an extra defence, like that at West Tarring – in 1450 the men of Tarring declared that they dared not go to market for fear the French might come and burn their village while they were away. In 1458 it was reported from Lewes Priory that sixty French ships had been sighted off the Sussex coast.

There were domestic upheavals. In 1381 the Poll Tax, levied on everyone over fifteen and amounting to more than several days' wages, caused the Peasants' Revolt – men broke into Lewes Castle, burning rent-rolls, stealing casks of wine. Brigands in the county's dense woodland poached the deer and robbed indiscriminately. Dissatisfaction with corrupt, ineffectual government was so great that in 1450 Sussex men of every class, including over twenty gentlemen, joined Jack Cade's revolt; later 400 pardons were issued. There was a levelling element in Cade's rising too – led by a carpenter called John Clipsham, a hundred men met in the woods outside Hastings, demanding that Henry VI be deposed and that all goods be held in common.

After the French raids and Cade's revolt, almost nothing of truly national importance took place in Sussex for centuries, not even during the Wars of the Roses or the Civil War, except for a certain amount of religious persecution. Despite being quietly prosperous from grain and wool, most of the county's dozen sleepy market towns were very small, some of them with less than 500 inhabitants. Its seaports continued to decay steadily. No doubt there were plenty of rich landowners and a fair number of enterprising iron-masters, especially when blast-furnaces were introduced. Yet until Victorian times smuggling was the largest industry here after agriculture, which shows how far removed the county was from central government. London may have been a mere fifty miles from the coast, but only as the crow flies – it did not find it easy to bring stubbornly unruly Sussex men to heel.

For long, for very long, Sussex was a backwater, the reason being its dreadful roads, which were among the worst in England. Those built by the Romans finally disintegrated during the seventeenth century, beneath the weight of the iron-founders' waggons. In 1724 Defoe commented 'the country indeed remains in the utmost distress for want of good roads'. As the eighteenth century progressed, turnpikes began to improve the situation, but often the improvements were not maintained. Travellers were also hindered by the complete lack of signposts, while proper maps did not exist; strangers needed guides, which were very hard to come by even in return for a day's wages since farmers did not care to spare their labourers' valuable time.

Inaccessibility made Sussex and its peoples different from those of neighbouring counties, with a peculiar character all of its own. 'We thought ourselves in the northwest part of England', wrote a shuddering Horace Walpole in 1749. 'The whole country has a Saxon air and the inhabitants are savage . . .' Only at the end of the eighteenth century did the turnpike roads really start to improve communications and make possible the rise of seaside watering-places. Even then, many parts remained surprisingly remote. Despite the coming of the railways, both Downs and Weald stayed more or less untouched until the advent of cheap motor-cars during the 1920s.

II
Pagan Sussex

As night falls, it requires very little effort for those who stand beside a downland tumulus in the screaming wind, or in the dank recesses of a wealden copse, to feel something of the religion of the pagan South Saxons – their belief in barrow wights, witch hounds and wood demons.

There are many ghosts in Sussex and the most enduring come from pagan times. It was no accident that this was the last part of England to be converted to Christianity. The solitude of the Downs and the darkness of the wealden forest have always inspired fear. The downland, with its barrows and its combes, can feel almost visibly haunted. So can much of the remaining woodland: South Saxons spoke of '*har heoltes feond*', the old woodland enemy; there was even a place called '*Egesawyda*', Terror Wood. Local legends here are frequently malevolent echoes of pre-Christian religion. Pagan customs were preserved by witches, black or white, and a few have survived into our own times.

The Lewes antiquarian, Mark Anthony Lower, born in 1813, recalled how during his childhood 'Nearly every unfrequented corner had its demon in the form of a black dog, while under every sequestered wooden bridge an old woman without a head was supposed to be engaged with a spinning wheel'. Even now, a headless lady who sat spinning on Pickwell Bridge over Turnham Gill is remembered at Henfield, where a wood was haunted by an animal about the size of a calf, with flaming eyes. (A legend used by smugglers to scare away excise men.) The animal was Black Shuck, '*Sceocca*', the hound of Woden, while the headless women were the Norns – the three weird sisters who spin the destinies of mankind. A hound like Shuck is still said to haunt Black Dog Hill, on the road from Ditchling to Westmeston. He was also known at Yapton, where he howled if doors were not left open for him to pass through. As late as the 1930s, the odd shepherd claimed that he could hear the 'witch hounds' in the sky – Woden's hounds hunting lost souls, the *Wild Jagd*. Often the old shepherds themselves looked like Woden, with his broad brimmed hat, black cloak and long staff.

Woden or Grim, God of Battle, is commemorated by at least three places – Wadhurst, Wannock and Wooton. Thor, the Thunder God, is known from two – Donnington and Thundersbarrow Camp. (After the conversion, the Church persecuted those who kept holy the fifth day, Thursday, in his honour.) Woden and Thor were not the only deities worshipped by the South Saxons. Tig or Tiw, God of Death, is probably commemorated by Tye Hill, Tie Oak and Tyes; Frea, Goddess of Fertility, just possibly by Frieze Oak and Friesland Wood, and Friday's Church may preserve a tradition that Frea was buried here, in one of three barrows.

A Saxon temple stood within a sacred grove from whose branches hung the bodies of men and animals who had been sacrificed to the gods. Captives were offered to Woden in this way, though they seem to have first been killed with a spear. (Woden hung from a tree for nine days and nine nights, sacrificing himself to himself to learn otherwise unattainable knowledge.) Ticehurst may be named after a grove of this sort – though the name is generally interpreted as 'kids' wood' (*Ticeshyrst*), it could instead by derived from 'the grove of Tig'.

From the evidence of place names, there were pagan shrines at Harrow Hill near Slindon, at East Hoathly and at Patchway (a small meadow in Stanmer Park). There may have been one on top of Mount Harry outside Lewes and another at the hill in Brighton on which stands the parish church of St Nicholas. Archaeologists have found ox skulls at Harrow Hill, which were offered to the gods during the autumn slaughter of livestock or at Yuletide. A Penitential (manual of penances) of about 690AD says 'If any go at the New Year as a young stag or a cow, that is, if he shares the habit of wild beasts and is clad in the skins of cattle and puts on the heads of beasts, any such who thus transforms themselves into the likeness of beasts are to do three years penance'.

Another animal sacrifice at these shrines was the horse, which the Northern religion associated with fertility. A phantom white horse used to gallop through the woods near Slindon. Did it come from the Saxon temple on Harrow Hill? There are tales of similar white horses which haunted St Nicholas's churchyard at Brighton, the moat of Bramber Castle and a lane at Tillington – the last being headless. A headless horse is also said to have been seen in Firle Park.

A well established tradition points to the existence of a pagan Saxon shrine on the hilltop called Chanctonbury Ring. As late as the last century it was believed that if you ran seven times round the trees on the summit the Devil would walk out from them and offer you a bowl of broth. This is a folk memory of autumn and yuletide meals when worshippers drank soup made from the sacrifices. A Christian Penitential lays down punishments for those who eat 'at the table of demons', who 'keep feasts in the abominable places of the heathens'. The trees were planted in the eighteenth century but must have had Saxon predecessors, a sacred grove surrounding a thatch and timber temple. (There had been Roman and Celtic shrines here before it.) The horror which Christians felt for such temples was fuelled by an account in the *Second Book of Kings* of pagan groves in high places destroyed by the Prophet Josiah.

It is likely that the South Saxons had other repellent customs besides human and animal sacrifice. In the Northern religion, virgins were sometimes ritually raped by the entire male community before immolation. From the evidence of Saxon graves elsewhere in England, wives were occasionally buried alive with their husbands, and female slaves with their mistresses.

To exorcise the old gods, the Christians built churches on temple sites, whether on hilltops, in woods, at crossroads or on barrows. (The pagan Swedes left bread and beer outside barrows because they thought that 'elves' – demons – lived inside them; probably the South Saxons did so too.) However, no church was built on Chanctonbury, which even today has an alarming name. Some who have spent a night near the Ring say that they have felt a sense of overwhelming evil, of being stalked by a malign presence.

Serpents guard the gold and silver which lies under the barrows and hill forts. The eighth-century saga *Beowulf* gives us an idea of how South Saxons thought of them, telling of barrow treasure guarded by 'the primeval enemy that haunts the dusk: the scaly, malicious worm which seeks out funeral mounds and flies burning through the night, wrapped about with flame'. It avenges thefts from barrows by spewing flame from its mouth, incinerating houses and sparing no living creature. Surrounded by tumuli, the South Saxons must have believed that dragons were plentiful in Sussex.

The best known Sussex dragon was killed by St Leonard in the forest named after him. It looked like a giant lizard. (Whenever the saint was wounded during their battle, lilies-of-the-valley grew from the ground on which his blood had fallen.) In 1614 a pamphlet by John Trundle claimed 'a strange and monstrous Serpent (or Dragon)' lived in St Leonard's Forest and had been seen within half a mile of Horsham. It was nine feet long, with red and black scales.

> He will caste his venome about four rodde from him, as by woefull experience it was proved on the bodies of a man and woman comming that way, who afterwards were found dead, being poysoned and very much swelled . . . Likewise a man going to chase it and, as he imagined, to destroy it with two mastive dogs, as yet not knowing the great danger of it, his dogs were both killed, and he himselfe glad to return with hast to preserve his own life.

Another monster, a great worm, was reported to inhabit Bignor Hill.

Worship of water-demons lies behind several Sussex legends. The Knucker Hole near Arundel is a large pond next to Lyminster church, which dates from Saxon times. It is said to have been the lair of a dragon, who liked eating pretty girls and had his eye on the King of Sussex's daughter, when he was killed by a gallant knight; there are several versions of the story – in one his head was cut off with an axe. Until quite recently the water, which comes from underground springs, was credited with healing powers and bottled. ('Knucker' derives from the Anglo-Saxon word *nicor* meaning water-demon.) In *Beowulf* the hero comes to a pool of this sort to kill a monster, Grendel's mother; as he looks down into it, he sees 'swarms of reptiles in the water, and strange dragons groping in the depths'. Yet a 'knucker' could grant favours; the Penitential calls vows made at springs 'sacrilege . . . diabolical'. There were other knucker holes in Sussex, at Lancing, Shoreham, Worthing and elsewhere – all supposedly bottomless.

As for the giants, Gill, who once hurled his hammer from the summit of Mount Caburn (an echo of Thor), is said to be buried in a long barrow called Gill's Grave near Glynde station, while a long barrow on top of Firle Beacon is known as 'The Giant's Grave'. The most famous giant is the Long Man of Wilmington, cut into the chalk on a slope of Windover Hill, between Lewes and Eastbourne. He has inspired many legends; the Firle giant supposedly threw a boulder to kill the Wilmington giant, who is buried beneath the hill. Some believe he is a Neolithic sun god. I myself think he was carved by Saxons and is Woden with his staff and spear. Whoever he may be, he looks like a baleful spirit wandering over the Downs.

Thirteen names derived from *puca* (goblin or demon) are given in *Place Names of Sussex*, 'suggesting that in local folklore Sussex was goblin-haunted to an extent without parallel'. The authors add that Puck lurked in 'rithes' (streams), springs, lanes and streets, hollows, nooks, hills, enclosures, meadows, clearings, mills and fields. The Welsh word for goblin is *pwca*, so belief in these demons may well date from Celtic times. The models for Kipling's *Puck of Pook's Hill* were malevolent and had to be propitiated; the Penitential fulminates at those who make vows to them at trees, stones or boundaries. There was nothing whimsical about a belief in 'pharisees' (fairies), whether called puck or pharisee. It was a memory of evil spirits whom the pagon

Saxons, and perhaps their British predecessors, had credited with extremely dangerous powers. Significantly, the nightjar, considered a bird of ill omen, was known as the 'puck-bird', while Puck was even used as a euphemism for Satan, though normally it was an appellation which belonged to lesser devils.

Manifestations still occur of a spirit whom the South Saxons would immediately have recognised as the *puca*, a mischievous presence sometimes confused with a poltergeist. There is a house near Lindfield, Walstead Grange, where sometimes he is in evidence. Prized objects go missing inexplicably, and are only retrieved after long and arduous searching; on one occasion a set of silver hair-brushes disappeared from a dressing table, to be discovered at the bottom of the orchard months later. Some people say they can feel a sense of illwill, if in no way threatening. This is a typical Puck haunting, which may have been known here from long ago. (Walstead is very ancient; *Walcanstede*, 'Walca's Place', is mentioned by King Eadwulf of Sussex in a charter of 765AD given to a thane called Hunlaf.)

There are many sinister legends about the Downs. 'Devil' occurs in many names – Devil's Dyke, Devil's Grave, Devil's Ditch and Devil's Bog. That of Devil's Dyke, a gap in the Downs which runs south-west from Poynings towards Hove, tells how the Fiend was digging a ditch to let in the sea and drown Sussex but was out-witted by an old woman with a candle; she tricked him into thinking the sea had risen so that he fled before he could finish his work. 'Devil' commemorates some unfriendly deity who is more than likely to have been Woden; the ditch and bank called the Devil's Ditch, from West Stoke to Halnaker, might better be named Woden's Dyke – like the Wansdyke in Wiltshire, it was clearly one of those boundaries prescribed by the Penitential.

Barrows, causeway camps and hill forts have always given rise to weird tales, no doubt ever since their construction – whether in the Stone, Bronze or Iron Age. The Devil's Humps are four barrows on Bow Hill sometimes called the Kings' Graves, while the Devil's Jumps are five barrows on top of Treyford Hill near Stoughton; the story goes that the Devil

(Woden) was jumping from one to another when he woke the sleeping Thor, who told him to stop it – whereupon the Devil threw a boulder which hit Thor in the belly. A long barrow on Cliffe Hill was known as the Warrior's Grave, perhaps its original name when it was erected in remote Neolithic times.

Many earthworks are said to have treasure buried beneath them, especially the Iron Age Forts. A knight in golden armour lies in a silver coffin under Mount Caburn. There are golden calves under Clayton Hill and the Trundle (where the calf may be heard bleating on certain moonlit nights), another silver coffin under Firle Beacon and a Roman in a golden coffin under the Long Man of Wilmington. There is treasure too beneath Cissbury Ring, Chanctonbury Ring, Hollingbury and Pulborough Mount. The golden calves are guarded by the Devil (Woden again?) and the Cissbury treasure by hissing snakes with bared fangs. At Chanctonbury the ghost of a South Saxon warrior searches frantically for his mislaid plunder.

Even in the last century it was believed that on Midsummer's Eve six skeletons arose from beneath the roots of an ancient oaktree on the Downs behind Broadhurst, the 'Midsummer Tree', and together danced wildly around it until cockcrow when they vanished. This is a memory of a pagan fertility rite, if not of something still more sinister.

Despite their conversion to Christianity, the South Saxons went on producing witches. In 1571 'Mother Margery' was evicted from her almshouse at Rye and driven out of the town for deeds 'such as any Christian harte would abhore to here spoken of much less to be used'. At least one of her enemies had hanged himself but the trouble ceased after she left Rye; raw beef was an ingredient in her spells, allegedly fed to demons. Margaret Cooper was not so lucky at East Grinstead the following year. The wife of a surgeon at Kirdford, she was accused of having bewitched two men and a woman so badly that they 'languished' and then died. She was found guilty and hanged. One way of deflecting a spell was to make the witch's blood flow by stabbing her in the buttocks with a knife (a method recommended in 1593 by Zaccharias, a wise man of Hastings). Bones from the body of John Breads, a murderer hanged at Rye in 1743 and gibbeted in chains, were stolen by old women as a cure for rheumatism – a remedy which would have been familiar to their Saxon ancestors.

Until the present century witches were credited with casting spells to make people fall ill ('wilting and withering'), with killing pigs and cattle, and with hag-riding – riding horses so cruelly by night that next morning they were found sweating and trembling in their stables. Witches stopped butter from churning, kettles from boiling, and immobilised carts; as late as the 1930s farm labourers scraped wagon-wheels with a knife to break spells. It was well known that they could turn into hares or cats; there are stories of hares hunted by hounds jumping through the windows of cottages which belonged to witches. Some years after the Second World War, a keeper shot a hare on the outskirts of a downland village; he and his dog chased it into a kitchen to find an old woman sitting in her chair, clutching her leg and moaning, with blood dripping from beneath her skirt. There are also tales of witches unable to die until other women would take their souls into their bodies. Many told fortunes and claimed they could see into the future.

The Penitential ordered that 'If anyone destroy a person by black magic, he must do penance for six years, three of them on bread and water'. It also condemned diviners who foretold the future from the flight of birds, and enchanters who made amulets or love potions. Such things happened within living memory – and all have been revived after a fashion.

It censures white witches no less severely. 'If any for the health of his little son pass through a cleft in the ground and close it after himself with thorns, let him do penance for forty days on bread and water.' This is not unlike a custom known in Victorian Sussex of passing a child with a hernia through the two halves of a sapling which had been split before sunrise; the sapling was then bound up, the hernia supposedly healing as the two halves grew together. Some believed that boils could be cured by crawling under a bramble which grew into the ground at both ends.

Kipling's 'Oak, Ash and Thorn' enshrines the old Sussex man's reverence for the ash tree which undid spells and guarded him against evil spirits; branches tied to the horns of a bewitched cow restored her to health, while a piece of ashwood carried in his pocket kept him safe. The oak (though not the holm oak) was also considered to be benevolent. Yet neither oak nor ash were so good as a thorn tree. An old Sussex charm for protection against thunder-storms – no doubt polished by some scholar parson – runs:

> Beware of the oak; it draws the stroke.
> Avoid the ash; it courts the flash.
> Creep under a thorn; it can save you from harm.

Perhaps this was shepherd lore.

Such beliefs seem laughably primitive, yet others no less misguided are creeping in with the decline of organised Christianity. One has only to look at the talismans dangling over car dashboards, or read accounts in the press of desecrated graveyards, to realise that paganism is returning. Recently a farmer near Cuckfield, a friend of mine, lost a fine black ewe. He was told by his manager that he would never see her again – she had been stolen for sacrifice on the Downs.

> From the hag and hungry goblin
> That into rags would rend ye,
> The spirits that stand
> By the naked man
> In the book of Moons, defend ye . . .

III

Chichester and the Rape of Chichester

One of the pleasantest ways to enter Sussex is by sea from the south-west, sailing into Chichester. The first sight of the cathedral spire from the coast has been compared with that of Chartres seen from the Beauce. The shore line of Chichester Harbour is seventeen miles long and is a paradise for birdwatchers and yachtsmen. Among the wildfowl on the harbour's northern extremity are such ducks as golden-eye and red breasted merganser, with every known wader – even avocets. Eighty years ago, the vicar of West Wittering was so alarmed by them that he put a notice on the church door begging his congregation to close it lest the birds fly round during services. Nowadays the Witterings, East and West, are mainly inhabited by men – and women – in yachting caps, yet their many bungalows have not banished charm from these villages.

The southernmost point of Sussex is Selsey Bill, 'island of seals'. Much of it has vanished beneath the sea including, so it is often said, St Wilfrid's monastery and Selsey Cathedral. There are tales of fragments of carved stone being dredged up in fishermen's nets, and many a fine purple passage has been written about 'the vanished minster under the sea'. However, recent research suggests that the site is still dry land, marked by the beautiful little thirteenth-century chapel of St Wilfrid at Church Norton; it is the chancel of a church the remainder of which was pulled down and rebuilt at Selsey one and a half miles away in 1865. This is the region known as the Manhood, flat and fertile, with water-logged saltflats. It reminds me a little of Holland. The many small channels which run through the marshes are known as 'rifes'.

Instead of sailing direct to Chichester, it is well worth while

23

putting in at Bosham Creek. At high tide, Bosham is unquestionably a great beauty; at low, with mud stretching as far as the eye can see, she is a dirty slut. The tribune Vespasian landed here in 42AD with the Second Legion after conquering the Isle of Wight; no doubt he received a fawning welcome from Cogidubnus but even the shrewd King of the Regni cannot have realised that one day this man would become Emperor of Rome. The oratory of a seventh-century Irish monk, Dicuil, is thought to lie beneath the church and there was certainly a royal manor here in Saxon times, if no one knows where the hall stood. Locals boast that Bosham shore was where King Canute commanded those impertinent waves to retreat. The church tower and the chancel are unmistakably Saxon, with one of the finest Saxon arches to survive. For many centuries there was a tradition that a small tomb held the body of 'King Canute's daughter'; opened in 1865 it was found to contain the bones of a girl of about eight. In 1064 the future King Harold sailed from Bosham on a voyage which ended in shipwreck and his being forced to take an oath of allegiance to William of Normandy – his departure is shown in the Bayeux Tapestry.

Being flat, south-western Sussex between the sea and the Downs is dominated by the tall cathedral spire, and yet on entering Chichester one's first feeling is not so much admiration for the cathedral as surprise at its rectangular Roman street plan, which is better preserved than anywhere else in Britain. The walls (medieval on top of Roman, with a single Roman bastion) are a mile and a half long, enclosing an area of about a hundred acres. A long street runs from north to south, another from east to west. The Roman city had an amphitheatre, a forum, public baths, a temple of Neptune and Minerva, and the governor's basilica (which may be under the cathedral). The walls were repaired by the Saxons as a place of refuge from the Vikings. Its strategic value was at once recognised by the Normans, even if Domesday Book valued it at only £15 compared to Lewes at £26. They built a wooden castle inside the walls, later replaced by stone but demolished by Henry III; its motte can still be seen, a low mound in Priory Park. However, the most important event in Chichester's history was the building of the cathedral.

A Saxon church dedicated to St Peter already stood here when the Normans moved the bishopric from Selsey to Chichester in 1075. (No diocese has a stranger coat-of-arms, a mitred bishop seated on his throne with a sword between his teeth.) The Norman Ralph de Luffa, who became bishop in 1091, began the cathedral which was not finished until 1240. Many writers claim it as quintessentially English, the 'most loveable of English cathedrals', 'exquisitely suited to Anglican worship although completed 300 years before the Reformation'. Yet to me it always seems that Ralph de Luffa's church is unmistakably French and just like a cathedral in Normandy – scarcely surprising when one realises how much of its white stone came from Caen, and that its basic design was inspired by the Abbaye-aux-Hommes at Caen, whose twin towers are repeated here. Admittedly, the massive, free-standing bell-tower, completed in 1436, is aggressively English.

Some visitors remark on Chichester Cathedral's subdued, muted atmosphere; E. V. Lucas thought it lacked 'radiance'. Were this so, it could compensate by the lovely things it contains. There are two wonderful limestone reliefs discovered in 1829, once part of a twelfth century screen. Awkward, almost primitive, yet deeply moving, they are the *Rising of Lazarus* and *Christ arriving at Bethany*; these are Saxon rather than Norman work, carved by someone who remembered pre-Conquest art – it used to be thought that they came from St Wilfrid's old minster at Selsey. Bishop Arundel's great Perpendicular screen is equally English; taken down and stored for a hundred years, it escaped when in 1861 the spire 'gently collapsed upon itself like a folding telescope', falling into the choir and nave. Through the screen one first glimpses John Piper's tapestry of the Trinity, hung upon a sixteenth-century screen of wood and concealing the retro-quire; a mass of blues, reds and greens, it makes a splendid reredos which enhances the liturgy. Over one of the side chapel altars there is a magnificent Graham Sutherland, *Noli me Tangere* – Christ appearing to Mary Magdalene after the Resurrection. There is also a red window of 1978, dominated by King David with his harp on a donkey, which was designed by Marc Chagall.

The acquisition of so many outstanding pieces of contemporary art was entirely due to the personal initiative of Walter Hussey, the remarkable dean here from 1955–77. It was he who commissioned the works of Piper, Sutherland and Chagall. Dean Hussey also encouraged the regular use of the cathedral for performances of music and drama, besides commissioning the 'Chichester Psalms' from Leonard Bernstein. He bequeathed his own superb collection of paintings to Pallant House [see below].

The cathedral precincts are those of a Trollope novel – two gatehouses, a bishop's palace, cloisters, a deanery, 'house of royal chaplains', a treasury and a vicars' close. The beautiful Chichester Roundel of about 1250 is in the palace chapel, a Madonna and Child painted in gold, silver and lapis lazuli by the chronicler Matthew Paris, if a most unlikely theory can be believed. At the exit to the cloisters one reads the following lines, often recalled:

> Thou wandering ghost
> Take home this rhyme,
> Next grave that opens
> May be thine

The vicars' close is a row of houses adjoining the cloister built for fifteenth-century vicars choral. (Vicars choral deputised for the prebendaries, taking their place in choir.) Lucas thought them far more attractive than the cathedral, because more human:

> that little terrace of ecclesiastical residences parallel with South Street, in the shadow of the mighty fane, covered with creeping greenness, from wisteria to ampelopsis, with minute windows, inviolable front doors and trim front gardens, which (like all similar settlements) remind one of alms-houses carried out to the highest power. Surely the best of places in which to edit Horace afresh or find new meanings in St Augustine.

Today's 'committed' clergy may have very different interests, but the close is just the same as when this was written in 1903.

Also in the precincts is a pleasant stone-flagged path called St Richard's Walk where a saint is said to have taken his exercise.

Richard of Wych (1197–1253) is the most celebrated Bishop of Chichester, and Sussex's patron saint. When the Pope appointed him to the see in 1245, King Henry III (who had appropriated its revenues) was so angry that he forebade anyone to house or feed him; at first Richard was dependent on charity and on his friend Simon, parish priest of Tarring. To visit his flock, he had to tramp the entire county on foot. An ascetic who wore a hair-shirt and refused to eat off silver, in a famous prayer he addresses Christ as 'Redeemer, Friend, Brother'. Merciless to usurers, corrupt clergy and priests who mumbled the Mass, he was a stickler for clerical privilege; when the men of Lewes dragged a thief out of sanctuary and hanged him, he made them cut down the rotting corpse and bury it in the sanctuary. Yet he was much loved and was canonised only nine years after his death. In 1273 his body was placed in a silver-gilt shrine in the retro-quire. Pilgrims flocked to it, especially on his feast-day, 3 April.

Fifteenth-century bishops persecuted Lollards, proto-Protestants, with enthusiasm. Thomas Bagley was burnt here in 1431 for his opinions but John Boreham escaped the stake eight years later though he owned a copy of the Gospels in English and admitted practising necromancy. Ironically, Bishop Pecock (a famous fulminator against Lollards) was deposed in 1458 for heresy (he had rewritten the Apostles' Creed) and imprisoned in a monastery for the remainder of his life. At the Reformation the bishops were impoverished, losing many of their powers over the city, though they remained men of spirit, such as that scourge of Papists, Dr Barlow, whose five daughters all married bishops. During the seventeenth century they included truly oustanding prelates – Richard Montague, Brian Duppa and Henry King.

After the cathedral, the city's most beautiful possession is undoubtedly the Market Cross, with its eight Perpendicular arches and a noble bust of Charles I placed there at the Restoration. It was built in 1501 by Bishop Storey, on the site of the Roman market place where the four main streets meet, its purpose being the 'succoure and the comfort of the Poore Peple', by providing a place where smallholders and fishermen could sell their provender without having to pay taxes. At first it angered the city's tradesmen but even they grew proud of it. 'In justness of design, symmetry of parts, and happiness of execution, the beautiful cross of Chichester will be allowed by the best judges to yield to none in the kingdom' wrote a local historian, Alexander Hay, in 1804.

Chichester's resemblance to Trollope's Barsetshire is striking. There is even a medieval hospital, St Mary's, which dates from 1290 and has been administered by the dean and chapter from the beginning. Outside, it looks like a cross between a tithe-barn and a church, with a vast, high pitched roof; inside, it is even more barn-like, with huge roof-beams — a great hall. An almshouse for old ladies, it contains seven little flats (each with bedroom and sitting room) together with a small chapel like a chancel. In the early days it also looked after poor travellers; those who feigned poverty and were found to have money in their pockets were flogged.

Under the Tudors, with a population of about 2,500 the city prospered. In 1572 nearly 150 vessels were operating from the harbour and there was a thriving trade with the Low Countries — the main cargo being wheat. There were also shipyards, tanneries, breweries and needle-makers' workshops.

When the Civil War broke out in 1642, apart from the cathedral close most of Chichester was for Parliament. The local cavalier squires seized the city in November. During the ensuing siege many houses were destroyed and the walls were badly damaged, while the cathedral was sacked when the Roundheads marched in. The needle industry never recovered.

Among Chichester's leading Parliamentarians was William Cawley, MP for Midhurst, who had inherited a brewing fortune and built a hospital for the aged poor which still stands. Having signed King Charles' death-warrant in 1649, he fled to Switzerland at the Restoration to escape being hanged, drawn and quartered. When he died, his son was suspected of smuggling his body back and burying it beneath the hospital chapel; a male skeleton in a nameless lead coffin was found here in 1883. The chapel is well worth a visit, a simple, touching little room.

When the eighteenth century began, Chichester's walls remained a mass of rubble, the streets were unpaved, and in winter the city was isolated by bad roads. Yet it prospered, as may be seen from the Georgian houses in the Pallants. (The name comes from the palings behind which red Sussex and Southdown sheep waited for market.) The streets here, a miniature replica of the main plan – north and south, east and west – were a rundown area of breweries, tanneries and squalid cabins with thatched roofs when, in Queen Anne's reign, Henry Peckham, a young wine-merchant who did so well out of port that he was called 'Lisbon Peckham', built a red-brick mansion in North Pallant with his crest of an ostrich on both gates – popularly believed to be dodos. (It was restored in the 1970s and now contains a superb collection of modern paintings – works by John Piper, Graham Sutherland, Henry Moore and Ivon Hitchens.) What makes Pallant House so interesting is that it gives a good idea of how a well-to-do Chichester merchant lived at this date. Others copied 'Lisbon Peckham', building new houses all over the city. They led a busy social life, with new Assembly Rooms behind the new Council House in North Street where routs were held and country dances made the floor thunder. Local squires moved in for the winter season. 'The domestic building in every part of the kingdom is greatly improved within the last few years; but in few places more than in Chichester' boasted Hay in 1804. Its houses were 'large, neat, clean and pleasant'. He adds that 'The pavement of the streets, and the spacious footpaths on each side, is kept exceedingly neat and clean'.

The city produced a poet famous in his day, William Collins (1721–59). There is an hilarious monument by Flaxman in the cathedral, well described by Hay. 'The poet is represented as recovering from a fit of phrensy, to which he was unhappily subject.' Hay quotes his epitaph approvingly:

Severely doom'd to penury's extreme,
He past in mad'ning pain life's feverish dream;
While rays of genius only serv'd to show
The thick'ning horror, and exalt his woe.
Ye walls, that echo'd to his frantic moan,
Guard the due record of this grateful stone . . .

The author of 'How sleep the brave' deserved better.

All that ruffled Chichester's tranquillity was an occasional battle between smugglers and excisemen, and the threat of French invasion.

The poet John Keats arrived at 20 Eastgate Square in January 1821, having come down from London by coach. A red-brick house of about 1780, now a shop, it is still there. 'I went twice at Chichester to old dowager card parties' he says in a letter. After a walk on a cold evening, he wrote in *The Eve of St Agnes* of the sensation:

Of one returning late
Past the echoing minster gate.

It was a quiet, modestly prosperous world which continued little changed into the present century. E. V. Lucas thought it a perfect example of an English country town, full of farmers and their wives on market days. 'But it is more than this: it is also a cathedral town, with the ever-present sense of domination by the cloth even when the cloth is not visible.'

Only W. H. Hudson failed to respond to its charm. In *Nature in Downland* he claims that a vile smell induced a depressive illness in its inhabitants called 'the chichesters'. He also alleged that most of the then population of 12,000 spent their entire time in the city's seventy public-houses – 'the perpetual swilling in Chichester is enough to turn the stomach of the most tolerant man'. His dislike may have been due to seeing a caged barn-owl in a pub kitchen; having at first agreed to give it to him for release in a suitable barn, the sluttish landlady changed her mind.

Recently Chichester has been pedestrianised. Save for the cathedral there is no imposing building, but from the Market

Cross one sees countless Georgian houses. If bomb damage during the Second War and slum-clearance have been the excuse for 'development', on the whole this has been reasonably sensitive. The Corn Exchange of 1832, with a great sheet of glass behind its Grecian portico, shelters a Macdonald's with admirable aplomb. The little city keeps its quiet charm – it looks best in the snow – while continuing to be a bustling county town and shopping centre. The Chichester Festival Theatre (opened in 1962 with Laurence Olivier as the first Director) attracts audiences from all over Britain.

Chidham, on a tongue of land between Thorney Channel and Bosham Creek, remains an unspoilt coastal village with a simple church which dates from 1220 and a fine eighteenth-century manor-house. It was famous for high yield wheat. (Wheat is harvested earlier in the plain than anywhere else in England.) Further east, South Mundham amid lanes and cornfields has been described as one of the best places to get the feel of the Selsey peninsula – flat as Norfolk but with the Downs and Chichester spire in the distance. When St Wilfrid was given the Mundham estate in the 680s he freed 250 slaves, who were probably British and possibly Christians.

Going north, Racton in the Ems valley is where the western Downs begin. Nearby, surrounded by gloomy trees, is a folly built in 1772 which looks like a Plantagenet castle. Not far away is Stansted Park. A royal hunting lodge in medieval times and later a Palladian mansion, it was rebuilt after a fire in 1900.

Colonel George Gounter of Racton helped Charles II to escape from England after his defeat at Worcester in 1651. The colonel wrote an account, found in a secret drawer when Racton House was demolished about 1830, which Harrison Ainsworth used in *Ovingdean Grange*. Gounter and his cousin, Captain Thomas Gounter, met the king in the grounds of Stansted Place. A 'tall man, six feet four inches high', he was disguised as a Roundhead. They took him towards Shoreham along what is now the South Downs Way. Ainsworth's reconstruction shows how little the landscape has changed:

> After quitting the forest and skirting Stansted Park, the Royal party pursued their way through a lovely and well-wooded district, until they came to the foot of an eminence called Bow Hill, and entered the narrow and picturesque vale denominated Kingly Bottom – so called from a battle between the inhabitants of Chichester and the Danes – and Charles failed not to notice the group of venerable yew-trees – venerable in *his* days, though still extant, with the trifle of two centuries added to their age – that adorn the valley. After this they passed Stoke Down, bestowing a passing observation on the curious circular hollows indented in the sod ... Avoiding Chichester, the king and his company pursued their way along the beautiful and well-wooded slopes of the Goodwood Downs ...

They crossed the Arun at Houghton (the same fifteenth-century bridge is still there) and the Adur at Bramber where they rode coolly through a troop of Ironsides.

At Westbourne, now a small village on the banks of the Ems but a minute market town until the eighteenth century, E. V. Lucas noted an epitaph to Jane Curtis, who died in 1719:

> She was like a lily fresh and green
> Soon cast down and no more seen

West Stoke has a dear little church of Saxon origin. However, though there was a church at Westhampnett in the eighth century, the present building may not pre-date the Norman Conquest. 'There is no doubt that it began its life as a Roman temple, at the side of Stane Street, and that upon this foundation the Saxons, inspired by the teachings of St Wilfrid, erected a church to the new faith' declared Lucas, nevertheless, in a rare fit of ill judged enthusiasm.

Further east, Boxgrove Priory has the finest monastic church in Sussex. A Benedictine house, it was founded in 1117 as a cell of the Norman abbey of Lessay. Only a few Norman arches and a roofless fourteenth-century guest-house survive from the monastic buildings, but the thirteenth-century nave and chancel (inspired by the retro-choir at Chichester) remain as a most dignified parish church. There is a magnificent chantry chapel, built in 1526 for Masses to be said for the soul of Lord de la Warr who died in 1554, a Gothic-Renaissance combination which gives the effect of a church within a church. (His lordship, an otherwise obscure figure, obtained leave of absence from the parliament of 1531–2 on the grounds of poverty – perhaps he had spent all his money on his chapel.) Another of Boxgrove's glories is its ceiling, decorated in the 1520s, before the monks had gone, with heraldic shields and twining foliage by a Flemish painter called Lambert Bernard.

The de la Warrs (or Wests) lived half a mile from Boxgrove at Halnaker House. The same Lord de la Warr who built the chapel rebuilt the medieval house but no more than a few fragments survive, together with the remnants of a thirteenth-century chapel. It was left to fall into ruin in 1800 by its owner, the Duke of Richmond, as soon as he had completed Goodwood to his satisfaction.

Halnaker Hill, celebrated by Hilaire Belloc, is crowned by a fine 'tower' mill, erected in 1740 to grind corn brought by the poor of the parish. In 1913 Belloc was shocked to see that it had fallen into ruin, writing:

> Ha'naker Hill is in Desolation:
>   Ruin a-top and a field unploughed.
> And Spirits that call on a fallen nation,
>   Spirits that loved her calling aloud:
> Spirits abroad in a windy cloud.

No-one knows why the sight filled the poet with so much melancholy.

The racecourse on top of the Downs, a mile and a half from Goodwood (see Ch. XIV), is dominated by the Trundle. The name is Saxon (*tryndel*, a circle) but this was an Iron Age hill-fort and before that a Neolithic causeway-camp of the people of the long barrows. As a fort, with three circular banks and ditches enclosing an inner area of three acres, it was probably the centre from which a chieftain ruled his estates, a place for tribal assemblies or a market, or all three. Its use as a Stone Age camp is harder to fathom – perhaps it was a pen for animals awaiting slaughter.

The Lavants – villages at the foot of the Downs – derive their names from the River Lavant, among the very few Celtic place names in Sussex.

Going north along the Lavant valley, one reaches Singleton. William Cobbett rode here in 1823. 'I got hither, down a long valley, along the *South* Downs, which valley winds and twists about hills, some higher and some lower, forming cross dells, inlets and ground in such a variety of shapes that it is impossible to describe; and the whole of the ground hill as well as dell, is fine, most beautiful, corn land, or is covered with trees or underwood' he writes in *Rural Rides*, and he was never lavish with his praise. Singleton belonged to King Harold (as it had to his father, Earl Godwin) and its church tower is almost certainly Saxon, and perhaps its tall nave too. The village is probably even better kept than in Cobbett's day.

Understandably, Singleton takes great pride in the Weald and Downland Open Air Museum nearby, covering thirty-five acres of a valley whose pleasant slopes are adorned by beeches. This contains a wonderful collection of buildings rescued from demolition, re-erected and restored. They range from charcoal burners' huts to wealden hall houses, from staddle barns to water mills; there are farm wagons, lined up as if ready to set off for work, and ancient breeds of livestock – Tamworth pigs and Red Sussex cattle of the sort which provided ox-teams.

Although the church in the pretty village of West Dean was burnt down and rebuilt in 1934, it still contains monuments to the Lewkenors, a once famous Sussex family. One of them was at the seige of Calais in 1347 while another rebelled against Richard III.

The Gothic West Dean Park, built by James Wyatt in 1804, was the home of that very odd figure Edward James – sometimes alleged to be a bastard of Edward VII – the friend of Magritte and Dali, who ended his days erecting fantastic palaces in the Mexican jungle. His one unflawed achievement was to give part of his park at West Dean as a site for the Weald and Downland Museum.

West of Singleton, on the Hampshire border, is Stoughton which has a genuinely pre-Conquest church. It is on the Downs and on the Roman road from Winchester to Chichester along which Caedwalla of Wessex and his war-band marched in 685 to defeat and kill King Aethelwalh of the South Saxons. The noble ridge of Bow Hill above Stoughton has four unusually well preserved bowl barrows, the Kings' Graves, which are supposed to be the burial mounds of Vikings slain by Sussex men in 900AD; in reality they date from the Bronze Age. Beneath Bow Hill is Kingley Vale, the finest yew forest in Europe, with trees 500 years old. It is famous for kestrels and wild orchids, though not in the bottom among the yews where nothing else will grow. Few can disagree with Lucas: 'Kingley Vale . . . always grave and silent, is transformed at dusk into a sinister and fantastic forest, a home for witchcraft and unquiet spirits.'

W. H. Hudson, who compared the vale to Chichester Cathedral, noticed that because of the abundance of their favourite food, yew-berries, it was a paradise for missel-thrushes in autumn. 'And do they feast! It is worse than a feast, it is a perfect orgy.'

The Mardens (or 'boundary hills') are small, isolated, downland hamlets. Approached through a farmyard, the Norman church at North Marden is no more than an elongated apse decorated by a tiny wooden belfry. A hundred years ago the parish numbered twenty-five souls; by 1900 there were only nine yet still enough to fill this minute temple of God. The thirteenth-century church at East Marden (whose village pump has a thatched roof over it) is disappointing. Wildham Wood nearby is one of the largest stretches of beech woodland to survive on the Downs. 'I walked by devious ways to East Marden', wrote Lucas in Edward VII's reign, 'between banks thick with the whitest and sweetest of sweet white violets.' He probably went by way of Wildham Wood which is still noted in springtime for *viola odorata alba*.

Faded cream wash and pale grey stone outside, the church at Up Marden, which also dates from the thirteenth century, has been described as possessing one of the loveliest interiors of any church in England. Like North Marden, it escaped the attentions of Victorian restorers. Small and rustic, it has a naive charm which is quite overwhelming. Yet in 1625 an angry vicar complained that the little church was 'so indecently and beastly kept . . . through the pigion dung and other filth in the same, that people are not able to endure the ill and noysome smell thereof when they come to the same, but are inforced to stop their noses or carry flowers in their hands'.

At Appledown, nor far from the Mardens, archaeologists have recently found graves with artefacts which seem to be Jutish in origin – indicating that the area may have been settled by colonists from the Jutes' kingdom in the Isle of Wight.

Just north of the Mardens, at Didling beneath the wooded slope of the most beautiful of the western Downs, is the lonely church of St Andrew, minute and charming – the 'Shepherds' Church' – and another which has escaped the restorers. Almost as small as North Marden, with smoke-blackened benches from the fifteenth century, and a crude Laudian Communion rail from the seventeenth fencing off the Holy Table, it is still lit by candles in iron holders at the end of each bench. An epitaph to Mary Aylwin, who died on 7 July 1756 aged twelve weeks and five days, calls her 'A harmless babe that only came and cried / in Baptism to be washed from sin, and died.'

You will find Up Waltham a few miles to the east even lonelier, just a farm, outbuildings and a church in a valley amid bare, rolling downland which can be very bleak indeed when the wind howls. 'A wonderful group' was Nairn's ecstatic reaction, 'like a monogram in flint'. The twelfth or thirteenth-century church of St Mary the Virgin, again tiny and unrestored, is no more than a nave and a round 'apsidal' chancel, with a quality of almost wistful antiquity. Cobbett thought its tower even smaller than another he had seen 'about double the size of a sentry-box'. He was horrified by the woman at the long-vanished toll-gate telling him that she made straw-hats from rushes. 'This woman ought to have my *Cottage Economy* . . . the Essay on Straw Plat.'

Up Waltham church was served from Woolavington a little further north, and in 1833 the new curate rode here to give his first sermon. He was Mr Henry Edward Manning, formerly a Fellow of Merton College, Oxford who was engaged to the parson's daughter. When his father-in-law died he succeeded him as rector of Woolavington (then known as 'Lavington'), where his wife died and was buried after a mere four years of marriage. In 1841 Mr Manning was made Archdeacon of Chichester, visiting every parish in Sussex. But in 1851 he went over to Rome and within a few years became Archbishop of Westminster. During his time at Woolavington he had converted a Catholic gardener and his wife to the Church of England. Meeting them again years later, he tried to bring the couple back to Rome. 'No, my lord' said the gardener. 'One change is good enough for us.'

The Hartings – East, West and South – in their setting of green hills and purple woods, have a big fourteenth century church with a pale-green copper spire. The old stocks and whipping-post are still outside. (The stocks were in use as late as the 1860s.) Reginald Pole, last Cardinal Archbishop of Canterbury, was rector here in Henry VIII's reign, if only as a pluralist who lived abroad, well out of his royal kinsman's reach. This was once a Catholic stronghold since the local squires, the Carylls of Lady Holt, were staunch Romanists. Their chapel, which they built on to the church in 1610, is now only a few crumbling stones though there is a monument to its builder inside the church. He was Sir Richard Caryll who died in 1616; like most of his family, his funeral would have been in the chapel at night, according to the old rite with tapers and hushed chanting – the rector tactfully turning a blind eye, and the villagers convinced that there were ghosts about. Under the Commonwealth, their house of Lady Holt was confiscated by the Roundheads, but the Carylls recovered it at the Restoration.

John Caryll of Lady Holt wrote *The English Princess or the Death of Richard III*, which Pepys described as 'a most melancholy play, and pretty good'. Sent to the Tower in 1679 during the Popish Plot, he later became James II's envoy at Rome, going into exile at St Germain-en-Laye with the king, who created him Lord Caryll of Durford. His nephew, another John Caryll, gave Alexander Pope the idea for his greatest poem, *The Rape of the Lock*. The last squire, John Baptist

Caryll, was ruined and after first selling his other estate of West Grinstead [see ch. VIII] he finally sold Lady Holt in 1767. He went to Italy, where he assumed his Jacobite title and was for some years Secretary of State to the King over the Water, 'Charles III' – Bonnie Prince Charlie – who made him a Knight of the Thistle. Lady Holt was pulled down shortly after his departure.

There seem to have been plenty of witches at the Hartings. One at least, Mother Digby of East Harting, had the characteristic knack of turning into a hare. A local squire's harriers were constantly checking at a drain outside her cottage down which the quarry disappeared. Eventually they caught a hare by the hind legs but it tore itself free. The squire burst into the house, to find an anguished Mother Digby rubbing her backside.

Treyford is a sad, hushed place, with two ruined churches. One built in 1849 was demolished in 1951, while the old thirteenth-century church is entombed in a small wood near the manor house, which is not easy to penetrate. It stood on a barrow, perhaps a Saxon shrine. There are five bell barrows just outside the village, the largest Bronze Age tumuli in Sussex, known as the Devil's Jumps.

At Durford there was an abbey of White Canons or Premonstratensians – so named from their mother house of Premontre near Laon. Nothing remains of it save for a few fragments in the garden wall of the farm on the site. However, they have left three monuments in their bridges across the western Rother; the best is that at Durford itself, with four round arches and great cutwaters, for not only did they build them, but they maintained them too. At the Dissolution, Durford was described as very poor, 'far in debt and in decay', yet not so poor that Sir William Fitzwilliam did not covet it. He added the canons' lands to his Cowdray estate.

There is a similar bridge at Trotton further down the Rother, built about 1300 by one of the Camoys family, who also built the long thin church with its small, cream-washed tower and truncated spire. A brass of 1310 commemorates

'Margarete', Lady Camoys; her hair is bound by a narrow fillet across her forehead, her head covered by a veil which falls to her shoulders, and her throat swathed in a wimple. Another brass, from a hundred years later, shows Thomas, Lord Camoys who commanded Henry V's left wing at Agincourt; in full armour, he clasps the hand of his wife, Harry Hotspur's widow Kate. On the west wall there are fourteenth-century paintings in red ochre of the Seven Deadly Sins and the Seven Works of Mercy – the angels are winged with bristling plumes.

A great Restoration playwright was born at Trotton, Thomas Otway, the curate's son. His *Venice Preserv'd* was much admired, but he became unhinged by an unrequited passion for the actress Mrs Barry, Lord Rochester's mistress, and 'languished in adversity unpitied, and dy'd at thirty-three'. Given a guinea when starving, he rushed out to buy a roll, choking on the first mouthful. 'His person was of the middle size, about 5 ft. 7 in., inclinable to fatness. He had a thoughtful, speaking eye.'

At Chithurst to the west a Norman church stands by the River Rother on a mound believed to have been a pagan shrine. Thirty years ago Ian Nairn described its setting as 'lush and intricate in spring, like a Pre-Raphaelite picture'. It is still the same in spring today, a mass of celandine and periwinkles.

Going back to the eastern side of the rape, Graffham is another pretty little village, beneath the wooded Downs. In the cruelly restored church, there is a wistful inscription to a mother and daughter who died in 1691:

> Death, to make recompence for what he'd Done
> In partinge two whose harts were joyn'd in one
> Att length the other tooke, and heere they ly
> Waiteinge the summons to Eternity.
> The indulgent mother first went to prepare
> A lodging for her daughter. She for feare
> Her daughter should be censured for her stay
> Courted her grave and gently fled away.

The church at Heyshott, under the Downs, has one of those odd little wooden belfries perched over the west end of the nave which are so characteristic of Sussex. Heyshott is a soothing, unspoilt village – Nairn commented on its 'harmonious' quality. Richard Cobden, the great advocate of Free Trade and of those harsh Victorian values which inspired Dickens's novel *Hard Times*, was born in a farmhouse here. Surprisingly, the working men of this village long remembered him for his kindness. 'Folks were real sorry when Mr Cobden died' an old labourer recalled at the turn of the century. ' 'E did a power for Heyshott, 'e did. 'E wor the best man what ever come here.'

On the same side of the rape lies Selham, its eleventh-century church minute and towerless, with a fine Saxon arch into the chancel. A Victorian rector, Mr Blackburn, set the royal arms of Plantagenet in the windows and told visitors 'Those are the arms of my children's ancestors'. The tiny buildings once served a remote community of pioneers in what were then the depths of the forest. The cosy pub here has the pleasant name of *The Three Moles*.

The chalk has been left behind; the soil is clay and sandstone. The name Midhurst (*middel hyrst*, the 'middle wood') is a memory of clearing the Weald. Although on a Roman road, it did not become a market town until the thirteenth century. W. H. Hudson liked it in 1899, describing it as 'a small, old and extremely picturesque town, which in its rough paved, crooked, uneven streets, ancient timbered houses, its curfew bell, and darkness and silence at night, seemed to have suddenly carried me back into mediaeval times'. It is not quite so medieval now, though it still has immense charm. A reserved place, its twisting streets have such homely names as Duck Street, June Lane, Knockhundred Row, Rumbold's Hill, Sheep Lane and Wool Lane. None of its buildings, including the church, is of any real distinction but the overall effect is undeniably pleasing. It was famous for its inns, notably *The Spread Eagle* (once a favourite haunt of Hilaire Belloc), most of which dates from Queen Anne's reign.

The magnificent ruins of Cowdray which dominate the town are described elsewhere. At its gates is Easebourne, in whose church is a splendid effigy of Henry VII's great-uncle

Sir David Owen, who began the rebuilding of Cowdray; he wears fifteenth-century armour, since he ordered his tomb forty years before he died in 1535. There is another imposing monument to Sir Anthony Browne, first Viscount Montague, who completed the house. His two wives are with him; beneath the effigy of the second, a most formidable lady who departed in 1609, are her proud name and parentage: 'Magdalen, daughter of William Lord Dacre, Knight, Lord Dacre, Graystock and Gylesland, & Lord Warden of ye west Marches of England for anempste Scoteland'. The harsh northern names sound alien and outlandish in these southern parts. The church was once that of Easebourne Priory, whose canonesses were a byword for naughtiness; in 1441 a visitation found them in debt because of the prioress's high living, which included trimming her habit with expensive fur; in 1478 the then prioress and two sisters were accused of gross immorality, hunting, and giving smart parties. Listing their sins, the *Victorian County History* suggests primly that 'this remote priory served as a kind of reformatory for young women of good family who had strayed from the path of virtue'.

In 1909 Cowdray Park and Easebourne were bought by Sir Weetman Pearson, who was created Baron Cowdray in the following year. The Pearson family soon left their mark on Sussex, employing a distinguished architect, Sir Aston Webb, to preserve the ruins of Cowdray and also bringing Elizabethan Parham back to life. (See Ch. VIII.) Nobody could disagree with Ian Nairn's eulogy of the beautiful condition in which the ruins and the surrounding park are kept, 'like everything administered by the Cowdray Estate'. The estate is the largest in Sussex, covering 17,000 acres, its farms and cottages recognisable by their yellow doors and window frames. For many years the park has been one of the world's most famous polo grounds.

Despite its high, narrow, Saxon aisle and pilasters, the church at Woolbeding is disappointing, but not the elegant Woolbeding Hall next door which dates from William and Mary's day.

Its garden has a delightful Italian fountain from the sixteenth century, once in the courtyard at Cowdray. Here lived, very briefly, Charlotte Smith, the county's best poetess even though she is largely forgotten, a friend of Cowper, Wordsworth and Romney. Born in 1749, the daughter of a well-to-do landowner called Turner, she grew up at Bignor Park as a Sussex girl. ('Ah! hills beloved! – your turf, your flowers remain,' she wrote later.) At fifteen she made a disastrous marriage to Benjamin Smith, the son of a prosperous West India merchant, who gave her twelve children. After her father's death, Benjamin's prodigality resulted in her spending seven months in a debtors' prison. She began to write verse and when her *Elegiac Sonnets* was a success, embarked on a career as a writer – her sole source of income. She leased Woolbeding, far above her means, and started a series of novels, the first of which, *Emmeline, or The Orphan at the Castle* was reasonably well received.

In 1788, after only two years, poor Charlotte moved out of Woolbeding to escape from the unfaithful, bad-tempered and sponging Benjamin – who eventually died in a debtors' prison. Until 1793 she lived at Brighton, where she moved in literary circles, becoming something of a 'democrat' who welcomed the French Revolution; her novel *Desmond* of 1792 was so critical of monarchy that Wordsworth suspected her of being a Jacobin agent. (A translation appeared in Paris, *Desmond, ou l'amant philanthrope*.) Her novels had only a brief vogue, but her verse was long admired, especially her sonnets – though some readers were disturbed by her gloom. She had much to be gloomy about and was so poor that a Brighton landlord locked her out of her lodgings and seized her clothes. She sympathised with others in the same plight, writing an ode to a young actor arrested for debt. The rest of her life was spent moving from one garret to another while her hands grew so arthritic that she had to dictate to a daughter; only her pen stood between them and destitution. There were no more novels after 1798. She died eight years later, working on her poem 'Beachy Head'.

Not far from Fernhurst, up in the High Weald, a 'Furnace

Pond' and a 'Minepit Copse' remind us that this was once a centre of the iron industry. Verdley Castle stood in the woods nearby. In the 1830s, according to Horsefield: 'One tradition reports it to have been a castle, demolished in an invasion of the Danes; another makes it a madhouse attached to the nunnery of Easebourne; a third a grange belonging to the monks of Shulbrede.' In fact it was a hunting tower built by the Bohun Lords of Midhurst during the thirteenth century, which their Browne successors let fall into ruin, so lonely that Camden's words soon applied – 'It is known only to those who hunt the marten cat'. Not a stone remains today. While there may well have been pine martens here, I have been unable to verify a report (in a recently published book on ghosts) that Verdley was haunted by the last bear to be killed in Sussex.

The Augustinian priory of Shulbrede was founded about 1200 when the High Weald really was a wilderness. Part of the prior's lodging survives as a house in a remote wooded valley; it keeps a sixteenth-century panel from the canons' time with paintings of talking animals who rejoice at the birth of Christ. In 1536, Shulbrede was visited by Dr Layton, one of the commissioners for the Dissolution; he reported that the prior had seven mistresses and the other brethren four or five each.

The rape's northernmost village is Linchmere, around a village green on a hill. Sadly, its medieval forest chapel was spoilt by Victorian restorers. Even so, although on the edge of Surrey, it has been saved from the neighbouring county's cloying cosiness. Sussex is still Sussex here, right up to the border.

IV
The Downs

The Downs are the heart of Sussex. The sea is merely part of the frame, the Weald mere background. As Hilaire Belloc said, 'Sussex is Sussex on account of the South Downs'.

They rose from under the sea, where their chalk was formed, a species of limestone composed of myriads of tiny shells which once housed minute marine creatures. Then they were carved by long vanished streams in an age when the climate was much wetter. These streams were too weak to reach the sea and disappeared down through the porous chalk, to form underground springs which lie on beds of clay far beneath.

Many writers have paid tribute to the colour and shape of these strange hills, which stretch from the Hampshire border to Beachy Head. Although never more than 800 feet high and usually only 500, often they seem like mountains. The same contours repeated over and over again create an illusion of unending distance, even of being at a high altitude. The views are wonderful; south, over the coastal plain and out to sea, or down on to the four rivers (Adur and Arun, Ouse and Cuckmere) which run through the downland, dividing it into five separate massifs; north, over the Weald and its woods – the woods of Kipling's 'Oak, Ash and Thorn'.

Above all, the Downs are secret, with a quality of ancient mystery. They belong to the dead. The late H. V. Morton – not, I would have thought, a man easily frightened – called them sinister, melancholy hills, 'haunted by dark, far off things', and in the rain 'a land empty of any but the most grotesque and ancient memories'. That great Sussex poet Ted Walker warns that when walking by oneself among their immense solitude 'you move among multitudes; and whether or not you believe in ghosts as such, you would have to be spiritually dead not to have a sense of the men of pre-history who lived and worked here'.

I know what they mean. Occasionally, I take an unmarked path from Itford Hill to Tarring Neville, just out of sight of the Ouse valley, through a thorn-choked combe, sometimes occupied by a solitary sparrow-hawk. Here I am always uncomfortably aware of being watched by unseen eyes. (Near here, on the lower slopes of Itford Hill, a Bronze Age hamlet was found in 1955, a community of perhaps twenty households.) The eerie atmosphere of such places was captured by Edward Thomas, who understood them:

> The Combe was ever dark, ancient and dark.
> Its mouth is stopped with bramble, thorn and briar,
> And no one scrambles over the sliding chalk
> By beech and yew and perishing juniper
> Down the half precipices of its sides, with roots
> And rabbit holes for steps . . .

The South Saxons gave many combes a wide birth, believing them to be the abode of demons, like that at Balcombe – 'The Evil Valley.'

Slopes and hangers as well as combes are thronged with phantoms. There are tumuli all over the downland, burial mounds of princes of forgotten peoples. Morton's fertile imagination saw trotting past the neolithic long barrows 'the ghosts of hairy men grasping stone axes, men driving their little sheep before them over the sweet chalkland'. There are more than a thousand small barrows from the Bronze Age, most of them near prehistoric highways and landmarks of great significance in their time; many once contained bronze weapons and gold jewellery. Then there are the causeway-camps and the Iron Age camps, the flint mines from whence came the warriors' axes and spear heads.

On sunny days, however, the Downs can have a joyful, liberating feel, and are J. H. Massingham's 'wild and inspiriting land, whose gates are a ticket of leave from progress and an introduction to the simpler and darker emotions of our being'. Undeniably, some find them exhilarating in certain moods.

Arthur Beckett, founder of the Society of Sussex Downsmen, could write 'on the Downs I generally carry a light bamboo pole. It is useful in climbing, but I take it for the furtherance of my pleasure in leaping furze bushes, for in the Downs country the moments of ecstasy that provoke such feats are many.' (This comes from a book which is supposedly about the Weald.) 'Throw off your starched dignity, put your cap in your pocket and bound across the brow of the hill and down the declivity into the next' he urges in *The Spirit of the Downs* (1909). 'Often have I in this fashion drawn the stare of the solitary shepherd moving slowly by the side of his browsing sheep.' Photographs of Beckett show a portly gentleman with a very red face.

Whether alarming or liberating, men have always acknow-ledged the loveliness of the downland hills. 'Though I have now travelled the Sussex Downs upwards of thirty years, yet I still investigate that chain of majestic mountains with fresh admiration every year; and I think I see new beauties every time I traverse it' Gilbert White wrote from Ringmer in 1773. 'For my part I think there is somewhat peculiarly sweet and amusing in the shapely figured aspect of chalk hills . . .'

No doubt, there have been one or two dissenters. 'We drove over Alpine mountains, drenched in rain' recalled a shudder-ing Horace Walpole after a visit in 1749. Dr Samuel Johnson positively disliked them. However, Walpole and the doctor form a tiny minority.

The shape of these unending bare hills is not easy to define. Kipling merely hints at it:

> No bosomed woods adorn
> Our blunt, bow-headed, whale-backed Downs
> But gnarled and writhen thorn —
> Bare slopes where chasing shadows skim . . .

John Cowper Powys thought of huge waves solidified into chalk and turf, while Massingham talks of sweeps, bluffs, unencumbered folds and crescents. Yet images of smooth, gracefully rounded hills ignore the hollows, combes, sheep paths and lynchets — terraces once ploughed by the Celts, carefully sited so as to catch the sun. Moreover the western range south of Midhurst is quite heavily wooded compared to the bare eastern range from Steyning to Eastbourne – if, admittedly, the latter is what the Sussex Downs mean to most people.

'They are an indescribable colour, that is not green and is not brown and is not gold, yet is a little of all these' says Esther Meynell. 'It is a colour which very few painters ever succeed in catching' she continues. 'And to express the softness of the Downs painters are too fond of a smudged horizon line – in any but misty weather the line of the Downs against the sky is always delicate and sharp.' Conan Doyle (in *Rodney Stone*) describes them as 'curving away in olive-green folds, with here and there the snow-white rift of a chalk-pit'. Becket prefers 'green-grey'. I myself would include purple, the purple in the deep hollows when they are misted over.

Where the Downs really differ from mountains is in being waterless. There is no such thing as a downland stream. (Unless you accept 'winterbournes' as a regular feature of the landscape, subterranean rivulets which only flow above ground during the very wettest of winters.) Kipling makes the Downs say:

> We have no waters to delight
> Our broad and brookless vales –
> Only the dewpond on the height
> Unfed, that never fails

Dewponds are flat, shallow depressions, carefully dug out of the turf and then lined with clay to stop the water sinking down into the chalk; they are filled partly by rain but mainly by the mist condensing. They are becoming rarer and rarer. Sheep must have been drinking from ponds like this since neolithic times, though they have to be remade by succeeding generations every few years.

All too often there is plenty of drenching mist to fill the dewponds, cold and grey. Sometimes the southern slopes may be basking in sunshine when the northern escarpment is shrouded in impenetrable fog, 'so that to cross the Downs is to go from November to April' Esther Meynell points out. She warns of being lost in sudden mists, of the risk of falling into unfenced combes. This is when the Downs are most like mountains, when the mist is lifted for a moment by a breeze and the curves of some far off slope appear, only to vanish again. Mist can make them feel very hostile indeed. Even the euphoric Beckett admits that 'in walking the Sussex Downs from end to end the pedestrian is at once struck by a sense of loneliness' – he had been caught by the mist. I have found myself in it at night, when all the old gods seemed to be out on the hill, thankful when the summer sun chased it away at five o'clock in the morning.

Then, in the dawn, one is aware that downland has its own music – that of larks singing, whose highest notes can sometimes be heard three miles away. W. H. Hudson describes it best:

> The song of the lark is a continuous torrent of contrasted guttural and clear shrill sounds and trills, so rapidly emitted that the notes, so different in character, yet seem to interpenetrate or overlap each other; and the effect on the ear is similar to that on the eye of sober or dull and brilliant colours mixed and running into one another in a confused pattern. The acutest note of all, a clear piercing sound like a cry several times repeated, is like a chance patch of most brilliant colour occuring at intervals in the pattern. . .
>
> Let the reader, then, who has not been on these downs in summer in a brightest, windless day, and listened to this sound – alone, since a companion's talk or even his silent presence would in most cases mar the effect – let him imagine if he can the effect of a great number of birds all round the sky pouring out their highest, shrillest notes, so clarified and brightened by distance as to seem like no earthly music.

It is often said that ploughing has altered the Downs beyond recognition but this is not true. Swathes of corn revert to pasture and at least a handful of sheep return. No doubt sheep farming has declined while much of the age old turf has been ripped away and scrub covers large areas. Yet the bones of the landscape remain.

Admittedly no one will ever again know the Downs so well as the shepherds, the real downsmen. Some people must remember working with them. Their life was beautifully described between the Wars, just in time, by Barclay Wills. He quotes a local poet:

> Alone he bides, a tall old man and lean
> With knotty hands, clasping his hazel crook.
> The old blue cloak, patched, worn and weather stained,
> Hangs to his leather leggings; at his feet
> His two dogs lie, and down the hill below
> In a long sickle line, the feeding sheep . . .

A little earlier, in the 1880s, Richard Jeffries had seen such a man, in a blue smock frock with a brown umbrella. The long blue cloaks came in after the Peninsular War, ex-army issue, while their huge umbrellas were generally green, fading to blue with age. Sometimes they wore long white overcoats, a Lewes speciality, while their broad brimmed hats were known as 'chummies'. 'One old shepherd, ancient of the ancients, grey and bent, has spent so many years among his sheep that he has lost all notice and observation' was among those whom Jefferies watched at a South Down fair – 'there is no "speculation in his eye" for anything but his sheep.'

Their dogs were collies, or else cross-breds with a very decided dash of collie. Earlier sheepdogs had been shaggier and darker. Apart from the weather, the shepherds' greatest enemies were foxes. These killed young lambs – they still do – eating the head first and then burying the carcase for the next meal.

It was a lonely life. As many as ten days and nights had to be spent on the hill at lambing-time, which in Sussex can be a colder season than in more northerly counties since it comes in February – the ewes lamb down earlier here because the dawn light returns sooner. It was also a life of real hardship. Generally the shepherd's sole shelter was a shallow hole dug into a bank, covered outside with furze bushes and lined with dried fern or straw. Very occasionally the farmer might build him a tiny one room cott with a fireplace (a handful survive in remote hollows) while latterly he sometimes provided a small wheeled shed of corrugated iron. Miserable wages were supplemented by taking gulls' eggs from the cliffs in spring, by trapping wheatears in the summer and moles in the winter, and by discreetly poaching the odd rabbit or hare. About 1900 Arthur Beckett met an octagenarian Sussex shepherd who informed him that he had not touched more than six pounds of 'butcher's meat' since his marriage some sixty years before, though he had eaten a good deal of pork since he always kept a pig in his garden. The old man's worst affliction was a rheumatic back, due to frequent drenchings in the rain; he had to have a mouthful of gin every morning just to keep him going, but he made a bottle last for six months.

The 'trade' of shepherding went from father to son and certain family names were associated with it – decent, kindly folk, as appears from their dignified toast:

> If I had store,
> By sheep and fold,
> I'd give you gold.
> But, since I'm poor,
> By crook and bell
> I wish you well

They were sociable when they had the chance, if this was only at sheep shearings, harvest homes and Christmas:

> Here stands our brown jug, and 'tis filled with good ale.
> Our table, our table, our table, shall increase and not fail.

This comes from a sheep-shearing song, often quoted:

> Here the rosebuds in June and the violets are blowing
> The small birds they warble in every green bough
> Here's the pink and the lily, and the daffadowndilly,
> To adorn and perfume the sweet meadows in June.
> 'Tis all before the plough the fat oxen go slow;
> But the lads and the lasses to the sheep-shearing go.

They could be whimsical. One fine old shepherd is said to have made himself an impressive set of dentures out of sheeps' teeth, which he fastened together with wire. He wore them only for going to church on Sundays; although magnificent in appearance, they were of no use for eating.

In 1858 Murray's *Handbook for Travellers in Sussex* declared that 'the South Down shepherds have all but shared the fate of the bustard'. Even so, at the end of the nineteenth century W. H. Hudson was still able to believe that 'The solitary shepherd with his dog at his feet will doubtless stand watching his flock on the hillside for some thousands of years to come'. However, in Hudson's day there were already far fewer sheep than in 1813 when there had been as many as 200,000 over an area about thirty-three miles by six between Eastbourne and Steyning. Gradually they were ceasing to be profitable. The small hornless Southdown produced very fine mutton but changing tastes found it too fat, so that the Southdown began to be replaced by a bigger, leaner, cross-breed. Yet this too failed to make enough money.

Although even today there are downland flocks of up to 3,000 sheep, it has become much too expensive to employ one man to look after a single flock full time. Wire prevents the sheep from scattering or becoming trapped in steep combes. A daily visit by Land-Rover is quite sufficient, except in the lambing season.

The last shepherd worked for Glyndebourne Farm up on Mount Caburn during the 1960s. I wonder if he knew the old sheep counting rhymes, such as that once used at Southease? 'One-the-rum, two-the-rum, cau-the-rum, coo-the-rum, sin-the-rum, san-the-rum, wine-barrel, jig-tarrel, tarrididdle, den.' (There are Celtic echoes here.) Did he carry a 'shepherd's crown'? This was a fossilised sea-urchin which the ancient shepherds had clenched in their fists to ward off lightning during thunderstorms, a custom dating from neolithic times.

The passing of the Sussex shepherds is symbolised by the fate of Pyecombe where their crooks were made. The haft was a hazel rod with the bark left on, the head being a section of old gun barrel, partly hammered flat and then curved. Although very near the London to Brighton road, until very recently this little hamlet – a medieval church, with a farm and a handful of cottages – kept much of its character. But now the road has been widened, exposing Pyecombe to the roar and fumes of unceasing traffic. There could be no more brutal testimony to the end of a way of life which had endured since the Stone Age.

Thankfully, the downland behind Pyecombe remains

surprisingly unspoilt. There are still thousands of sheep on the Sussex Downs and Findon sheep-fair is still held annually at Nepcote, on a green beneath Cissbury Ring.

Not only the shepherds, but the men who worked on the downland farms or on those at the foot of the Downs, led a hard life. 'When I were a young man it were work from fower in the marnin' till sunset, an' naun to eat but a bit o' fat pork fur brakfurst, an' bren-cheese [bread and cheese] fur dinner 'cept it were harvest-time' an old labourer told Beckett. Women and children 'leased' [gleaned] during the harvest, picking up ears of corn. A family might collect as much as eleven bushels, the husband being allowed to thresh it in his master's barn, after which he took it to the mill to be ground into flour; eleven bushels made eleven sacks of flour, baked into bread in the cottage's brick oven. Men let themselves go at harvest suppers. Beckett says they invariably drank themselves into a stupor, those few of their comrades who stayed sober taking them out and laying them in rows on straw, 'like so many pigs that have become pork' until they recovered sufficiently to resume drinking. He comments that love of beer is in the Sussex man's blood.

It is only fair to point out that Sussex countrymen drank such vast quantities of beer because of the way they had to work. 'Beer was regarded as a daily beverage and no one realized more than the old farmers the value of its restorative qualities in the hay or harvest field, and the stone beer jars, lying in the cool shade of the hawthorne hedge at the field's corner, were never allowed to run dry' Bob Copper tells us in *A Song for Every Season*. 'There is nothing in the world that can quench an honest English thirst like honest English beer; when the load of hard, dirty, repetitive work begins to weigh heavily on the shoulders, beer will strike new heart into a man and spur him on to fresh efforts.'

Beckett is more charitable towards the aged:

The faces of the old men are generally mild and patient, weather-beaten and often ruddy. It is pathetic to notice how tired these old men often appear; their watery eyes wear an expression of chronic fatigue, which is evident in their every movement. Fatigue has as much to do with the bend of their bodies as age. But in spite of their many hardships they are a wonderfully cheerful and philosophical race, and the grizzled hair, unkempt beards and knotty limbs may be taken as the outward signs of ruggedness of character.

When this was written in 1909 there was no old age pension. Most old men and women ended in the workhouse, separated from their spouses – one Sussex couple walked hand-in-hand into the village pond and drowned themselves rather than face it.

Contrary to popular opinion, the Downs were ploughed before the Second World War (and not just in Celtic times). During the struggle against Napoleon, Britain was unable to import corn from Europe. The price of bread rocketed in 1809, when there was a very real threat of famine; due to ploughing between then and 1814 some downland near Eastbourne and Jevington still has unusually coarse grass which sheep find unpalatable. 'To this day downland farmers can identify steep slopes unploughed since the Napoleonic Wars' wrote Peter Brandon in 1974.

More and more downland went under the plough throughout the first half of the nineteenth century until corn prices fell. Among those who farmed it was a Quaker, Martin Robinson, who in 1853 came to Saddlescombe, a little hollow in the Downs six miles from Brighton, and whose daughter Maude has left an enchanting account, *A South Downs Farm in the Sixties*. Her father 'saw in the primeval turf a field for enterprise, for it was in the palmy days of corn-growing' she tells us. However, 'Ours was also a sheep farm – "A sheep to an acre" was the old rule:

and on the 900 acres were kept three flocks of 300 sheep each. They were folded on the arable land by night, but all the day long each flock was followed by a shepherd with his shaggy dog and polished crook. In the sixties the shepherds were a race apart. One of ours was named Thomas Shepherd, and another Fred Wooler, as if their ancestors had followed the calling since surnames were invented. So absorbed were they in the welfare of their flocks that when we started sending milk to Brighton the shepherds regarded every crop grown for the cows as infringing the rights of their sheep.

Her father used six ox-teams, six to twelve oxen being harnessed in pairs, each with a birchwood yoke; in the past they had sometimes been harnessed in single file, though only in wet clay country to avoid disturbing the soil too much. Their iron shod hooves pulverised the earth, with a slow, screwing tread. Traditionally, red Sussex bullocks formed the teams, large, bony animals, but towards the end of the nineteenth century a bigger breed, long-horned black Pembrokes, were brought in droves from South Wales and found to be stronger. According to Maude: 'The pairs were chosen as nearly of a size as possible that the heavy wooden yokes might be level, and their names were always one with a single syllable and one with two: "Hawk and Pheasant", "Quick and Nimble", "Crisp and Curly", "Peart and Lively", and if one name was called the two responded.' She had heard the oxman call 'Peart' when the team was lying down in the thick straw in the yard whereupon up would jump Peart and Lively with him, standing side by side to be harnessed.

Each yoke consisted of a heavy oak cross-beam with two bows of green ash to fasten around the pair's neck. Some still hang as ornaments in public houses, as in that fine old hunting pub *The Sussex Ox* at Milton Street near Wilmington. The goad was a hazel wand, tipped with metal, which was invariably 8ft 3in long so that it could be used as a measuring rod when not in use. Shoeing was a difficult business since the animal had to be turned on its back, with its feet fastened to a wooden tripod, for the 'cues' or ox-shoes to be nailed onto its hooves. The team could do work of which horses were incapable, hauling enormous loads such as entire windmills – as at Brighton in 1797 when eighty-six oxen pulled one nearly two miles, from Regency Square to Dyke Road. Dewponds were puddled by driving a team round and round the bottom of a pond after it had been lined with clay, the animals' hooves breaking up the clay. Above all, oxen were cheaper than horses. They needed neither grooming nor expensive harness while they ate rougher food; oat-straw and swedes instead of oats, hay and bran. Broken to harness at about two-and-a-half years old, they were worked until they were seven when they were sent to the fattening stall, finishing up as excellent beef.

In the tenth-century dialogue of Abbot Aelfric, a ploughman tells the abbot how he goes out with his oxen at daybreak and has to plough an acre each day, with only an iron-tipped goad to help him; in addition, the ploughman has to fill their bins with straw, water them and muck out the stalls. Bob Copper, who quotes this in his book, *A Song for Every Season*, says it was precisely the same job as that of an ox-man in 1900. 'So for over a thousand years man and beast had teamed up in exactly the same manner to wrest a living from these acres of downland soil.' In fact, they had been doing it since the Bronze Age. In 1400 there were 466 working oxen on the Earl of Arundel's Sussex manors and only sixty-seven horses.

Steam tractors meant the end of ox-teams. 'Our old ox-man wept when the last team was sent away to the butcher, and he had to turn to horses and other farm work' Maude remembered. Barclay Wills, that lover of ancient Sussex custom, saw what was probably the last team of all working at Exceat in about 1926. The oxen were fitted with nose-nets to stop them grazing when on grass. Wills was told how much stronger they were, and how much cheaper to feed, than horses.

'What would modern young people think of the utterly quiet life on the Downs in winter, shut in by snow or rain, with no neighbours to associate with'? asked Maude Robinson. Yet she describes a contented existence:

The long winter evenings were always made cheerful and happy by our parents. The substantial tea – the last meal – was at six o'clock, and almost all the food was home grown. A grist of wheat was sent to Ballard's white windmill at Patcham and brought back as flour. From this the large loaves were kneaded and baked in a perfect cavern of an oven in the old Tudor end of the house, the large plain cakes in the same way, and we had plenty of jam from the fruitful garden. The butter also was home-made, but not the cheeses which always figured at teatime, sometimes Dutch cheese like a magenta football, for which we children had a special appreciation. The table cleared, two good oil lamps were placed upon it, and we all sat round at our different employments, father with his book and paper and with his tired feet to the blazing fire, and mother with her over-flowing workbasket for eight active country children made abundance of sewing.

Although transport and television have transformed life since then, only a few miles from Brighton or Eastbourne even today a feeling of remoteness remains in some downland hollows where farm-houses have been built to escape from the terrifying wind – as they have since the Bronze Age. During the late 1940s, a family strange to the area moved into an exposed farm up on the Downs and cut down the holm-oak trees which served as a wind-break; they committed suicide as did the two families who followed them.

Maude was a good ornithologist. 'In the sixties the unmistakeable croak of the raven was not infrequently heard' she tells us, adding that in 1885 they were nesting in a small plantation on Wolstonbury Beacon; the reason for their disappearance had been the law that all carcases of dead animals must be buried. 'In the sixties the shepherds were accustomed, after removing the skin, to throw the dead sheep into any hole or copse, to the delight of foxes and disgust of the violet-pickers.' She thought that this was why hooded crows had also vanished, though she had never heard of any nesting on downland. As today, the kestrel was the commonest bird of prey. 'No less than fourteen kestrels have been seen at once, poised in the air over a ridge where the little land lizards, called "Effuts" by the country people are plentiful and a favourite food of these hawks.'

In former times the most typical downland birds had been the great bustard, three foot long (the shepherds' 'wild turkey'), and the wheatear. William Borrer was told by his grandfather, who died in 1844, that he had often hunted bustards with greyhounds:

He used to go out early in the morning, after a foggy night, to look for them feeding in the wet turnips, when they were frequently so thoroughly soaked as to be unable to fly. He generally found them in little parties of five to ten, and sometimes took five or six in a morning, commonly young birds, though occasionally he had known an old one to be caught, but they avoided them as much as possible, as when overtaken by the dogs, they fought savagely and had more than once damaged the greyhounds.

They were most numerous on a part of the Downs between the Dyke and a place known as Thunder's Barrow.

They died out about 1825, though a migrant was shot on downland near Eastbourne as late as 1876. None have been seen this century. Attempts are being made to re-introduce this splendid bird on Salisbury Plain – one hopes for a similar scheme in Sussex.

The beautiful little wheatear is still with us, once Sussex's greatest delicacy. In 1882 Borrer heard of an immense number being trapped in a single day by a shepherd at East Dean near Beachy Head. 'I think they said he took nearly a hundred dozen, so many that they could not thread them on crow-quills in the usual manner, but he took off his frock and made a sack of it to put them into, and his wife did the same with her petticoat.' They were caught with a horsehair noose in a tiny T-shaped burrow dug in the turf, some parts of the Downs being riddled with these traps. Ideally they were wrapped in vine leaves (if available) or else baked in a pie, and eaten in Sussex, since they went bad too soon to reach London tables. Wheatear trapping was forbidden by the Bird Protection Act of 1897.

While Arthur Beckett considered the wheatear, with its lovely grey and white feathers and black wings, to be *the* 'Bird of Downland', he included 'among birds proper to the Down Country' the yellow hammer, the dartford warbler and the stonechat. I have never even seen a dartford warbler while sadly I notice a decline in the number of stonechats. Beckett thought the skylark so plentiful as to be beneath notice yet it is the bird walkers remember best because of its persistent song, which to me is inseparable from grassy slopes and fresh, keen winds.

'Butterflies abounded', Maude Robinson recalls. 'Strong-winged Fritillaries rushing by, Chalk Hill Blues, often mistaken for harebells, as they perch on slender grass stalks, dainty Small Coppers and Burnet moths, metallic green with scarlet spots . . .' She might have added marble whites and adonis blues, together with red admirals, painted ladies and peacocks. In April 1988 I saw a Camberwell beauty on Itford

Hill, chocolate wings bordered with cream and blue, but then learnt that a man in Brighton had been buying imported pupae and releasing the butterflies when they hatched. A friend of mine has recently seen the little Duke of Burgundy fritillary on downland.

As for downland flowers, the round-headed rampion, with as many as forty tiny blue flowers in a single head, is known down here as 'The Pride of Sussex'. Then there is viper's bugloss; one can well understand why adders are supposed to enjoy basking beneath this tall and handsome plant. However, the county's real glory are wild orchids – not just the early purple, spotted, pyramidal, bee or dwarf, but the lizard, spider, frog, tway-blade, musk and tress. Too often their sites are destroyed by ploughing, though it is amazing how they will reappear years later. Alas, fewer sheep to crop turf means that wild thyme is far less universal. Even so, the absence of pesticide on wide areas of downland ensures an almost vulgar profusion of wild flowers in spring, with those carpets of cowslips which are an almost forgotten memory in other parts of England.

'Under the September sun, flowers may still be found in sheltered places, as at the side of furze, on the highest of the Downs' Richard Jefferies tells us in *The Southern Shepherd*. 'Wild thyme continues to bloom – the shepherd's thyme – wild mignonette, blue scabious, white dropwort, yellow bedstraw, and the large purple blooms of greater knapweed. Here and there a blue field gentian is still in flower; "eggs and bacon" grow beside the wagon tracks.'

The downland tree *par excellence* is the beech, which makes up most of the hangers on the lower slopes. Juniper too abounds in the combes – much sought after for making pokers, juniper pokers being the best for stirring a fire. There are countless thorn trees, a mass of white in spring.

Everyone who roams the Downs is fond of certain corners in particular. One of mine is the lost hamlet of Balsdean, on the very edge of Brighton yet so hidden in a hollow that I can think myself back in the days before the South Saxons. Not far from Rottingdean, unapproachable by road, it is near Bullock Hill and lies beneath the spur known as the Bostle. Sheltered from the harsh downland winds, it may have begun as a Bronze Age settlement and was undoubtedly an Anglo-Saxon hamlet, a site which has not yet been excavated – except by badgers. As late as 1579, the vicar of Rottingdean would walk or ride up here to take a service, and the nave of a little Norman chapel survived until the beginning of this century although it had sunk to being used as a cowshed. Until quite recently I could make out the path which led to Lewes, now obliterated by ploughing.

William Borrer, the grand old man of Sussex ornithology, records how in 1845 he bought the corpse of a greenland falcon, most majestic of all birds of prey, which had been shot near here. Peregrine falcons may sometimes be seen flying over the surrounding hills; during the last few years they have returned to Sussex, terrorising pigeons and skylarks, and nesting at a site whose whereabouts are a jealously guarded secret.

My favourite vantage point is the magical Itford Hill, from where I watch the cross-Channel ferry coming into Newhaven harbour or look down onto the Ouse Valley, to see the river below twisting between the hills. Once I spotted a hen-harrier up here, a rare bird of passage in Sussex – during his long life old Borrer saw one only three times.

In the 'thirties J. H. Massingham wrote a haunting description of tramping from Alfriston along the ridgeway to Firle Beacon:

> As I walked the grey clouds parted and instantly the long ridge parallel to Firle's and arching the valley from Wilmington to the sea, the scalloped cliff-line that at last broke off the long smooth journey of the downs from the west, and the flying green butresses resting their bases on Cuckmere Vale, became dappled in a series of luminous browns, swept with the violet of the shadows passing them . . .

He calls it a sight of which 'the resurrected dead in the barrows, watching through forty centuries, could never tire.'

Nowadays there are always other people walking on the Alfriston to Firle ridgeway, though it is worth trying very early in the morning, or in foul weather beneath the beating rain.

When I want real loneliness, however, I know that I must keep off the South Downs Way. Yet, if I look hard enough, without too much trouble I can still be sure of finding that ancient solitude known by the shepherds.

V

Arundel and the Rape of Arundel

A first astonished glance from the train will make you think that you are in France. There, in profile, a great Gothic castle and cathedral crouch over a beautiful little town standing in a flat, marshy plain. From a distance they look superb, and have been called with justice one of the great town views in England. The view is even better from the south-east, looking over the Arun and across the marshes from the Black Rabbit Inn at South Stoke – from where Turner painted the castle battlements. However, close to, Arundel is disappointing. The castle was rebuilt during the nineteenth century (in what Nairn calls 'unfeeling Windsor castle style') while the cathedral dates from the 1870s and is an unexciting pastiche. The town itself is marred by ugly new flats.

Guarding the Arun gap through the Downs, the hill here was a natural centre for a rape. King William gave it to Roger de Montgomery, together with the rape of Chichester, making him lord of eighty-four manors. Earl Roger built a castle around which a town and a port grew up. In 1240 it was acquired by the Fitzalans, who became Earls of Arundel. When they died out in the male line in 1580, Arundel was inherited by Philip Howard, Earl of Surrey, son of the Duke of Norfolk and of the Fitzalan heiress, and a Catholic martyr who has been canonised. The Howards suffered for their faith but recovered their dukedom at the Restoration. (Not all Dukes of Norfolk were Roman Catholics, though they have been so since 1851.)

Badly damaged during the seige of 1644, the castle was 'slighted' in 1649 – blown up with gunpowder. Left roofless for more than a century, it was partially restored about 1718. The old Norman keep on the motte remained a ruin and was used as an aviary for owls; a white owl seen fluttering at a window was taken for a warning that someone in the Fitzalan-Howard family was going to die. (All over Sussex a 'screech-owl' was commonly regarded as a messenger of evil.) There was more rebuilding at the end of the eighteenth century in the 'Gothic' style, though most of this has been pulled down.

The castle in its present form, and the cathedral, are the creation of Henry, fifteenth Duke of Norfolk, who succeeded in 1860 when he was thirteen. He inherited staggering wealth, with estates all over England, together with ground rents in London and Sheffield. When he died in 1917, according to his biographer he 'already seems to be of another race, another civilisation'. His way of life combined spendour with simplicity. Dinner was announced by trumpets and a steward with a wand, walking backwards, preceded him into the dining room as he went in with his guests – sometimes to dine on swan. Yet his beard was unkempt and his clothes so shabby that a lady arriving at Arundel Station mistook him for a porter and gave him her case to carry. 'Here, my man, is a penny for you' she said when he had brought it to her cab. 'The first I ever earned' he answered. He was buried as 'The late Most High, Mighty and Most Noble Prince'. (His son was styled in the same way at his own funeral in 1975.)

Duke Henry took great pride in his ancestors. The first duke died at Bosworth Field, fighting for Richard III. His son, the Earl of Surrey, routed the flower of Scotland at Flodden while another Earl of Surrey wrote the first English sonnet. The first Earl of Arundel and Surrey died for his religion in 1595, as a result of years of imprisonment in a dungeon at the Tower of London that was so foul smelling that gaolers were reluctant to enter it. 'Wonderful it is how much he lost, and with what quietness of mind he endured all adversities' a contemporary Jesuit wrote of St Philip Howard.

The castle is both medieval fortress and Victorian country house. From the former there remain a Norman keep and gatehouse and a thirteenth-century barbican. During the Regency, the Tudor long gallery was turned into one of the most beautiful libraries in England. Almost everything else is from Duke Henry's time. Work on Arundel Castle continued for thirty years. The architect, Charles Alban Butler, has few admirers yet some of the rooms are magnificent, such as the chapel, the dining room and the soaring Baron's Hall.

The architect of the cathedral was also the inventor of the cab, J. A. Hansom. It is unexciting, to put it mildly, save for a striking altar to Philip Howard which is adorned by his coat-of-arms. Every June a floral carpet transforms it on the feast of Corpus Christi, when the floor is decorated with a myriad flowers in many patterns – a tradition imported from southern Italy by Duke Henry. After Mass, escorted by black-robed Knights of Malta (who often include the present Duke), the bishop processes through the streets amid clouds of incense, so that Arundel takes on a Mediterranean tinge. This is the worship of Persephone, not of Woden.

The best building in Arundel is the collegiate church of St Nicholas, which dates from about 1380, adjoining the ruins of the 'college' where its priests lived until the Reformation. A glass wall divides the chancel from the nave, replacing the brick wall built by Duke Henry after the vicar disputed control of this Catholic area of the church. Here are the tombs of the Howards and the Fitzalans.

As premier dukes of England, the Howards are well known. The Fitzalans have been forgotten. They descended from Alan who fought at Hastings and were the greatest magnates in Sussex. Earl Richard (nicknamed 'Copped Hat') fought at Crécy. His son was beheaded for plotting to murder Richard II while another earl died at the siege of Harfleur. Earl John, called 'The English Achilles', was mortally wounded at Beauvais in 1435 and refused medical aid from chagrin at his defeat. (An armoured effigy lies on top of his tomb, a shrouded skeleton beneath.) When another peasants' revolt threatened Sussex in 1549, the last Fitzalan earl was able to prevent it without using force, because the smallholders had such respect for him.

Apart from the church of St Nicholas, the other outstanding building (so far as I am concerned) is that fine old hostelry, the Norfolk Arms, a cheerful red-brick building from the late eighteenth century. Maltravers Street and Tarrant Street are pretty enough, with some nice Georgian houses, but the town is beginning to combine the suburban with the feudal. Once Arundel was a port where smugglers fought with excisemen on wharves; until the Edwardian era ships as big as 400 tons sailed up the Arun from Littlehampton – some were still being built here. Nowadays the principal traffic is tourist buses. Constable's verdict stands. 'The Castle is the cheifest [sic] ornament of this place – but all here sinks into insignificance with the woods and hills' he commented in 1836. On the day he died, 31 March 1887, he was working on his last, never to be completed picture, a view of *Arundel Mill and Castle*.

Going back to the flat coastal plain is, for me at any rate, always disappointing. The landscape lacks the beauty of Downs and Weald, though some find it pleasing enough. However, at Yapton in the south west of the rape, one is consoled by finding a shining example of that handful of Sussex churches which escaped 'restoration' during the nineteenth century. It dates from the end of the twelfth, boasting a tie-beam roof with kingposts over the nave and aisles whose external walls are only five feet high. There is a wonderful font of black marble, reminiscent of a Roman well-head. The village is largely spoilt though there are some good cottages. But Yapton is worth visiting for its church alone.

At Poling, further east, the hall and chapel of a thirteenth-century commandery of the Knights Hospitaller (later called Knights of Malta) survive as part of an elegant little Georgian house, Fairplace Farm. It is known that in 1338 the commandery contained two knights (one being the commander, Peter atte Nasshe), a chaplain, two clerks – one of whom lived out – and four officials and servants. Their job was to administer their order's lands at Poling, Easebourne, Midhurst, Up Marden, Islesham and Rumboldswyke, with others at Shipley and Compton which had recently been acquired from the Templars. Part of the revenues went towards the house's upkeep but the bulk were sent out to the

Holy Land, then to Rhodes and finally to Malta. It continued until 1540, the Knights being the last religious order to be dissolved by Henry VIII. Externally, the farm preserves the commandery's outline most convincingly. Indeed, some people claim to have heard the sound of ghostly chanting here while others think they have seen phantom knights who haunt the surrounding fields.

Castle Goring, near Goring in the south-east corner of Arundel Rape, was built by Biagio Rebecca about 1790 for the poet Shelley's grandfather, Sir Percy Bysshe Shelley. It is among the very oddest houses in all England, perhaps in all Europe. The north front, in flint and stone, is eighteenth-century Gothic in style, partly castellated and with several of its windows in the 'Perpendicular' style. But on going round to the back, a startled visitor is confronted by a house in white stone and white brick which is half Palladian, half Neo-Classical. The overall impression is of a majestic practical joke although that was surely not the intention of the architect or his patron.

Returning inland towards Arundel, Burpham is well worth a detour, along a beautiful road which leads nowhere. Lucas thought it the quietest village within a few miles of London. 'It must be enchanted, for apparently it has not changed for centuries', wrote Esther Meynell in the 1940s. 'It might still be living in the seventeenth century, even, in some respect, in an earlier century'. Sadly, Burpham is no longer quite like that, having since become much too tidy and gentrified, yet even so it still keeps plenty of charm, together with its superb views of the Arun, Arundel and the Downs. Few realise that Burpham was the predecessor of Arundel, a Saxon *burh* with its own mint which was abandoned at the Norman Conquest. Its earthworks survive, and give some idea of the exact size of a *burh*; during the 1970s archaeologists uncovered a whole range of Saxon buildings inside them.

Amberley Castle has been described as a fortified manor house, but it is far more of a fortress than Arundel. In 1377 Bishop Rede of Chichester, fearing that French pirates might sail up the Arun, surrounded his favourite country mansion by a curtain wall (partly destroyed) with towers and a gatehouse; a moat and the adjoining marsh gave added protection. Although never besieged, it was sacked by Roundheads to punish a notorious Cavalier who lived there, John Goring – later in trouble for having 'drunk a toaste to Prince Charles and the confusion of Parliament'.

Lucas said that Amberley was 'sheer Sussex', while Esther Meynell spoke of its 'sturdy and simple charm'. There was a side to life here of which they may have been ignorant. A booklet which I bought at the church, *Dear Amberley*, gives details of inquests held in 1872–75 at the Houghton Bridge Inn, a nearby public house:

> In September 1872, Elizabeth Merritt 'whilst in the act of tightening her stays' dropped dead in her bedroom at Houghton Bridge. In the following December, George Gearing went wassailing and had two quarts of beer at the Cricketers. Three of them then drank a pint of elderberry wine, and returned to 'Mr Ratley's shop' where they had half a pint of wine each. Gearing then set off for home for Watersfield along the railway line. Later 'blood and material' were found on a train driven by Job Luxford at Ford. A plate-layer, Leggat, at 6.45 am, found 'first a walking stick, 5 or 6 yards later a boot with a foot in it, 15 yards on the body of the deceased whom he knew, and 30 yards on, the other leg.' The verdict at the Bridge Inn was 'accidentally run over by a train having fallen asleep across the line whilst in liquor'.

Only a few years later, the landlord of the Bridge Inn was fined for adulterating his whisky; he may have done so out of concern for his patrons – more than one native of Amberley drowned in the river when drunk. The endearing defence of an intoxicated local lady Anne Fossey, who had put up a fierce fight after being arrested in 1888, was 'I am very passionate'.

Amberley Wild Brooks in the Arun valley, under the Downs, are water-meadows – Sussex 'levels'. Embanked, these flood in winter but are drained in summer by deep dykes and can be grazed. A nature reserve, in part they are owned by the Sussex Trust which in 1977 fought off an attempt to drain them permanently by the then Southern Water Authority. During winter they are host to all kind of wildfowl, especially duck – mallard, pintail, teal, pochard, shoveller and widgeon – as well as a flock of Bewick's swans. In summer, redshank breed here while you find such uncommon plants as frogbit, water pepper, marsh horsetail, water parsnip, arrow head and adder's tongue fern. Also the yellow water lily or 'brandy bottle', so named from its oddly shaped seed-pod.

Virginia Woolf called Amberley 'an astonishing, forgotten, lovely place between water meadows and downs'. If scarcely forgotten today, it remains surprisingly unspoilt.

At first sight, Pulborough is disappointing, despite being beside the Arun, but climbing a hill you are suddenly among old houses, all faded pink brick and cream coloured Sussex stone. They are grouped around a Perpendicular church, built in the years after Agincourt, on the site of a Roman villa.

Stopham Bridge, rebuilt in 1423, is the finest medieval bridge in Sussex, though its setting is marred by the ugly modern bridge nearby which takes the traffic. This is beautiful country, lush slopes alternating with water-meadows. The Barttelot family came to Sussex with the Conqueror and have been at Stopham for a very long time indeed; the Norman church here is interesting mainly because of their monuments. The floor of the nave is carpeted in brasses, one of which commemorates John Barttelot who fought at Agincourt. The family have a long military tradition: every squire of Stopham since the Peninsular War has been a regular officer; a Barttelot was killed in the Boer War (at the head of the Petworth Volunteers), another during the Great War and a third in Normandy in 1944, while the present baronet was Colonel of the Foot Guards.

The little church at Hardham, just a nave and a chancel, dates from about 1100 and is one of the best things in the county because of its contemporary wall-paintings. White-washed at the Reformation, these were uncovered in 1866. The work of monks from Lewes Priory, they may have been inspired by some Saxon miniatures in a pre-Conquest manuscript of the poems of Caedmon. Nearly the whole scheme, two tiers on each wall, remains intact save for where windows have been inserted. A 'bacon and egg' palate of red and yellow ochre, lime white and carbon black, together with an unusual blue green was used as the artists were limited to pigments from the neighbourhood. (The green is copper carbonate, probably made from malachite.) Although faded, these pictures of scenes from the story of Adam and Eve, the life of Christ, and the Labours of the Months, are still very beautiful. There are similar paintings by Lewes monks at Coombes, Clayton and Plumpton, but these are the finest.

Near Hardham church, in an adjoining field, lies a Roman posting station beside Stane Street; three ripple patterned flue-tiles from it are in the church's external walls, in the north-western corner.

The refectory of Hardham Priory, half a mile away, was converted into a handsome farmhouse. The shell of its chapter house stands next to it, with three delicate, pointed arches dating from about 1250 when the priory was founded by Augustinian canons. The house is blessedly unrestored while the site has never been excavated. If only a fragment, this is an unusually attractive survivor from monastic Sussex, redolent of Tennyson's 'Old summers when the monk was fat'. The canons must have led a pleasant existence here among their water-meadows. They had well filled fish-ponds; at a stock-taking during the fourteenth century 2000 pickerell (perch), 3000 roach and 4000 eels were counted. In 1527 there were only four brethren. Two years later, their prior was found guilty of poaching Lord Arundel's deer.

I have a bad blind spot when it come to Roman remains. At the age of eleven, I was forced by my father to read the works of Livy in translation, which induced life long boredom with the Classical past. Yet very occasionally its associations stir my sluggish imagination, as they do at Bignor:

> Then, 'twas before my time, the Roman
> At yonder heaving hill would stare:
> The blood that warms an English yeoman,
> The thoughts that hurt him, they were there

Houseman was writing of Shropshire, but in Sussex, Bignor Hill and what lies below it have precisely the same effect on me.

You go to Bignor from Hardham through leafy lanes to flat farmland beneath the Downs. Here, under sheds which look like farm buildings, are what in my opinion are the most eloquent Roman remains in all Britain, far more inspiring than the palace at Fishbourne. It is a great Roman villa with two courtyards covering four acres, owned and displayed by the descendants of the farmer who found it in 1811 when ploughing with his oxen. It reached its zenith during the fourth century when it was self-sufficient, with its own forges and a kiln for tiles. There were over sixty rooms, including slave quarters. The soil here is very good, capable of growing large crops and, since it was only a few hundred yards from Stane Street, the corn could easily be taken to Noviomagus for export. Obviously its owners lived in luxury, to judge from the hypocaust which provided their central heating, the luxurious baths (one can see the steps down which they walked for their cold plunge), the fountains, and the costly mosaics. The tesserae, tiny cubes of stone or glass which make up the mosaics, are delicately coloured; tawny red, buff yellow, cream, slate blue and olive green. There are vivid scenes of gladiators, a dolphin, a Medusa, a Ganymede being carried off by a fierce eagle, and a strangely mournful Venus.

There is also a brooding Winter who haunts me. She is portrayed as a hooded woman, with the bare branch of a tree behind her head. If the owners came from the Mediterranean, they must have dreaded winters here and their exposed existence at the foot of the Downs. Bignor Hill is still worked, as it probably was in Roman times, and the wind in its trees can be bitterly cold.

E. V. Lucas was convinced that this was 'the residence of a Roman Colonial governor of immense wealth, probably supreme in command of the province'. It is much more likely that ordinary landowners or their bailiffs lived here, men who were expert farmers, a group of related families rather than a single magnate. The villa was abandoned before the end of the fourth century. Perhaps its owners were murdered by Saxon raiders or mutinous slaves, or fled to Noviomagus. Until the day they died, any survivors must have remembered those mosaics – especially 'Winter'.

Ever since it was sketched by Constable, Fittleworth has

attracted visitors. 'The woods hang from excessive steeps, and precipices, and trees are beyond everything beautifull [sic]' he wrote. 'I never saw such beauty in *natural landscape* before.' A big straggling village, it has a tall, mysterious water mill and two fine medieval bridges over the Arun.

The Swan Inn, one of the pleasantest in Sussex, dates from Tudor times. Lucas says that in his day artists were as much charmed by a warm welcome as by its views – 'one of those inns in which one stumbles down into every room, and where eggs and bacon have an appropriateness that makes them a more desirable food than ambrosia'. The hotel register contains a note by Rudyard Kipling boasting how in 1902 he has just motored thirty miles in a mere three hours. The old gibbet-like inn sign straddling the road was taken down in 1963 – it showed not only a swan but a naked Leda, who was draped with a cloth when it was learnt that Queen Victoria might drive past.

During the last century the wife of the Fittleworth rector, Mrs Latham, wrote down 'scraps of homely conversation', later published as *Some West Sussex Superstitions lingering in 1868*. This little book is among the most important sources for the county's folklore and magic. After a fine chapter on 'Ghosts, Goblins, Witches and Fairies', it tells of disgusting charms used as 'cures' – a live spider wrapped in butter for jaundice or a paw cut from a living mole for toothache. Nine mice roasted to a cinder and powdered were drunk in a glass of ale to combat debility, while 'a slice of the liver of the dog that bit you, to be boiled and eaten' was the remedy for hydrophobia. A goitre was healed by stroking it with the hand of a man who had been hanged. All the local witches believed firmly in the effectiveness of their charms.

Fittleworth's greatest claim to fame is a cottage in the woods called Brinkwells, where Edward Elgar came in May 1917 to escape from depression brought on by the Great War. His wife Alice found it, telling a friend: 'I am in the garden & before my eyes lies a wonderful deep wood & low hills beyond & then the Downs, larks are singing as there are some fields as well, & a nightingale is heard sometimes, & in the evening the nightjars go whirring around on the fringe of the wood.'

Elgar himself was no less enthusiastic, reporting 'It is divine: simple thatched cottage & a soiled studio with wonderful view: large garden *unweeded*, a task for 40 men.' Two years here worked miracles for his health and his music. Here he wrote both his great cello concerto and his piano quintet; the latter's weird, unearthly beginning was inspired by some blasted trees on a plateau just above the house, popularly believed to be a band of Spanish monks who had been struck dead for practising black magic. Brinkwells is still unspoilt, mercifully unmodernised, in the same lonely wealden setting which the Elgars knew, carpeted in spring with primroses, bluebells and wood anemones – Sir Edward's beloved 'wind-flowers'.

You should make a detour to see the church in Burton Park, one of the few in Sussex to have escaped the dead hand of Victorian restoration. A Tudor (but pre-Reformation) painting next to the north window depicts a red bearded lady standing on her head. This is St Wilgefortis, a noble Portuguese virgin who, having taken a vow of chastity, avoided marriage to the King of Sicily by growing a beard and moustache – so infuriating her father that he had her crucified upside down. She asked God that all who remembered her martydom should be delivered from any encumbrances, and became known as 'St Uncumber'; women anxious to be rid of their husbands prayed at her shrine, offering a pinch of oats on her feast-day (20 July). There is also a wall-painting of the arms of King Charles I dated 1636, which somehow escaped the Roundheads' attentions – it bears the injunction 'Obey them that have the rule over you'.

I myself think that Petworth is the prettiest town in the entire county. Its little streets are full of charming houses, Tudor and Georgian. But everything is overshadowed by THE house, the greatest and most beautiful mansion in Sussex. [see ch. XIV.]

Coates in the wealden heathland south of Petworth has a Norman church remarkable for an east window of just two simple lancets. There is a small wooden belfry, typical of

Sussex, perched over the back of the nave and a magnificent cedar of Lebanon in the churchyard. Inside, there is a monument to the first Duchess of Abercorn (Louisa Jane Russell) who died in 1905 after being photographed with a hundred of her children, grandchildren, great-grandchildren and great-great-grandchildren. Near the church stands one of the loveliest manor houses in Sussex, small and seventeenth-century – all cream stone, heavy Horsham tiles and mullioned windows.

Wisborough Green is set in the rolling Weald, among meadows bordered by shaws (strips of woodland) instead of hedges. It lives up to its name, with what must be the finest and best kept village green in the country. Once its church owned relics of the Apostles and a cross containing 'Milk of the Virgin'. (Earth from the grotto at Bethlehem which turns white on exposure to the sun.) There is a well preserved fragment of thirteenth-century wall-painting, with a crucifix and the Apostle James. The altar-stone here is said to be made out of one of a circle of pagan standing stones, a miniature Stonehenge, which stood on the site of the church.

The road between Wisborough Green and Billingshurst crosses the River Arun and the Arun Canal which runs beside it, narrow, sluggish streams with overgrown banks. Once it was busy and bustling here. 'At this [crossing] there are large *timber* and *coal* yards, and kilns for *lime*' William Cobbett recorded in 1823. 'This appears to be a grand receiving and distributing place.' Although the canal has been cleaned up, and there is what may have been a warehouse, the site is deserted.

Not far away is the Blue Idol at Coolham, a sixteenth-century black and white farmhouse. In 1691 the eastern end became a Meeting House for the Quakers who had been meeting at Coolham for the last ten years; it has a gallery, a fireplace and a stand for the preachers. William Penn, the founder of Pennsylvania, had been among the latter. It must have been lonely in the woods. 'The *Country* Life is to be preferr'd; for there we see the Works of *God*', wrote Penn in *Some Fruits of Solitude*.

Persecution had inclined Penn to solitude. A Chichester court record calls him 'a factious and seditious person'. Disliked as trouble makers who refused to pay their tithes and heckled the parson, these early Quakers had not yet acquired their reputation for benevolence. The Friends had been active in Sussex since 1655, led by their founder George Fox, whom a contemporary described as 'a man that God endued with a clear and wonderful depth, a discerner of others' spirits, and very much a master of his own'. In the 1680s there were a dozen meeting houses in the county, but only five families attended the Blue Idol a hundred years later; from 1786 until 1869 it was disused – 'idle' – and painted blue. Hence its name.

Although its outskirts have been 'developed', Kirdford retains many graceful little houses. It has a good church with a fine, solid, fifteenth-century tower and, in a window, some fragments of medieval glass from local furnaces – dark ruby red, rose, pale green, and peacock blue. For, from the fourteenth century to the sixteenth when it was ousted by iron, this was a centre of the Sussex glass industry. The greensand country had all the right ingredients: charcoal for furnaces, bracken for potash, and fine quality sand. The glass-houses were sited on top of wealden hills, using every gust of wind. Not only stained glass was made, but bottles, bowls, goblets and 'urynalls'.

Kirdford has had its tragedies. It was the home of the wretched Elizabethan witch, Margaret Cooper; the gossip in the village before her trial must have been terrifying, neighbours being scared out of their wits. A famous slab in the churchyard commemorates three fatal accidents in 1838, all within seven weeks; six boys suffocated by burning green wood in a windowless room, a man killed in a fall from his horse, and a boy crushed by a farm cart. Less harrowing is a quaint warning against the Demon Drink, which 'turns the body into an hospital', inscribed on a stone set in a wall opposite the church. Ironically, it was erected by an alcoholic vicar.

Lurgashall among the woods of the High Weald is yet another Sussex village which is almost too pretty, with a beautiful, triangular green. The church here, which once belonged to Lewes Priory, is tall and narrow with a Saxon arch; fragments of a mural on the south wall include the arms of Lewes Priory painted by the monks. A delightful wooden cloister was built on to the south wall during the sixteenth century, apparently as a meeting place for parishioners after Mass, though it later became the village school.

Some of the houses in these northern parts use black Burgate stone from Surrey, in contrast to the creamy stone of West Sussex. Most are occupied by commuters or week-enders. Very occasionally one sees a labourer's cottage with the labourer still living in it, and therefore badly maintained. Stockbrokers (and sometimes underwriters too) can at least afford to paint them. 'God bless the sensitive stockbrokers of West Sussex' wrote Ian Nairn appreciatively.

Not far from Lurgashall, further up among the trees and almost in Surrey, is Blackdown, a hill 900 feet above sea level. Here is Lord Tennyson's beloved but unlovely retreat, Aldworth House, which he had built in 1869 on a site formerly called Black Horse Copse – Nairn dismisses it as 'a fussy small hotel'. A shaggy man who smoked a rank pipe all day long and drank a bottle of port *with* his dinner – sometimes a bottle and a half, not to mention sherry and champagne – the poet was not noted for cleanliness, but he was so pleased with the new house's running hot water that at first he bathed five times a day. He immortalised the view from Blackdown over the Weald with:

> Green Sussex fading into blue
> With one gray glimpse of sea.

The 'gray glimpse' was Pevensey Bay. He died at Aldworth in October 1882. 'Lord Tennyson', the old vicar of Lurgashall told his corpse, 'God has taken you, who made you a Prince of men'.

VI
The Weald

For all Belloc's pessimism about the future, anything he wrote on Sussex is worth reading. He conveys the essence of the Weald, something which often eludes lovers of the Downs. 'A man with leisure desiring to understand what is left of the ancient kingdom now in peril of death had best wander inland for a fortnight, taking no direction but exploring from village to village, avoiding towns and sampling the whole Weald from the Hampshire border to Kent.' This is good advice, even today:

> The explorer will remember the unbroken woods, the isolated clearings, the primeval tracks, now metalled and now green, the little patches of swamp, the clay pools and the short oaks, the abrupt sandstone ledges crowded with pine, the bare Downs beyond seen between such trees, and the large levels of the four rivers which, between them, make up the county, and explain the history of its soil and of its families, and the peculiar tenacity with which it has so long maintained its soul under all modern vicissitudes.

Travelling northwards up the rapes into the Weald, one sees how much less is the population, villages becoming fewer and small – large areas, one as big as sixteen miles by ten, have only hamlets and farms. Settlement has always been concentrated on the coast, apart from such modern conurbations as Haywards Heath or Gatwick-Crawley. These seemingly interminable blocks of housing give the impression that central and northern Sussex are entirely built up, which is far from being the case. Many villages have escaped enlargement and absorption, farms and cottages are often surprisingly isolated in woodland areas. However, a good deal of the Weald always had wide tracts of bracken or gorse. Clay and sand, some of it waterlogged though without extensive marshes, this only became worth cultivating when the population expanded. Such forests as Ashdown or St Leonard's have plenty of scrub and heathland. It should not be forgotten that 'forest' meant an area of land, not necessarily wooded, in which forest law applied – orginally their primary function was as game parks to supply the privileged with food.

Even in the Bronze Age, men living at the northern foot of the Downs were beginning to push their way into the Weald, but any land they may have brought under cultivation was abandoned when the Romans left. By the eighth century, a growing Saxon population needed more food and started clearing trees and scrub by burning and axework, then by grazing cattle, sheep, goats and, above all, pigs. Yet in 892 the *Anglo-Saxon Chronicle* could still record that the Weald of Kent, Surrey and Sussex was a forest 120 miles wide [actually 90] and 30 deep, most of it being in Sussex. It held wolves and wild boar and probably bears. Some settlements in the northern Weald were so remote that they were not listed in Domesday Book. However, by the thirteenth century entire new market towns were springing up, the most northerly being Horsham. One can still trace the clearances in fields separated by shaws, or thin belts of woodland, instead of hedges and by small churches which once served pioneer communities.

The Weald had been conquered by the time of the Black Death in 1348. Fewer mouths to feed (the population may have dropped by half) meant that settlement came to an abrupt halt; many villages contracted or were deserted. No new hamlets were begun after that date and few farms, so that large areas of the Weald remain as they were in medieval times. Shaws as much as 30 feet deep contain tall trees which give the landscape a park-like appearance, while fields are small and resemble woodland clearings; in the High Weald, narrow lanes can seem like pathways through a forest. For centuries the timber was carefully tended, especially oak, which was needed for houses, providing shingles as well as beams, and for ships. Thirty-six acres of woodland went into the Tudor warship *Mary Rose*; far more were cut down to build a man o'war of Nelson's time which required not less than 2,000 full grown oak trees.

*

'Coppicing' was cropping a wood regularly by cutting down trees at ground-level. In a well managed wood some were left for future use as timber. From prehistoric times this was a vital part of the economy, changing the woods' appearance yet ensuring continuity. No longer dark and humid but light and open, they were full of bluebells and primroses in the spring. During the eighteenth century, however, landowners began to grub out trees for replacement by arable land, or else let them grow to their full height as stands of timber. Recently there have been signs of a revival in coppicing. Should wood-burning stoves become popular, a need for firewood might well help to preserve the traditional wealden landscape.

Richard Jefferies gives a vivid picture of an ancient wealden industry which even now is not altogether extinct:

The brown charcoal-burner, upright as a bolt, walked slowly round the smouldering heap, and wherever flames seemed inclined to break out cast damp ashes upon the spot. Six or seven waterbutts stood in a row for his use. To windward he had built a fence of flakes, or wattles as they are called here, well worked in with brushwood, to break the force of the draught along the hill-side, which would have caused too fierce a fire. At one side stood his hut of poles meeting in a cone, wrapped round with rough canvas. Besides his rake and shovel and a short ladder, he showed me a tool like an immense gridiron, bent half double, and fitted to a handle in the same way as a spade. This was for shifting charcoal when burned, and separating the small from the larger pieces. Every now and then a puff of smoke rose from the heap and drifted along; it has a peculiar odour, a dense, thick smell of smothered wood coal, to me not disagreeable but to some people so annoying that they have been known to leave their houses and abandon a locality where charcoal burning was practised . . .

The demand for charcoal had largely disappeared with the passing of the wealden iron industry during the eighteenth century. [See Ch. XII, 'Sussex Iron'.] Even so, in Jefferies' day goldsmiths continued to use it for soldering, preferring that made from the thick bark of the butts of birch trees. (At the butt or foot of a birch the bark grows much thicker than the rind higher up, which is thinner than on other trees.) Sheffield Park was the last mansion in Sussex which was still heated entirely by charcoal, though some houses went on warming plates with it. The main demand a hundred years ago seems to have been for hop-drying.

There were other humble industries in the Weald. 'The wood cooper follows his trade in a rude shed, splitting poles and making hoops the year through, in warm summer and iron-clad winter', observed Jefferies. 'His shed is always pitched at the edge of a great woodland district.'

At least a tenth of Sussex is still wooded, mainly by deciduous trees. For centuries the oak was so common that it was called the 'Sussex Weed', but it is much less common since the terrible gale of 16 October 1987 when nearly three million trees perished in the eastern half of the county alone. Oaks, which never bow to storms, suffered most of all, and the old practice of planting an oak for each one felled has long been abandoned. Numberless beeches went down as well, mature beeches being very brittle. Elms have been wiped out by Dutch Elm disease (to the dismay of coffin-makers) while ash has been decimated during hot summers by a malady known as 'dieback'. Large areas of woodland have disappeared beneath housing estates or factories. Even so, Sussex remains the second most heavily wooded county in England.

Besides the great trees, the woods of the Weald contain birch, hazel, yew, wild service, alder and wild cherry. There are hornbeams (whose wood burns like a candle) and the sinister holm-oak, an evergreen whose timber is only fit for firewood; little undergrowth grows beneath its thick foliage which shuts out the sun all year round. Where there are beechwoods there are often whitebeam and the wayfaring tree. Characteristic flowers include bluebells, wood violets, Solomon's seal and orchids – the common orchid, the bird's nest orchid and the white helleborine. The rarer and more glamorous butterflies are silver-washed fritillaries, white admirals and purple emperors.

Among the birds of the wealden woodland are nuthatches, marsh tits, warblers – even an occasional nightingale – lesser spotted woodpeckers and nightjars. Ravens and honey buzzards, which flourished during the last century, have vanished though the common buzzard has made a modest comeback, breeding again in both East and West Sussex. (The local word for a buzzard was a 'puttock'.)

The woods are full of deer, fallow, roe and muntjac – some of the fallow deer are dark skinned, without spots. Once there were pine martens, the last recorded being killed by foxhounds near Holmbush during the 1860s. Red squirrels had died out by 1955.

There are four main regions – the north-west, the forest ridge, the south-east and the low clay plain. The first is a land of pine, birch, gorse, bracken and heath, landscape of a sort one associates more with Surrey. The forest ridge is high country, among the most thickly wooded in the county, full of little streams; an area of small ridges and valleys which can only be explored on foot and where it is easy to lose the way; this, for me, is the classic Weald. The south-east is a more managed landscape, more open, with deep valleys and small meadows, a countryside with many isolated farms. The low clay is the eastern plain, once the marshland of the Andredsweald, but it was reclaimed long ago and it now has many tall trees.

During the Middle Ages there were six great forests: Arundel, Ashdown, Dallington, Waterdown and Worth, all save Arundel having been part of the Andredsweald. There were lesser forests and, after the Norman Conquest, deep parks; sometimes outside the forests, the latter were fenced hunting reserves for deer – many of them were 'disparked' in Elizabethan or Jacobean times and turned into farm land.

Only Ashdown, at the centre of East Sussex, survives in anything like its medieval form. Once it covered 15,000 acres; in Norman times it had 'pannage' (acorns and beechmast) for 7,000 pigs, but by the end of the thirteenth century it could feed less than 3,000 – evidence of deforestation. During Edward III's reign it became a hunting chase of John of Gaunt and was called 'Lancaster Great Park'. Woodland and barren heath alternate in this wilderness of 6,400 acres, the largest in the county, much of it resembling Exmoor. The terrain consists of rolling folds and dips, an extraordinary patchwork of dense woods, moor and arable, full of ancient, unmetalled roads, of hammer ponds and marlpits. 'The most villainously ugly spot I ever saw in England' was Cobbett's opinion of it in 1822, but he disliked any landscape other than good farmland.

In its time, it has been a refuge for smugglers, highwaymen, poachers, rogue gipsies, vagabonds of every species and – more respectably – charcoal burners, who up to the Second World War lived in huts next to their kilns. In earlier times there were smallholders of the very poorest sort, eking out a wretched existence in tumble-down shacks made from turf and branches, dependent on such scanty common rights as windfall timber, bracken and grazing. Some areas disturb and frighten those with sensitive imaginations. Perhaps one should look for the 'Terror Wood' of the South Saxons somewhere within the confines of Ashdown Forest.

St Leonard's Forest, also in central Sussex, once stretched over 9,000 acres at its widest extent. Although much more broken up by parks and gardens, in some parts it can nonetheless feel even lonelier than Ashdown Forest. Among its many alarming legends is that of a headless ghost, Squire Paulett, who jumps up into the saddle behind anyone foolish enough to ride alone through the forest at night. The source of the River Arun is here, a lake of great beauty. With its shaws and its fine stands of timber, this is still very much forest country, despite farms, villas and modern housing.

There is plenty of ghyll woodland here. A 'ghyll' (a Norse word apparently imported from the far North of England in about 1400) is a long, narrow river valley or ravine which has steep sides overgrown by moss and fern, and a fast running stream at the bottom. Sheepwash Ghyll is a particularly attractive example.

St Leonard's has two offshoots to the north, Holmbush Forest and Peasepottage Forest. Although mainly oak and beech, they also contain sweet chestnut. The Forests of Balcombe, Worth and Tilgate to the south are very small but beautiful enough. Beech woods, they suffered badly during the great gale of 1987.

A pleasant feature, especially in East Sussex, is the 'Wealden House' which had developed by the fourteenth century – a hall with rooms on each side which jut out and overhang at first floor level. They are built of oak and chestnut beams with infillings of brick, flint and clunch, crucks forming an arch in the centre. Their windows were unglazed, with shutters to keep out wind and rain, though sometimes these had panes of horn or oiled cloth. Smoke went out through a hole in the roof, not a chimney; often such houses are dated by the discovery of blackened beams in the attic. The most famous examples are Stonehill at Chiddingly, which Nairn considered the 'perfect timber-frame house of the fifteen century', and The Old Shop at Bignor from about the same time – painted by countless Edwardian water-colourists. Many are disguised by the addition of Georgian facades in brick. Probably hundreds more await discovery.

There are also moated houses in the Weald, their moats' function being two-fold: to protect their owners' flocks from thieves, and as fish-ponds – 'stews' for carp, pike and bream. There is a good example at Buncton under Chantonbury Ring, not far from the church. Some moats surrounded several acres, enclosing an entire complex of farm buildings, as at Orfold Farm near Wisborough Green.

Towards the end of the nineteenth century, luxurious villas began to be built in the Weald, a fashion which continued up to 1939. 'Here, till recently, was a wild heath with fine groups of fir trees', Augustus Hare says of Haywards Heath. 'The land has been cut up and sold in small portions . . . and is now a colony of Cockney villas, and the roads both to Lindfield and Cuckfield are lined with lamps'. But even Hare would have been impressed by the mock medieval manor house of Nymans, built for Colonel Messel at Handcross near Cuckfield. Although burnt to the ground in the 1940s, amid their magnificent gardens its ruins are comparable to Cowdray.

*

'Today the Weald is – except for some precious enclaves – commuters' country' wrote Sir Nikolaus Pevsner in 1965. 'Wherever there is a suitable railway station, cars wait during the day in the large parking places for their masters returning at six or seven in their town clothes.' Yet today there are still many places which are unsuited to commuters and surprisingly few cottages to house them. I wonder if Pevsner ever strayed more than a few yards from his own car? I doubt it. Some years later, Peter Brandon explained why the Weald receives so much less attention than the Downs, and why it was impossible for someone such as Pevsner to understand it on a fleeting tour. 'Even now, to make an intimate acquaintance with the Sussex Weald one has to travel on foot by reedy ponds, across damp, rushy fields, fern-covered slopes, extensive woods and along unused footpaths.'

Although Rudyard Kipling is best known for his love of the Downs, he was enchanted by 'the secret Weald' too and had a surprising knowledge of it. His poem 'The Way through the Woods' is one example:

> It is underneath the coppice and heath
> And the thin anemones.
> Only the keeper sees
> That, where the ring-dove broods,
> And the badgers roll at ease,
> There was once a road through the woods

The Weald inspired his 'Tree Song' – 'Sing Oak, and Ash, and Thorn, good sirs' – and much of 'Puck's Song':

> See you the ferny ride that steals
> Into the oak-woods far?
> O that was where they hewed the keels
> That rolled to Trafalgar.

You do not have to look very far to find Kipling's ferny ride or even his road through the woods.

Only by walking the Weald in Brandon's way – which was Belloc's way and no doubt Kipling's way as well – can you ever hope to appreciate just how wooded the county remains and just how hidden. Admittedly, you may look over all Sussex from the Downs and drive enjoyably through wealden lanes. But to travel through the Weald on foot gives a far more vivid impression of its astonishing variety of landscape and of its mystery. It is no less secret than the Downs. No one who explores it properly can remain unmoved by its beauty.

VII
Bramber and the Rape of Bramber

Bramber Rape was dominated by what is now a small village, barely more than a street. Yet Bramber has been both borough and port. The Conqueror gave the rape to William de Braose, its other key points being Steyning up stream and Shoreham down stream. Only a tall corner of the keep still stands on the great motte, once a mighty stronghold. From the bailey, a grassy amphitheatre with wild service trees and strange black rabbits, you can see across the Weald to the North Downs. The castle's command of the rape was reinforced by a line of lesser fortresses, from Edburton to Knepp. It controlled the River Adur, which in Norman times lapped at its walls, and where merchants and fishermen on their way to Steyning would land to sell their wares. A town grew up, the castle chapel becoming a church dedicated to St Nicholas of Myra – patron of sailors. But the river silted up in the early 1100s and spoilt the little port.

The Black Monks of Sele Priory, on the far side of the Adur, were wardens of the bridge here. A comfortable looking house which they built in Bramber during the fifteenth century survives, the one building of note other than the ruined castle and truncated church. The former was blown up in the Civil War in 1646, while the church – which had become a gun emplacement – lost its chancel when the castle wall fell on it. By then Bramber had ceased to be a town in all but name, though as a classic rotten borough it went on returning two MPs until the Reform Bill of 1832 when there were only a hundred inhabitants.

Long ago, the castle was haunted by the wan phantoms of two emaciated young children, who wandered down the motte and through the streets during the Christmas season. Some said they were the children of William de Braose, lord of Bramber, starved to death by King John to punish their rebellious father. But they have not been seen for many years. Nor has the spectral white horse which used to gallop round the moat.

At first Old Shoreham was the port closest to the sea, and during the early twelfth century the Normans rebuilt its Saxon church (though their work was to be almost ruined by the Victorians). However, as the haven in the estuary here began to silt up, another port was established at New Shoreham nearer the coast, a move which was celebrated by the enlargement of its church in about 1170 into one of the largest and most noble Romanesque buildings in Sussex. Visiting Southampton, the Arab geographer Idrisi heard of 'the important town of Shoreham', the second port on the South Coast. However New Shoreham was mortally wounded by the silting up of the Adur and by erosion from the sea which swallowed many houses together with a Carmelite friary.

'Most of the town of New Shoreham has been washed away by the sea, yet is still a prosperous place' reports the *Universal Magazine* in 1760. It:

> has a collector and other officers to take charge of the customs here, being a very good harbour for vessels of considerable burden, and many ships are built both for the Navy and merchants. The ships' carpenters and ships' chandlers, who are pretty numerous, with all the tradesmen depending on that business, seem to have settled here chiefly because of the great quantity and cheapness of timber in the country behind them, and the river, though not navigable for larger vessels, serves to bring down the floats of it from Bramber, Steyning and the adjacent country . . .'

The yards built small naval vessels into the nineteenth century, such as HMS *Scorpion* in 1804; a sloop of 227 tons, she mounted sixteen guns. The last ships from the Shoreham yards, two barques of 800 tons, were launched in the 1870s.

Further west along the coast from Shoreham is Worthing. Personally, I find it dull, with its remaining traces of elegance overshadowed by a modern shopping centre. Yet it still keeps a little Georgian theatre in Anne Street where Mrs Siddons acted, even though the building has been used as a warehouse for well over a century. Once a lonely little fishing village, its career as a genteel seaside resort began in 1798 when King George sent his daughter Princess Amelia here for her health. Now a big town, it has gobbled up the surrounding villages. Among them is Broadwater, whose Norman church – Worthings' original parish church – has been spoilt by restoration.

Another village swallowed up by Worthing is West Tarring, whose High Street still makes it feel like a village. The church, with a notably tall tower, is yet another victim of Victorian restorers. The incumbent here from 1834 to 1878 was the antiquarian, John Wood Warter, author of *The Seaboard and the Down; or my parish in the South. By an Old Vicar.* However, Tarring's real interest lies in the Old Palace, now the parish hall, formerly a palace of the Archbishops of Canterbury, a lovely little building which dates largely from the thirteenth and fourteenth centuries. St Thomas a'Becket often stayed here, at an earlier palace on the site, and is credited with having planted – supposedly about 1162 – the adjoining fig tree orchard. It is sometimes said that St Richard of Chichester planted it; certainly he, too, frequently visited West Tarring.

The great neo-Gothic chapel of Lancing College, 94 foot tall and grandly sited on a hill across the river from Shoreham, is called the 'Cathedral of the Downs', though other Sussex churches dispute the title. Like Arundel Cathedral, it is less impressive when seen close to. (When a boy there, Evelyn Waugh described the school as 'our flint-girt fortress'.) On the same side of the Adur is Coombes, once a substantial hamlet but now just a farm with two or three cottages on a grassy slope. Inside the tiny unrestored church, one of the loveliest interiors in Sussex, there are murals by the Lewes monks like those at Hardham. Coombes is enchanting, even if it faces a hideous cement works on the other side of the Adur.

Not far away is Botolphs, another deserted hamlet, with a tall church which is partly Saxon. Although an East Anglian, Abbot Botolph was clearly a much loved saint in Sussex. No doubt his popularity stemmed from his role as a patron of river crossings, and protector of sailors, travellers and farm workers. His relics were much prized in Saxon England.

Steyning was once known as the 'Port of St Cuthman', but during the twelfth century the Adur became unnavigable. (Archaeologists have recently found the wharf.) Deceptively small outside, the church astonishes one by its vast interior, even more impressive than New Shoreham. Curiously, it is dedicated to St Andrew and not to Cuthman, the patron saint of Steyning. A wandering mystic pushing his crippled mother in a wheelbarrow, he arrived here during the eight century; when the wheelbarrow broke, he took it as a sign from Heaven and built a church. Many miracles have been worked by Cuthman, and Sussex Catholics still pray to him on his feast day. England's first royal family, the Cerdicings, had a manor at Steyning which they may have acquired from the Kings of Sussex; obviously there was a royal hall here, but so far its site has not been found. King Ethelwulf, father of Alfred the Great, is buried in the church, where a slab with a double incised cross may once have covered his grave. Prospering from royal patronage and riverine trade, it acquired a mint during the tenth century. It continued to prosper even after the end of the port.

In *The High Path* that fine Sussex-bred poet Ted Walker describes Church Street, Steyning, as an anthology of the county's vernacular architecture. 'There are timber-framed houses with plaster-and-wash, a brick-tower, leaded lights, cobbled aprons, tile-hung fronts, knapped flints, roofs of hand-made tiles, overhanging upper storeys, an absence of straight lines, an abundance of nooks and crannies, oak beams and wrought iron-work' he writes. 'On a summer's afternoon, with swallows and martins wheeling, Church Street is still one of the best sights to be had of "typical" (i.e. *un*typical) England.' 'Brotherhood Hall', the grammar-school in his day, began as the Fraternity of the Holy Trinity – the gables overhanging its windows date from the final years of Elizabeth I's reign.

*

Sompting, to the south of Steyning, is famous for a Saxon church with a 'Rhenish helm' roof which I had always thought pre-Conquest – I am mortified to learn that it is a fourteenth-century addition.

Travelling west along the road to Arundel, you come to Clapham, a nice little village. Along a muddy lane you will find a medieval church and a rambling Elizabethan manor next to an enchanting wood where a pine marten was trapped as late as 1841. During the fifteenth century, Clapham was acquired by the Shelleys, a branch of the poet's family. They lived at Michelgrove on the Downs two miles north, a great mansion which is said to have resembled Hurstmonceux. The church contains some fine monuments to them, notably one in stone and three in brass. That in stone is to Sir William Shelley, Chief Justice of the Court of Common Pleas, who died in 1549. A quaint bas-relief set in the chancel wall, it shows him with his wife, and their seven sons and seven daughters; he wears the close fitting hood which judges wore before they adopted full-bottomed wigs. One of the sons, Richard, became a Knight of Malta and Grand Prior of England. A valued servant of Henry VIII, whom he entertained at Michelgrove, Sir William was sent to demand the surrender of York House (later Whitehall) from Cardinal Wolsey. The brasses (of 1526, 1550 and 1580) are those of Sir William's father, son and grandson, the father in a tabard emblazoned with whelk shells.

The Shelleys were stiff-necked Papists. One of Sir William's grandsons was condemned to death for involvement in the Throckmorton Plot of 1583 to replace Elizabeth I by Mary, Queen of Scots, but somehow survived; he had been overheard plotting with another conspirator in the woods nearby. In 1676 it was reported that there were still fourteen Papists in the parish. However, in 1716 the then Sir John Shelley 'renounced his recusancy', closing his chapel, and abandoned Catholicism.

The penultimate Shelley to live at Michelgrove never recovered from the death of his adored wife in 1772 at only twenty-three – 'a loss felt by all who had the happiness of knowing her, by none to be compar'd to that of her disconsolate, affectionate, loving and in this world ever-lastingly miserable husband, Sir John Shelley'. His son sold the house to the neighbouring Norfolk estate in 1800, and it was demolished about fifty years later.

Salvington is remarkable only for having been the birthplace of the great Jacobean jurist, John Selden, in 1584. E. V. Lucas considered him 'the writer best endowed with common sense of his day', quoting with approval from Selden's *Table Talk*: 'Of all people Ladies have no reason to cry down Ceremony, for they take themselves slighted without it. And they were not used with Ceremony, with Compliments and Addresses, with Legs and Kissing of Hands, they were the pitifullest Creatures in the World.' Dangerous stuff in today's feminist climate. By contrast John Aubrey's account of the paragon, which Lucas dared not quote, is much more acceptable. 'His father was a yeomanly man, of about fourty pounds per annum, and played well on the violin, in which he took delight, and at Christmas time, to please him selfe and his neighbours, he would play to them as they danced.' A charming vignette of Sussex life in the olden days. However, Aubrey then goes into detail about Selden's career as steward to the Earl of Kent 'whose Countesse, being an ingeniose woman and loving men, would let him lye with her, and her husband knew it. After the Earle's death he married her. He did lye with Mrs Williamson (one of My Lady's women), a lusty bouncing woman, who robbed him on his death-bed. I remember in 1646 or 1647, they did talk also of my Lady's Shee Blackamore.'

Cissbury Ring staggers by its size, 65 acres enclosed by a ramp and a ditch three metres deep, which must have been dug with antler picks or ox shoulder-blade shovels. Constructed about 250BC, it was a tribal centre and perhaps a town too, though one wonders where its inhabitants found their water – dew-ponds would not have been enough. Hummocks which look like fallen buildings are filled in flint-mines from an earlier period; a Cissbury flint has been discovered as far away as the Eastern Mediterranean. The views from here are marvellous. Ignoring the sprawl of Worthing, to the south they include Selsey Bill and the spire of Chichester Cathedral, with Chanctonbury Ring to the north. If some downland nearby is under plough, most is as it was in the shepherds' day. An admirable policy of grazing sheep in the camp and on its slopes keeps scrub at bay so that the old springy turf flourishes, with wild thyme and fleawort. There are adders, slow worms and viviparous lizards, all preyed on by the kestrels overhead.

Below, Findon sheepfair continues on the green at Nepcote every September, just as it has done since the thirteenth century, though Findon itself has become a garden suburb.

Chanctonbury Ring is named from the beeches which crown its summit, visible for miles around. Many were destroyed in the 1987 gale, leaving a sadly tattered crown. Here, too, the views are magnificent. It has had an Iron Age hillfort, a Roman temple and a pagan Saxon shrine. Nearer our own time, the satanist Aleister Crowley offered disgusting little sacrifices to Old Nick here. The Ring retains a sinister reputation.

There is a good Norman church below Chanctonbury, at Buncton. Standing in the fields, it is reached through a wooded gully, a reminder of the time when it was a place of worship for settlers clearing the Weald. Unspoilt, small but massive, its walls contain Roman tiles from an untraced villa somewhere near by, while the outside of the chancel is decorated with arches and chequered masonry brought from Sele Priory at the Dissolution.

Also below Chanctonbury, at the end of a long wooded valley beneath the ridge, is Wiston, a great Tudor mansion of which only the Elizabethan east front survives. It has suffered the ultimate indignity of becoming a conference centre, but once it was the home of a race of heroes, the Shirley family. Sir Hugh Shirley, Grand Falconer of Ireland, acquired it by marrying the Braose heiress late in the fourteenth century. Hugh was killed by the Earl of Douglas at Shrewsbury in 1403, in mistake for Henry IV; he had purposely dressed himself in the royal armour to protect the king. Hugh's son, Ralph, fought at Agincourt. During the reigns of Elizabeth and James I, three Shirley brothers were among the most colourful and most unfortunate adventurers in British history.

The eldest brother, Sir Thomas Shirley, MP for Steyning, saw himself as a crusader, embarking on a career as a privateer in the Levant. Captured by the Turks, he was imprisoned at Constantinople before being ransomed for an enormous sum of money. He trudged home on foot, to be unjustly accused of fraud and imprisoned in the Tower. He was imprisoned yet again, for debt, was forced to sell Wiston, and died a ruined man.

Sir Anthony, the second brother, fought at Zutphen against the Spaniards. In 1595–6 he raided the Portuguese in both Africa and America, ravaged Jamaica and Cuba, and then sailed home by way of Newfoundland. Two years later, he arrived at the Persian court as a self-appointed ambassador, seeking an alliance with the 'Great Sophy' against the Turks. He then turned Papist, entering the service of Spain and becoming 'Admiral of the Levant Seas', was disgraced and died a beggar at Madrid.

The third brother, Sir Robert, who had accompanied Anthony to Persia as 'co-ambassador', remained to train the Persian army (which placed an order for Sussex cannon) and married a Christian Circassian – Teresia, daughter of a kinsman of the Sophy. He returned to England in 1608 as the Sophy's envoy, wearing Persian robes and a turban with a gold cross. 'She had more of *Ebony* than of *Ivory* in her Complexion' says Fuller of Teresia in his *Worthies*, 'yet amiable enough, and very valiant, a quality considerable in that Sex in those Countries.' Robert went back to Persia where, dismissed by the Shah, he died at his house in Kasbin in 1628. (Teresia retired to Rome, edifying all by her piety.)

Wiston was bought by John Fagge, the son of a prosperous merchant of Rye. A devout Puritan, during the Civil War Fagge supported Parliament and became a Roundhead colonel, but he played his cards so well that he was knighted at the Restoration. The heiress of the Fagges married a Goring, and it was Charles Goring who in 1760 planted the beech clump which was to become Chanctonbury Ring on what was at that time a bare hilltop.

At Ashurst a funny little church dating from the early twelfth century was enlarged in about 1180, and again in the following century, for a growing congregation. Once it was a chapel for Saxon swineherds who spent the summer months here in rough shelters but wintered with their pigs nearer the safety of Steyning. Amid heavily wooded country, it can still feel remote in winter. On the border of the rape, West Chiltington has good twelfth- and thirteenth-century wall paintings of scenes from the lives of Christ and the Virgin; although mercifully unrestored, it is too much to claim – as some have – that here one recaptures the atmosphere of a medieval church better than anywhere else in Sussex.

Henfield is a large, untidy village, long and straggling, but sufficiently proud of itself to have applied for a coat-of-arms in 1991. The church is impressive outside, disappointing within. 'Ignorant clergy have – more in this country than in most – been permitted to amuse their leisure and seek temporary exaltation for themselves by restoring away all the interest of their churches.' One can only agree with Mr Augustus Hare, though a *very* good thing has escaped the restorers here: the monument to a grandmother and her grandson. Mrs Anne Kenwellmersh, who died aged sixty-eight in 1633, had been 'A Vertvovs & woorthy matron of piety'. Perhaps it was she who composed the epitaph of her grandson, Meneleb Rainsford. He had predeceased her in 1627, aged eight:

> Great love hath lost his Ganymede I know
> Which made him seek an other here below
> And findinge none not one like vnto this
> Hath ta'ne him hence into eternall bliss
> Cease then for thy deer Meneleb to weep
> God's darlinge was too good for thee to keep
> But rather ioye in this great favour given
> A child on earth is made A Saint in heaven

Dressed like a grown-up, with baggy breeches and a deep turned down collar, poor Meneleb holds a round Puritan hat in his hand.

The church at West Grinstead, deep in the Weald, is part Norman and part from the late Middle Ages with a fifteenth-century wooden porch. There is a fine brass of yet another Sussex man who fought at Agincourt, Sir Hugh Halsham, in plate armour from top to toe, together with that of his wife, Jocosa. The early nineteenth-century pews have the names of parishioners' farms painted on them in white letters: 'White Soan', 'Priors Bine', 'Little Champion', etc. A monument by Rysbrack commemorates William Powlett, a captain of horse grenadiers who died in 1746 – some say that he is the headless Squire Paulett who haunts St Leonard's Forest. An imposing house next to the church, Glebe House, which dates from about 1600, has an almost northern dourness despite its rose coloured brick.

Another monument in the church here commemorates a Caryll squire and his brother, a Benedictine monk who died in 1686. These were the Carylls of South Harting, who moved from their East Sussex estate at Shipley to West Grinstead Park on acquiring it in the seventeenth century. Devout Catholics, they kept chaplains disguised as servants. One was Archdeacon of Sussex during James II's reign.

Their friend, the poet Alexander Pope, was much indebted to the Carylls for something which only Sussex squires could provide – contraband claret. 'I beg you to do me a familiar or rather domestic piece of service' he wrote to John Caryll in August 1717. 'It is, when a hogshead of good French wine falls into your hands – whether out of the skies or whatever element that pays no customs – that you would favour me with about twelve dozen of it at the price you give.' He received a consignment in January and another in March, after which he thanked Mr Caryll 'for the care and circumspection shown in the affair'. He had no qualms about patronising smugglers, adding 'as wine may be reckoned a part of that by which we live, so the necessity under which all polite people lie of drinking, and of drinking only French wine, must render us blameless in the conscientious point, though criminal in the letter of the law.'

He visited the Carylls frequently. In 1728 he wrote gratefully of spending an old fashioned Christmas with them:

I am strongly inclined to think there are at this very day at Grinstead, certain antique charities and obsolete devotions yet in being; that a thing call'd Christian cheerfullness, incompatible with Christmas pies and plum-broth, whereof frequent is the mention in old sermons and almanacs, is really kept alive and in practice at the said place: that feeding the hungry, and giving alms to the poor, do yet make a part of good housekeeping in a latitude not more remote from London than forty miles; and lastly that prayers [Mass] and roast beef, do actually make some folks as happy as a whore and a bottle.

During another visit here, sitting under a tree in the park, Pope wrote part of the *Rape of the Lock*.

The last of the Carylls had to sell his West Grinstead estate in 1749. However, the family left an enduring memorial. This is the Priest's House, a seventeenth-century cottage encased in Georgian red brick, the oldest post-Reformation Catholic presbytery in England.

Soon after the Gunpowder Plot, the Carylls had built the presbytery as a safe house near their mansion, outwardly a home for a land agent. It had a walled up, windowless room where Mass could be said away from prying eyes, entered by a secret door reached through the chimney, while there were priests' holes for emergencies. During Charles II's reign, John Caryll, overcome by remorse at having briefly conformed to the Church of England, endowed the little house with £600 to provide for three priests; the first occupant was Dom Serenus Cressy, a Benedictine and chaplain to Queen Catherine of Braganza. Bishop Challoner found 150 Catholics here in 1741. When the Carylls went they gave the house to Challoner, ensuring the community's survival. Even the mansion which replaced the Carylls' has fallen into ruin and been demolished.

Going north, one comes to another ruin, Knepp Castle, a mere corner of a Norman keep. Built to guard the road between Bramber and Horsham, it became a favourite hunting lodge of King John. Like Bramber it was 'slighted' during the Civil War and nothing more mournful can be imagined. Yet only a quarter of a mile away there is a new Knepp Castle, which Nash designed in 1806 for the Burrells, who are still there. 'Gothick', with a round tower at its back, it stands beside a vast sheet of water which was once a hammer pond. It was burnt out in 1904, eight Holbeins perishing in the blaze, but the rooms were restored, embellished with Georgian fireplaces bought from decayed Irish mansions.

The Protestant Burrells, who took the place of the Carylls, are one of the great Sussex families. Like the Carylls, they made their fortune from iron at the end of the sixteenth century. The most interesting of them was Sir William Burrell who died in 1796, a Fellow of the Royal Society of Antiquaries famous for the forty volumes of notes he made for a definitive history of Sussex, which he never wrote, and which are now in the British Library.

Shipley is approached through lonely lanes, amid wide fields bordered by hedges or shaws. Hilaire Belloc lived here beneath a windmill and it is good to see how his hope that the old Sussex might survive in patches has come true – very little is spoilt at Shipley. The Knights Templar built the church in 1125, tall and narrow, with massive arches and a tower like a small fortress. The upper reaches of the Adur were navigable by small boats from Steyning. In the church lies Sir Thomas Caryll who died in 1616; he has a fine marble head with a pointed beard and wears elegant armour. A rich ironmaster who was also a Papist and would not attend the services here, he was able to worship as he pleased at his remote manor of Benton's Place, far away from any main road and only accessible along muddy tracks.

Cowfold Church is surrounded by pretty little houses. There is a treasure inside: the superb, canopied brass of Dom Thomas Nelond, twenty-fifth Prior of Lewes, who died in 1433. Despite his tonsure, Nelond was not just a churchman but a great Sussex magnate. Also buried in the church is Richard Pearce, 'gent' who died in 1714 aged ninety-four, seventy-two years after he had 'received a wound through his body at Edgehill fight as he was loyally defending King and country'. William Borrer lived at Brook Hill, Cowfold, with a collection of stuffed birds; among them, according to Hare were 'the very rare Glossy Ibis found at Piddinghoe; a Crane from near Newhaven; and a Ger Falcon from Rye'. Borrer claimed that he had once seen fourteen golden orioles perching on a thornbush on Henfield Common.

There are living monks at Parkminster, not far away – white habited Carthusian hermits – though they are seldom glimpsed. The tall spire of their charterhouse, the only one in England, has been described as being to the Weald what the spire of Chichester is to the western coastal plain. Foreseeing the laws which would drive them out of France in 1901 the fathers at the Grande Chartreuse decided to build a refuge in England. A sternly Protestant landowner near Cowfold believed that he had sold his estate to a friend of the Tsar, a Russian general who had come to inspect it with a letter from the Imperial embassy in London. So he had, but the general at once returned to his cell at the Grande Chartreuse. Carthusians, who never eat meat and have only one meal a day, nonetheless drink alcohol – a glass of wine or half a pint of cider per day. Many have lived to very great ages; in 1948 the Ministry of Health, intrigued by a flood of centenarian death-certificates, sent a team to investigate but it could find no explanation. Today, the charterhouse contains a dozen choir-monks who each live as a hermit enclosed in a solitary cell and who, save for services in their church, meet only once a week. Their cells, which are really small cottages with four rooms, are grouped around a vast cloister; the scanty daily meal, prepared by lay-brethren, is delivered through a hatch in the cell door.

Warminghurst, some miles to the west, has a delightfully unspoilt wealden church, which once served a vanished thirteenth-century village. Miraculously, both inside and out, it escaped the dead hand of Victorian restorers and keeps fittings which date from the days of King Charles II or the Georges. William Penn worshipped in this 'steeple house' before he became a Quaker. In 1904 E. V. Lucas thought Warminghurst 'one of the most retired hamlets in Sussex', and thankfully it remains much the same.

Further north, Nuthurst is among wooded valleys on the edge of St Leonard's Forest. Spoilt by a devastingly thorough 'restoration' during the last century, the church's main feature of interest (to me) is a spindle bush which is said to grow in the churchyard hedge; such bushes were planted over witches' graves and a woman is known to have been buried here at dead of night during the 1640s – the burial of a witch. However, I have been unable to find the bush despite a determined search. In 1558 a Nuthurst churchwarden, Mr Richard Lewkas, left a kindly bequest to the parish: 'I will that in the case Almighty God do take any of my four daughters before they be married, that then my overseers do deliver a cow to the churchwardens of Nuthurst to make a drinking once a year with bread and beer for the poor people there at a time convenient, and for the churchwardens to renew the cow as she waxes aged.'

The Normans built a small castle at Nuthurst, about a mile to the west of the village – Sedgewick Castle. No more than a mound topped by a wooden tower, which was surrounded by a stockade and a moat, and garrisoned by a mere handful of men, it would nonetheless have served to hold down the conquered Saxons besides guarding the vital road link between Bramber and London. During the thirteenth century it was completely rebuilt in stone, being given a keep and curtain walls. Today, only a few fragments remain among the undergrowth.

This is a landscape full of those narrow river valleys called 'ghylls' in North country style. Many were damned in the seventeenth and eighteenth centuries, in order to make the long hammer ponds which drove tilt hammers beating out molten iron. One such is Hawkins Pond in St Leonard's Forest, surviving as a magnificent serpentine lake. Another, not far away in the same forest, is called simply 'Hammer Pond'. There is an especially beautiful example at Lower Beeding. Next to a lonely reed-fringed stretch of water, with lilies and wild duck, the forge house here still stands by the bay which dammed the hammer pond. Once this tranquil spot was full of noise and smoke, the woodland cut down for miles around to provide charcoal.

Not far from Horsham, Itchingford ('Hechengefeld' in Old English) was served by Black Monks from Sele Priory, who rode through the forest along the old Roman road and spent the night at the Priest House beside the church. This is a brick and timber building only ten feet wide which dates from the fifteenth century; small as it is, it was enlarged about 1600 after which it became an almshouse until the 1850s. The churchyard yews provided bows for the Hundred Years War. When the church was restored in 1865 a skull was found hidden on a tie-beam. It was discovered to be that of a Jacobite, Sir Hector Maclean, who had been hanged, drawn and quartered at Carlisle in 1715 though no one knows who brought it to Itchingfield.

Horsham was 'a very picturesque little country town' when Augustus Hare knew it a century ago. 'It is quiet, except when enlivened by its market, which has much local celebrity.' Now it is commuter country, a dormitory suburb. The best things to survive are the streets known as the Causeway and Carfax, which bound all that is left of the great triangular green built over in Victorian times. A thirteenth-century church by the river at the bottom of the causeway dominates this oasis, with a spire shingled in Horsham slabs and a tower once used as a prison for Lollards. Inside a life-sized stone effigy commemorates the last Lord de Braose who died in 1395; his daughter's marriage to a Shirley brought Wiston to that family. There is also the tomb, in black and white marble, of a lady who was clearly much loved. Elizabeth Delves died in childbirth in 1654 when she was only twenty-five:

> dvtiful as davghter, affectionate as a wife, tender as a mother, discreete in her family as a Mistris charitable in the relation of a neighbour, also of a sweet & afable disposition & of a sober and winning conversation . . . Her sorrowfull husband (sadly weighing such a considerable losse) erected this monument that an impartiall memoriall of her might bee the better communicated to posterity.

The tranquillity of Carfax may give the impression that the old Horsham of long ago was a gentle, kindly, place. In reality the little town saw some of the most ghastly spectacles in the entire history of Sussex, since the county assizes were held here from 1307 to 1830 and there were countless executions – it is surprising that there is not a phantom standing at every street corner. Whenever a judge was expected, thousands swarmed in to what they playfully called 'Horsham Hanging Fair', arriving in farm-carts and camping on the Common. Sometimes the bodies of those hanged were flayed, their skins being tanned to make souvenirs or charms for curing wens. The last public execution here was on Easter Sunday 1844 in front of a crowd of 3,000, when John Lawrence was hanged for beating a Brighton policeman's head in with a poker. Next year the gaol was demolished and hundreds paid 2d to see Lawrence's body awaiting reburial.

More than hangings took place. In 1735 a suspected murderer was put to the *peine forte et dure*, in the prison-yard but in full view of the public, being pressed to death under boards piled with stones for refusing to plead guilty or not guilty; he had pretended to be dumb. Women were burnt at the stake after being strangled, the penalty for murdering a husband. The last to die here in this way was the octogenarian Widow Cruttenden in 1776; she had cut the throat of her simple-minded spouse, forty years younger than herself, and then mutilated his corpse. Lesser punishments included 'burning in the hand', the fate of the bigamist William Thompsett in 1777, or being whipped at the cart's tail around the market-place 'until the body be bloody', which was the penalty for petty larceny. There was also being placed in the pillory in Carfax, to which a man's ears might be nailed. No less cruelty was shown to animals – a bull was baited to death in Carfax as late as 1813.

Everybody likes mellow Slinfold. Nairn even liked a new estate on the west of the village, 'this happy marriage of old and new'. Inside an unworthy Victorian church lies a battered effigy with a wimple, a thirteenth-century lady from Dedisham Manor nearby; originally a moated mansion, it declined into a mere farmhouse. There is a hammer pond in Roman Woods next to Dedisham, so called because of the Roman staging-post on Stane Street which ran past the manor.

In its day Slinfold was notorious for witchcraft. On one occasion a 'wise woman' told the locals that they could recover a church bell which had fallen into the marsh at Alford Dene a few miles to the west, by using a team of twelve white oxen – but only if they remained silent throughout. They had almost pulled it up when a gleeful yokel cried 'We've got back the Alford Dene gurt bell!' whereupon it disappeared for ever.

Two villages on the Surrey border which deserve a visit are Rusper and Warnham. Rusper (where there was once a nunnery of Benedictine 'dames') looks nice enough, with a good church containing the elegant brass of a married couple from Edward III's time, but is too near Gatwick for comfort; another runway would make it uninhabitable. Mercifully, Warnham, even nicer, is further away from the airport. In its Norman church there is an exuberant Jacobean monument to the Papist ironmaster Sir John Caryll who died in 1613, with his wife and nine children.

Field Place, a handsome Georgian mansion just outside Warnham, was the ancestral home and birthplace of the poet Shelley, who belonged to a younger branch of the Michelgrove family. This was where he began his first long poem, *Queen Mab*. He was surely thinking of Sussex when he wrote:

> Away, away, from men and towns,
> To the wild wood and the downs –
> To the silent wilderness . . .

VIII
The First Great Sussex Houses

Many great mansions were built in Sussex from the fifteenth century onwards, especially in Tudor times. Most of them were deep in the Weald. It is impossible to describe each one, so I have chosen five of the finest: Bodiam, Herstmonceux, Cowdray, Parham and Danny.

Bodiam may seem a surprising choice since it is everyone's idea of a medieval castle. Arising from a superb moat studded with water-lilies, on which it seems to float, it is very like Edward I's Welsh fortresses, with a great curtain wall, seven feet thick, strengthened by drum-shaped towers at the corners and square ones between, together with a massive gatehouse which had a barbican, a portcullis and two drawbridges. Yet this was a house as well as a castle, with suites of rooms around its courtyard, some of them in the towers; they contain not less than thirty-three fireplaces. 'It is remarkable, among all contemporary buildings, for the number and extent of its internal comforts' observed Lord Curzon.

Built in 1385, five years after the sack of Winchelsea, Bodiam's function was 'defence of the adjacent country against the king's enemies' – to guard against French raiders who, it was feared, might sail up to Bodiam Bridge, where the Rother was nearly a quarter of a mile wide and navigable. In those days the site was among marshland, and next to a small riverside harbour. Born in the year of Crécy, its builder, Sir Edward Dalyngrigge, had made a fortune from loot in France. A distinguished soldier, he was Captain of Brest in 1388 and Keeper of the Tower four years later – a job which he soon lost for being too lenient with the Londoners. What is almost certainly his brass may be seen in Fletching church.

When the last Dalyngrigge died, Bodiam passed to his nephew Sir Roger Lewknor, head of a great Sussex family now extinct. This was about 1470. The castle made its only known appearance on the stage of history when Roger's son Sir Thomas Lewknor joined the Duke of Buckingham's disastrous rebellion against Richard III in October 1483; the king at once sent orders to besiege the castle and a spot called the 'gun garden' is said to mark where the royal cannon were sited, but the garrison surrendered without a shot being fired. (The defence's real weakness was the moat, which could have been quickly drained by breaking down the embankment which divides it from the Rother.) It was confiscated, a constable being appointed. This was a certain Nicholas Rigby who in November 1487 was described as 'late of London, gentilman, alias one of the servants of Sir Richard, late Duke of Gloucester' and also as 'late of Bodyham, Co Sussex.' However the Lewknors did not recover it until 1542.

Bodiam has almost no other history. Far from being 'slighted' by Sir William Waller during the Civil War as a potential Cavalier stronghold, it was simply left to moulder into ruin though it was inhabited until the end of the seventeenth century. Predictably, it appealed to 'Gothick' taste, even to that of the savage Lord Thurlow, who wrote about 1780:

> The owl now haunts thee, and oblivion's plant,
> The creeping ivy, has o'er veil'd thy towers . . .

in his unreadable poem 'On beholding Bodiam Castle.'

The age of Sir Walter Scott found it still more attractive. In 1829 Ambrose de Lisle Phillips and Kenelm Digby met at Bodiam at midnight, having ridden there in full armour by the light of a full moon. They were lucky to find it still standing. The castle had only just been saved by Mad Jack Fuller of Brightling, who bought it for £3,000 to save it from being demolished and its stone used as building material.

The great Marquess Curzon, not a sentimental man, fell in love with Bodiam, calling it 'the most romantic and, notwithstanding its rather austere appearance, the most fairy of

English Castles . . . unequalled for picturesque beauty among the Castles of our own or almost any other country', extolling 'that air of feudal romance' and 'the ancient and solitary beauty of the scene'. He did more than praise; in 1919 he began a sympathetic restoration and then gave it to the nation.

Although not so majestic, in its way Herstmonceux is as romantic as Bodiam, standing amid its own serene moat. The only red brick castle in Sussex, its faded carmine contrasts wonderfully with the green of Pevensey Marsh on one side and wooded country on the other, enhanced by Tudor gardens — set off in turn by a rhododendron dell and a lavender garden.

'Were it called Hurstmonceux House or Place, or Manor, or Grange, all would be well' grumbled E. V. Lucas (using the old spelling) who, because it was built of brick, could not accept that it was a castle. Yet it was impregnable against besiegers without artillery, such as Frenchmen coming up through the Marsh. It had a daunting gatehouse and a drawbridge, while in the walls there were arrow slits and loop-holes for guns.

It is a monument to plunder and graft. Sir Roger Fiennes, who fought at Agincourt and was Treasurer of Henry VI's household, made one fortune out of loot during the wars in France and another from corruption at home. (His brother, Lord Saye and Sele, was beheaded by Jack Cade's men for doing the same thing, his body being drawn naked through London at a horse's tail.) With this ill-gotten wealth, Roger rebuilt the manor house where his ancestors had lived since Edward II's time. He may have been inspired to use brick by châteaux he had seen in France or Flanders, for this was the first large edifice in England to be built in brick since Roman times. Some think that the masons were Flemings because the bricks look Flemish, but there is no proof.

In shape a large square, the battlemented walls encircle four courtyards which have a series of interconnecting rooms around them, including a great hall and a chapel. There is an octagonal tower at the angles, with polygonal intermediate towers along the battlemented walls. The gatehouse is the outstanding feature, 85 feet tall, with an imposing entrance arch flanked by two slim towers.

Sir Roger's son became, by marriage, Lord Dacre and for a century the Lords Dacre of the South were among the leading Sussex magnates. It seems their broad acres aroused envy. Thomas, Lord Dacre, 'a right towardlie gentlemen', was one of the jury which tried Anne Boleyn and among those who welcomed Anne of Cleves to England. In 1541, when he was twenty-four he fell out with his neighbour, Sir Nicholas Pelham of Laughton. On 30 April, Dacre and his cronies sallied forth from Herstmonceux to kill some of Pelham's deer. Caught by game-keepers in Pikehay field near Horselunges Manor, they came to blows; Dacre mortally wounded one of the keepers, John Busbridge. Arrested and tried by his peers, he was sentenced to death. So certain were his gaolers of a pardon that they postponed the execution for three hours. It did not come, and he was hanged at Tyburn, his lands being forfeit to the Crown. Camden, the Elizabethan historian, heard that Lord Dacre died because of his 'great estate, which greedy courtiers gaped after, causing them to hasten his destruction'. But his heirs recovered Herstmonceux in 1558.

Some of the Fiennes may be seen in the parish church nearby, which looks over the Pevensey Levels. There is a very fine armoured brass of the builder's father, with an inscription in Norman French to *William ffienles Chevalier* who died in 1402. Two magnificent effigies commemorate the eighth Lord Dacre and a son who pre-deceased him. They supposedly date from the 1530s yet wear Milanese armour of fifty years earlier – apparently they were appropriated from Battle Abbey at the Dissolution and are really two knights of the Hooe family.

The Dacres sold the castle in 1708 to a family called Naylor. The ghost stories date from the time of the Naylors' occupation. Lady Grace Naylor, a sister of that greatest of all Sussex magnificoes, the Duke of Newcastle, had a lovely daughter also called Grace, who was starved to death by a jealous governess in 'The Lady's Bower' – a room with an oriel window, on the east side, which she haunted for many years. Then there was the 'Drummer', a phantom nine feet tall who stalked along the battlements beating a tattoo on a drum; some said it was the shade of a Lord Dacre in hiding, who drummed to keep off the would-be suitors of his supposed widow. (The drummer has long been claimed as the inspiration for a scene in Addison's play, *The Haunted House*.) Many have thought that these ghosts were a device of smugglers to frighten revenue men away from the ruined castle which was used as a hiding place for contraband, but they were seen before 1777, when the Naylors demolished it.

Anxious to provide for her children and contemptuous of the old furniture and pictures which Horace Walpole had made a pilgrimage to see, the then Mrs Naylor – the owner's second wife – persuaded her husband to abandon Herstmonceux and sell the collection. She then built a new house for herself with the proceeds, Herstmonceux Place, half a mile away. Ironically, when her husband died she found she had done so on entailed land, so that the house reverted to his son by his first marriage.

Until the early twentieth century, Herstmonceux stayed a beautiful ruin, as desolate as Bodiam, but in 1911 Colonel Lowther started to restore it, the work being completed in the 'thirties by Sir Paul Latham. It was occupied from 1948 until very recently by the Royal Observatory. Perversely, I wish it had been left as it was – I like ruins. No county boasts more graceful ruined mansions than Sussex; besides Bodiam, there are Slaugham, Brambletye near Forest Row, Nymans at Cuckfield and Cowdray.

Just outside Midhurst, in the water-meadows of the western Rother and with the Downs in the distance, Cowdray is reminiscent of Hampton Court, though built of sandstone instead of brick. Replacing a castle of the Bohuns, it was begun by Sir David Owen who had married their heiress in 1492. (He was a bastard son of Owen Tudor, Henry VII's grandfather.) It was then bought by William Fitzwilliam, Earl of Southampton – one of those courtiers of Henry VIII who glare so warily from their portraits. When Fitzwilliam died in 1592, he bequeathed it to his half-brother Sir Anthony Browne of Battle Abbey, Standard Bearer of England and another Tudor favourite. These three built Cowdray round a vast quadrangular court, with a great hall and gatehouse which were obviously modelled on Hampton Court.

The Brownes, Viscounts Montagu, who lived at the house till its destruction, stayed faithful to the old religion. Even so, they did very well out of the dissolution of the monasteries, securing no less than five; a Black Monk cursed Sir Anthony when he took Battle – 'by fire and water his line should come to an end'. Queen Elizabeth paid a notably successful visit to Cowdray in 1591. She shot several deer with a crossbow, watched others torn to pieces by hounds for her delectation, was entertained with pageants and country dancing, and knighted six gentlemen. One breakfast consisted of three oxen and 140 geese. She was so pleased by her visit that she embraced Lady Montagu, who exclaimed 'O happie time! O joyful daie!' Old Anthony died later that year; a contemporary wrote 'Though he were a great Roman Catholic, yet the Queen, finding him faithful always loved him and in his sickness went to visit him'.

Cowdray was occupied by both Cavaliers and Roundheads during the Civil War. Waller's troops looted the house but did not dare to 'slight' it for fear of enraging the tenantry; the Lord Montagu of the day was fined heavily for his loyalty to King Charles and had his plate stolen. The fourth viscount, no less loyal to James II, was the first Papist to be Lord Lieutenant of Sussex since Tudor times. His brother, an equally staunch Catholic who succeeded in 1708, shot his chaplain for beginning Sunday Mass without him, and had to spend the rest of his life hiding in a priest's hole six feet square in the keeper's lodge – his wife would put on a white dress when visiting him, hoping to be mistaken for a ghost.

During the eighteenth century Cowdray began to attract antiquarians. 'Our greatest pleasure was seeing Cowdry' Horace Walpole declared in 1749. 'We see here how our ancestors lived' said Dr Johnson to Boswell after they had driven over from Brighton. 'The house is a square building, and at each angle is a Gothic tower, which produces a good effect when viewed from the rising grounds' reported George Walpoole in 1784.

> The large parlour, or room at the hall, is of Holbein's painting; where that great artist has described the exploits of king Henry VIII before Boulogne, Calais, his landing at Portsmouth, his magnificent entry into London, &c . . . Here is a long gallery with the twelve apostles, as large as life; another very neat one, wainscotted with Norway oak, where are many ancient whole-length pictures of the family in their proper habits.

It was clearly a house of enormous charm; the bedrooms had such delightful names as the 'Red Damask Bedchamber', the 'Old Chintz Bedchamber', the 'Velvet Bedchamber' (where Queen Elizabeth had slept). the 'Yellow Bedchamber' or the 'Red Bedchamber'.

The medieval chapel, dating from Sir David Owen's time, was sumptuously decorated, with a Baroque altar-piece by Amigoni. The courtyard was graced by an exquisite Italian fountain, allegedly by Benvenuto Cellini, and admired by Horace Walpole. (Now at Woolbeding Hall.) 'The park is very noble, having a great variety of grounds in it, and is well wooded with firs, pines and other evergreens, which are grown to a large size; and here are some of the largest chestnut trees in England' George Walpoole tells us. 'The vallies in the park are well supplied with water, which keeps in a constant verdure.'

But in 1793, to quote a contemporary, there 'passes away in fire, water and sorrow the glory of Cowdray Castle'. On 24 September a careless workman left untended in an upper room a charcoal brazier which fell over. Soon the entire house was in flames and very little of the priceless furniture, pictures or tapestry could be saved. 'That loveliest and perfectest of all ancient mansions' lamented Horace Walpole.

As if in fulfilment of the monk's prophecy, before a messenger could reach him with the news, the 24-year-old Lord Montague drowned on 15 October in an insane attempt to shoot the falls at Schaffhausen on the Rhine, despite his valet attempting to restrain him by force. His cousin, the next and last Lord Montague, a Franciscan friar, received a dispensation from the Pope to marry but did not find a bride until 1797 and died the same year without fathering a child. What was left of Cowdray had already passed to his predecessor's sister, the Hon. Mrs Poyntz. She lived in the porter's lodge at Cowdray until 1815, the year when her two young sons drowned in front of her in the sea at Bognor.

Today the house's mellow sandstone shell stands amid long grass, a riot of wild flowers in spring. Guarded by an imposing gatehouse, it keeps much of its ancient splendour. Deer still roam the park as in Tudor times.

A mile or so to the west of Storrington, Parham stands in a park full of aged oaks and cedars which has been called 'pure Tudor' in its disordered, unarranged appearance. An abandoned Saxon village lies beneath the turf, while the ancestors of its fallow deer once supplied Westminster Abbey with venison, for this was a grange of the Black Monks of Westminster from the tenth century until the Dissolution of the Monasteries; the grange's buildings form part of the east wing. Henry VIII granted the manor to the Palmers, who built the present house in 1577. E-shaped, all of grey sandstone, it is typically Elizabethan, with mullioned windows, a tall great hall, an upper hall, a great parlour, a great chamber, and a long gallery 160 feet long in which to take exercise during rainy weather. These rooms are surprisingly cosy and cheerful on wet days, contrasting with the bracken and ancient timber of the sombre park outside and with the glimpses of bare downland. There is a priest's hole off the Long Gallery which was used as a refuge by one of the conspirators in the Babington Plot of 1586. Ironically, there is a well founded tradition that once Elizabeth dined here on her way to Cowdray in 1593.

In 1601, Parham was brought by Thomas Bysshop of Henfield, who was made a baronet by James I and whose descendants were to live here for three centuries. After inheriting Parham, his eldest son, Sir Edward, was in serious trouble with the law for killing (presumably in a duel) Henry Shirley, a local playwright and one of the Wiston family, who had called on him to demand money; he only just escaped a sentence of being 'burnt in the hand'. Edward became one of Sussex's leading Cavaliers. He helped to defend Chichester against the Roundheads in 1642 and rode with Hopton's advance guard when it seized Arundel at the end of the following year, after which he was a hostage for the castle's surrender and then a prisoner of Parliament in the Tower of London.

There is a painting at Parham of Sir Edward's youngest brother, Henry Bysshop of Henfield, holding a small dog. It commemorates his having hidden in a priest's hole in the Parsonage House at Henfield when the Roundheads were searching for him; his noble companion refrained from barking lest they be discovered.

Henry had an odd career. Although he began as a royalist, he tried to join the Parliamentarians but his landlady forgot to deliver the petition and in 1644 he was proscribed as 'a Papist and delinquent', his property being sequestrated. He then spent two years in Virginia, on a plantation near the James River which he had recently bought. At the Restoration he became Postmaster General, and invented the post mark.

During the eighteenth century the park was 'improved' by removing the little village of Parham, though its Tudor church was allowed to stay; in George IV's time it was refitted in the Gothic style, and still retains a comfortable pew for the squire, equipped with a fire-place – for which in winter he must have thanked God sincerely. Sir Cecil Bysshop, who inherited the title Lord Zouche from his mother, raised a troop of yeomanry during the Napoleonic Wars which, when it was raining, he drilled in the Long Gallery.

The most interesting owner of Parham during the nineteenth century was Sir Cecil's grandson, Robert Curzon, Lord Zouche, the travel writer, whose *Visit to the Monasteries in the Levant and Armenia* was immensely popular in Victorian England.

In 1922, Parham was sold to the Pearsons, who restored it magnificently. The house contains some superb pictures. One is Robert Peake's portrait of Charles I's brother, Henry Prince of Wales who, had he lived, might have averted the Civil War. Another is a marvellous Stubbs of a stuffed kangaroo, an animal Stubbs had never seen alive. There is also a magnificent Gainsborough of Major Norton Knatchbull in his red uniform and a painting by an artist called Barlow of a long forgotten Sussex sport, bustard shooting.

Danny, which Sir Thomas Goring started to build in 1582 just outside Hurstpierpoint, is another E-shaped Elizabethan house. (The E-design is not in honour of the queen, as was formerly supposed.) Built in brick which has mellowed to a soft red, instead of stone, and decorated with blue brick-work, it has fine mullioned windows, tall bays and gabled roofs. The south wing was given a beautiful Georgian facade during the 1720s, with nine bays in the same red brick.

This was a Cavalier house, the home of George Goring, Earl of Norwich, who was one of King Charles's most devoted and least capable supporters. A former MP for Lewes, he was Captain of the Royal Guard and later the general who surrendered Colchester in 1648. Clarendon thought him 'frolicsome', Pepys 'something of a buffoon'. His son George, Lord Goring, who was born at Danny, was another of Charles I's generals, a Cavalier of the brutal and debauched sort. He died in Madrid in 1649, in the deepest poverty. All the Gorings' estates had been sequestrated, Danny and 160 acres being bought by Mr Courthope of Whiligh near Ticehurst. Despite being a favourite of Charles II, old Lord Norwich never regained the estates.

Born in 1616, George Courthope had had colourful adventures as a young man in Italy and the Levant. At Mytilene he was arrested by the Turks as a Venetian spy, only escaping the bastinado by a heavy bribe – afterwards he heard that news had reached England of his having been strangled in Turkey. Although an MP for Sussex during Cromwell's regime, he sent money to the exiled Charles II, and in consequence was knighted at the Restoration and allowed to keep Danny.

Henry Campion, a gentleman from Kent, married the

Courthope heiress in 1702 and Campions have lived at Danny (or nearby) ever since. Fittingly, they had been a Cavalier family. The armour of Sir William Campion, who was killed fighting for his sovereign during the Civil War, hangs over the fireplace; there is a portrait of him in the drawing room. In 1728 the south front of the house was given a Queen Anne facing, which enhances the house's overwhelming elegance. History was made here this century when Lloyd George and his war cabinet had several meetings in the Great Hall in 1918, drawing up the terms of the Armistice on its long oak table.

In the background, Wolstonbury Hill towers above Danny Park, smooth as a green egg. I first saw the lovely house from it. Returning to the coast from London, it always cheers me to see Wolstonbury from the train, a reminder that one is returning to the Downs.

IX
Protestants and Papists

Lewes is the last place in England, probably in Europe, where to the dismay of ecumenists the Pope is regularly burnt in effigy. This takes place every 5 November, the day of the old service for 'the happy Deliverance of King JAMES I and the Three Estates of England, from the most traitorous and bloody and intended Massacre by Gunpowder; and also for the happy arrival of his Majesty King WILLIAM on this day, for the Deliverance of our Church and Nation', as the *Book of Common Prayer* used to put it. On England's most colourful bonfire night, members of the town's bonfire clubs march through the streets in thousands, dressed as Roman legionaries, knights in armour or Red Indians, and carrying flaming torches. Forty-one of the 288 martyrs burnt in Queen Mary's reign suffered in Sussex, most of them at Lewes. Surprisingly, during Elizabethan and Jacobean times the county was a stronghold for Catholics as well as Protestants.

There had always been Lollards in the Weald, proto-Protestants who insisted that the true path could be learnt only from Scripture and thought that the Pope was Antichrist. They had originated in the fourteenth century in response to John Wyclif's teaching. Most were small craftsmen, persecuted, secretive, illiterate and barely able to read their tattered, handwritten Bibles. But they welcomed the new ideas coming out of Germany, buying books from seamen at Rye.

In October 1554, one of the foremost gentlemen in Sussex, Mr Edward Gage of Firle, burst into the house of a Flemish brewer in Black Lion Lane at Brighthelmstone, Dirck Carver, to arrest him as he was at prayer with a friend. After spending many months in Newgate gaol, he was brought before Dr

Bonner, Bishop of London, to be tried for heresy. Carver told him tactfully 'Your doctrine is poison and sorcery'. He was taken to Lewes and burnt in a barrel in the High Street in July 1555, shouting at spectators, 'You shall burn in Hell perpetually'. He became a local hero. His 'house' can be seen at Brighton, a reconstruction of the eighteenth-century brewery which stood on its site.

Two years later, according to Foxe's *Book of Martyrs*, 'In the town of Lewes were ten faithful servants of God put in one fire on the 22nd of June'. A huge gridiron, on which they were said to have been roasted, was displayed till quite recently in the kitchens of Brighton Pavilion.

The most attractive of the martyrs, perhaps because we know most about him, is Richard Woodman of Warbleton in the Weald. Born in the late 1520s, by Queen Mary's reign he was a successful yeoman farmer and iron master; his income of £56 was that of a small squire, while he had received some education – 'Yea, I can read Latin but I understand very little'. In 1554, he rebuked his parson for reviving the Mass at Warbleton. The church is still there, not far from Hailsham, with bolts on the tower door which are said to have been made by Woodman himself – his house is near the churchyard. The priest complained to the authorities and Woodman spent eighteen months in prison, including eight weeks in Dr Bonner's 'cole-house'. Then, much to his surprise, he was released. He continued to evangelise and was reported to Sir John Gage who sent men to arrest him while he was ploughing. They had forgotten to bring a warrant, so he was able to escape to the woods, living 'even under a tree, and there had my Bible, my pen and mine ink, and other necessaries, my wife bringing me meat daily'. He then fled to Flanders, 'but I thought every day seven years ere ever I were at home again', which was within three weeks.

He avoided arrest until denounced by his father and brother who owed him money. One morning his small daughter came running in, crying 'Mother, mother, yonder cometh twenty men!' He hid in a loft concealed by chests. 'We know he is in the house and we must search it, for we be the sheriff's men' they told his wife. 'Let us have a candle.' When they found his hiding place he jumped from a window and, without shoes, ran down a lane full of cinders, his pursuers chasing with drawn swords, shouting 'Strike him! Strike him!' He fell into a hole and was caught. Bound with a dog-leash, he was taken to the Gages' house at West Firle, then to the Marshalsea in London for questioning by the Bishop of Chichester.

'I am sorry for you, and so are all the worshipful men of your country' Bishop Christopherson told him. 'For it hath been reported to me that you have been a man of good estimation in all the country, amongst the poor and rich, till now of late.' He invited Woodman to dinner, doing his best to save him. The prisoner refused to compromise. 'I see it is but folly to talk with you' said the Bishop. Poor Woodman was one of the ten who died on the gridiron.

It was an odd coincidence that Carver and Woodman, Sussex's two most famous Protestant martyrs, should both have been arrested by the Gages, who remained staunchly Papist for generations. Edward's father, Sir John, had been Comptroller of the Household to Henry VIII, who also made him Captain of the Yeoman of the Guard and Constable of the Tower. A 'man more ready to serve God than the world', at one point John Gage contemplated leaving his wife to become a Carthusian monk. This did not stop him from being a zealous commissioner for the dissolution of the monasteries and acquiring Alciston, the richest of Battle Abbey's manors – an abbey of which his maternal grandfather had been steward. When Mary came to the throne, she appointed Sir John Lord Chamberlain. He was the gaoler of both Lady Jane Grey and Princess Elizabeth. He died in 1556. On his tomb at Firle and on that of his grandson, are carved two verses from Job in Latin: 'For I know that my redeemer liveth, and that he shall stand at the latter day upon the earth: And though after my skin worms destroy this body, yet in my flesh shall I see God.'

When Elizabeth became Queen and the Prayer Book replaced the Missal, the bishop and at least a quarter of the Sussex clergy were removed or resigned. However, all six of the country's peers stayed faithful to Rome, as did many squires – Gages at Firle and Bentley, Carylls at West Hartington and Shipley, Kemps at Slindon, Leedeses at Steyning, Scotts at Iden, Shelleys at Clapham, Shoysewells at Etchingham, Thatchers at Westham and Threeles at Bexhill. John Gage's grandson's choice of the same epitaph as his grandfather hints at the alienation of these recusants from their environment. Not only were they fined for refusing to attend the Anglican services in the parish church, but they were always distrusted by their neighbours, as potential traitors who might welcome Spanish or French invaders for religion's sake.

Few Papists carried dislike of the new religion to the point of political opposition. The exceptions were Henry Fitzalan, Earl of Arundel, the county's Lord Lieutenant, though his politics had as much to do with dynastic ambition as piety, and his neighbour at Petworth, the Earl of Northumberland. Both men were implicated in the Ridolfi Plot of 1569 – to replace Elizabeth by Mary, Queen of Scots and bring back Catholicism. (Mary was to marry Thomas Howard, Duke of Norfolk, who was Arundel's son-in-law.) In the event, Norfolk and Northumberland were beheaded, but Lord Arundel escaped with imprisonment.

The real leader of the Sussex recusants was Viscount Montague, of Cowdray and Battle, who in 1559 spoke out in the House of Lords against the breach with Rome. However, Queen Elizabeth liked and trusted him, so he was left in peace – as at first were most Catholic landowners. He kept several priests at Cowdray, among them a former Archdeacon of Chichester, Fr Alban Langdale, and a Carthusian monk, Dom Anthony Clerke. On Langdale's advice, Montague occasionally attended the new services. This compromise, that of many Sussex recusants, deflected persecution.

In 1568, the Chancellor of Chichester informed Sir William Cecil: 'Almost all places in our part of the world are full of Papists and Popishness.' Two years later it was reported, 'In the church of Arundel certain altars do stand yet to the offence of the godly . . . In many places they keep yet their chalices, looking for to have Mass again . . . Many bring to church the old Popish Latin primers, and use to pray upon them all the time when the Lessons are being read and in the time of the Litany.' Fr Moses 'sometime a friar at Chichester', was going from one gentlemen's house to another with news and letters, 'being much suspected in religion'. Battle was 'the most Popish town in all Sussex'.

Life grew much harder for Catholics after Pius V excommunicated Queen Elizabeth in 1570. They, too, acquired martyrs. Thomas Pilcher (or Pilchard) had been born in Battle in 1557. A Fellow of Balliol, he left Oxford in 1580 to study for the priesthood at Rheims. Returning to England, he worked in the West Country, but on a visit to London in 1587 was recognised in Fleet Street and arrested, to be hanged, drawn and quartered with much cruelty only an hour after his sentence – disembowelled while still alive. He was canonised with Philip Howard.

By the 1580s laws against recusancy (refusal to attend services in the parish church) were being enforced much more strictly. Between 1587 and 1592 John Gage of Firle had to pay the huge sum of £2,160 in fines, besides going to prison. He was not the only Sussex recusant to be imprisoned. New and stricter priests, trained abroad, who frowned on 'church papists' who went to Anglican services, made it difficult to avoid fines or prison sentences. Catholics were no longer appointed JPs and were excluded from the public life of the county. Persecution intensified when there was a threat of Spanish invasion as in Armada year, all Catholics being under suspicion as potential collaborators. During 1588, two priests from Littlehampton, Edward James and Ralph Crockett were hanged, drawn and quartered at Chichester, while for giving shelter to a priest, Edward Shelley of Bentley suffered the same fate at Tyburn.

Old Lord Montague died in 1592. His widow Magdalen, who survived until 1609, was not so tactful. On great feastdays, Mass in her house at Battle was celebrated by priest, deacon and subdeacon 'with singing and musical instruments'.

When rumours came of a Spanish landing in Sussex and the town was panic stricken: 'My lad. Montague's people seeing the towne of Battel in that uprore and miserable state rejoiced, and shewed signes of joy; in so much that the people fel to greate exclamations and cursinges of them openly in the streates.' Her grandson 'Anthony Mary, Viscount Mountague' was to be imprisoned in the Tower for nearly a year on a baseless charge of involvement in the Gunpowder Plot.

Not all were mirrors of piety. In a letter to Queen Elizabeth of June 1592 the priest hunter Topcliffe described a church papist called Anthony Copley as 'that most desperate youth', adding that 'Copley did shoot at a gentleman last summer, and did kill an oxen with a musket; and in Horsham church threw his dagger at the parish clerk and stuck it in a seat of the church. There liveth not the like in England for sudden attempts . . .' This young man was the son of another notorious recusant, Sir Thomas Copley of Roffey near Horsham, a former MP for Gatton, who had died in exile for the sake of his religion, while his sister had married one of the Gages of Firle. Anthony himself spent a good deal of time in exile – at Rome, and in Spain and Flanders. A friend of the Jesuit poet Robert Southwell, he wrote verses dedicated to Lord Montague in which he claimed to be 'disastr'd for virtue'. Topcliffe was right in detecting a born conspirator. Copley returned home in 1603 and was soon arrested for plotting to replace James I by Arabella Stuart, presumably with a view to bettering the lot of English Catholics. He was found guilty but pardoned. Just the sort of man for Guy Fawkes, he was lucky not to get involved in the Gunpowder Plot.

At that time about forty Sussex villages contained small Catholic communities. As a persecuted minority they have left few records but very occasionally a 'priest's hole' comes to light, as one did at Slindon in Victorian times – beneath the floor, it led to a secret passage which enabled the priest to escape through the cellars. Harassment was unrelenting. Some recusant gentlemen went abroad, such as Mr Edward Gage of Bentley in 1606 after two spells in prison, or Sir Thomas

Leedes of Steyning the following year – 'a great harbourer of priests and fancier of priestholes'. Yet the number of Sussex Catholics rose during the first half of the seventeenth century, even if only six leading families stayed faithful by 1641, out of eleven at the end of Elizabeth's reign. They continued to harbour priests, who made converts. Protected by the Montagues, Midhurst sheltered a comparatively large Catholic community ranging from gentry to labourers, though generally recusants lived in isolated groups, like that at Up Marden which in 1641 refused to contribute to the relief of Irish Protestants; a priest must have visited them from Cowdray, saying Mass at some lonely farmhouse. Besides Lord Montague, their leaders were Sir John Caryll and Sir John Shelley who in 1639, responding to an appeal by Queen Henrietta Maria, raised money from their co-religionists to finance Charles I's invasion of Scotland.

The Civil War saw increased persecution. A Franciscan friar from Midhurst, Thoman Bullaker, was executed at Tyburn in 1642. Several recusant squires, such as Caryll of Lady Holt and Kemp of Slindon, had to pay swingeing fines. Henceforward Sussex Catholicism declined, save for a brief moment of optimism when James II appointed the then Lord Montague as Lord Lieutenant of the county. Landowning families died out or conformed, families whose houses had provided vital Mass-centres.

Although the death penalty for being a priest was removed from the Statute Book during the 1680s, fines and taxes for recusancy were doubled. The last straw was the failure of the Jacobite rising in 1715. The Gages and the Shelleys turned Protestant, closing their chapels, as did the Duke of Norfolk and Lord Montague later in the century. Only at Easebourne, Slindon and West Grinstead did tiny congregations struggle on until Emancipation came in 1829.

If Catholicism had been strong in West Sussex, from the very beginning of the Reformation the eastern half of the county inclined to another form of Christianity. Rye had a close association with Tenterden where a Lollard community had been uncovered in 1511, while its trading links with the Netherlands ensured a steady supply of books espousing the new German ideas, and of English Bibles printed abroad. In 1536 a Dutch Anabaptist was burnt in Rye market place; during the following year twenty men from Rye and Winchelsea were accused of heresy. Thomas Scambler, who became vicar of Rye in 1547, was married in Rye church; deprived of his living under Queen Mary, he lay low in London, surviving to be made Bishop of Peterborough by Queen Elizabeth. In 1564, Bishop Barlow of Chichester reported to the Privy Council that 'Rye, Hastings, Lewes and Brighthelmstone are governed with such officers as be faithful favourers of God's word and earnestly given to maintain godly orders'. On several occasions Rye offered a safe haven to the ships of the Sea Beggars, Dutch Protestant privateers fighting Philip of Spain, while it gave a warm welcome to Calvinist refugees from France; for over twenty years the town sheltered the largest community of Huguenots in Elizabethan England.

In the towns and Weald of East Sussex both burgesses and gentry were overwhelmingly Puritan, convinced that they were predestined to inherit heaven; rigid keepers of the Sabbath, their churches heard interminable sermons, their houses constant family prayer and Bible readings. They owed much to Richard Curteys, Bishop of Chichester from 1570 to 1582, who insisted that all Sussex clergy should be able to preach fluently and satisfy the demand for sermons, so that 'salvation might ride into the hearts of men'. Rye and Lewes became Puritan strongholds.

Rye was a 'godly town' from the start. In 1581 the Corporation issued a 'Decree against Whoredom'; any unmarried woman who bore a child was ordered to wear a green and yellow partlet, a species of pinafore. However, at that date its mayor and jurats accepted prelacy and obeyed the bishops. Five years later, they complained of 'a small secte of pvrytanes, more holy in shewe than in dede', imprisoning a tradesman who claimed that 'my Lorde of Canterbury is but the Pope of Inglande, and that the Booke of Common Prayer which he aloweth to be sayde in the Church is but masse translated and dumdogs to reade it, for those ministers that do not preache they call them dumdogs'. Even so, Puritanism gradually took over the entire town and by 1610 the mayor himself was a Puritan.

In the countryside, Puritan squires had ousted the Papists from their monopoly of the Bench by 1590 at latest. They insisted on having ministers of their own way of thinking in their parish churches. Such names as Fight-the-Good-Fight-of-Faith White (Ewhurst), Safety-on-High Snat (Uckfield) and Fly-Fornication Richardson (Waldron) appeared all over East Sussex. There was much stress on belonging to the Elect, and a certain amount of intolerance. At Rye, Samuel Jeake protested when a minister addressed a Papist woman as 'Dear Sister' at her burial, asking 'What concord hath Christ with Belial?' He deplored the offering of prayers for a girl who had fallen ill after giving birth to a bastard, insisting that the Saved must not mingle with those cast away: 'What fellowship hath righteousness with unrighteousness?'

If often a harsh creed, it was not necessarily sanctimonious. Those who subscribed to it had a touching belief in God's providence. 'Afflictions are his love tokens and it is our duty to see it soe' wrote a friend of Jeake when he was sick.

Just as Catholics had been shocked by the changes at the Reformation, so Puritans were outraged by the innovations of the first High Church bishops of Chichester, Dr Richard Montagu and Dr Brian Duppa, between 1628 and the Civil War. These two opposed the doctrines of Geneva no less than those of Rome. 'I am none of that fraternity – no Calvinist, no Lutheran, but a Christian' wrote Montagu. A former chaplain to King Charles, he enforced a meticulous celebration of the Prayer Book liturgy; the congregation had to bow their heads at the name of Jesus, stand at the Creed and kneel at the Communion. Rogation Day processions were brought back, the Passing Bell was tolled. While arguing that 'the pure English Church is a sound member of the Catholick Church' unlike the Roman, he secretly explored the possibility of reunion with Rome. Montagu lived very simply at Aldingbourne, the bishops' summer palace, 'without state or retinue', spending much of his time at Petworth where he rebuilt the parsonage.

He introduced surplices and a 'Holy Table' or altar at the foot of the chancel, fenced off by Communion rails, all of which horrified Puritans. Worse still, his successor at Chichester, Brian Duppa (Prince Charles's tutor) demanded that parishes spend substantial sums of money on restoring and maintaining their churches. This infuriated gentry and townsmen alike.

The Civil War was a time of persecution for High Churchmen. The Commonwealth banned the Prayer Book and a fair number of 'Prelatist' priests were evicted from their livings. Towns like Rye became even greater models of Puritan observance, where there were fines for breaking the Sabbath, for profane swearing and for drunkenness – 'a city set on an hill', a minister called it admiringly. But the Restoration brought back the High Churchmen and the Prayer Book. In their turn scores of dissenting ministers were evicted, on 24 August 1662 – 'Bartholomew Tide' – while the gentry abandoned the Puritan persuasion.

Christianity in Sussex, whether Catholic, Anglican or Puritan, has never been more gracefully articulate or produced finer minds than in the century between the Reformation and the Restoration. The Catholics could boast Dr Gregory Martin of Guestling who died at Rheims in 1582, the principal translator of the Douai Bible, whose work helped to shape the King James Version; the Anglicans had such poet divines as Henry King, Bishop of Chichester; while at Rye the Puritan Samuel Jeake wrote powerfully on the 'Elixir of Life'. Moreover, there was genuine nobility in the witness borne by all three traditions, each of them producing heroes.

Yet decline was in store for every one of them, and no one remembers their heroes:

> The Wind blowes out; the Bubble dies;
> The Spring entomb'd in Autumn lies;
> The Dew dries up; the Starre is shot;
> The Flight is past; and Man forgot.

So wrote the banished Bishop King in 1657.

X
Lewes and the Rape of Lewes

The best way to approach Lewes is the route taken by the first Saxons and Normans, along the River Ouse which forms its eastern boundary, walking through water-meadows and marshes no less lonely than the Downs or the deep Weald. Hamlets are few and far between, and occasionally unexpected birds are seen, such as bearded tits. In Saxon times the estuary reached as far as Lewes and even today its little communities often look out in winter over wide sheets of flood-water.

The Ouse is not an exciting river but has undeniable charm, even at low tide. In the early Middle Ages it was known as the 'Mid-wind' because it divided Sussex into East and West. The derivations of its present name range from a mumbled 'Aqua de Lewes' to an undignified 'Ooze'.

The landscape from Newhaven to Lewes was a favourite with the poet Coventry Patmore. 'I do not know of a lovelier walk of eight miles' he wrote in 1886. 'During the last half of the walk Lewes is always in sight; and if there is the setting sun upon it and the evening is calm, the views have a quality of quietness, peace, humility and pathos, which I have rarely seen elsewhere.' Some walkers would still agree with him.

The Romans always knew a good site for a villa and there is no truth in the theory that in their time all East Sussex was a vast Imperial estate inhabited only by slaves – a villa lies beneath Newhaven police station. As its name implies, the port of Newhaven was founded as a new harbour, in 1539 when the Ouse was diverted to drain the marshes. Soon it overtook Seaford, the former outlet, though for 300 years it continued to be dominated by Lewes. A rare moment of fame came in 1848 when the deposed King of the French, Louis

Philippe, and his queen took refuge here from the Revolution of that year. (By then it had ousted Brighton as the principal Channel ferry port.) Augustus Hare described Newhaven as 'An ugly, dirty, little town and smoky port, with dangerous drinking water', but he admired its Norman church which stands on a hill. What other charms the town ever possessed are obscured by light industry though the coastline with green, white-topped cliffs may look attractive enough when approached from the sea.

Walking up the river in solitude, one meets many herons. Piddinghoe (properly pronounced 'Puddenhoe') is enchanting from a distance, a small hamlet whose Norman church stands on a mound which may be a Saxon burial ground. Its ancient tower is round, perhaps because of the difficulty of building it square in flint, the only stone available; some think it was used as a beacon for the ships which once went up and down the Ouse. In Norman times Piddinghoe was a fishing port and it still keeps a nautical look, with small boats moored by the bank. Closer inspection brings disappointment – the houses here have been 'gentrified', with smart front doors and carriage lamps.

At Rodmell further up-river, old Sussex has been no less overlaid by the new, even if there are beautiful views of the Downs. Only twenty years ago someone could write of its 'air of tranquility, often dreamed of but rarely discovered today'. It must have been exquisite when Leonard and Virginia Woolf settled here in 1919, and it was still unspoilt when Virginia drowned herself in the river in 1941. A few pretty houses remain, with a Norman church, an ugly old workhouse and the shell of a smithy. The best thing is the pink-washed Monks House, a rambling seventeenth-century cottage where the Woolfes lived, which can be visited; it has a beautiful garden, presided over by a fine bust of Virginia. But the village which sheltered those sensitive souls has been suburbanised like Piddinghoe.

A mile on, one's spirits lift at Southease, which stays as it must have been when the Woolfs first knew it – they thought of moving here during the 'twenties. Just a few old houses on a slope above the marshes, there is no more beautiful hamlet in the county; of all places in Sussex I should like to live here. It has a simple Norman church with a round tower like Piddinghoe (and a thirteenth-century bell), and also stands on what may have been a pagan shrine. The one memorable event in its history was a chance visit during the 1830s by Queen Adelaide when she rode over from Brighton. Virginia Woolf often went through Southease to start her tramps over the Downs, crossing the marsh and the Newhaven road to climb Iford Hill – past Iford Farm which was once a remote farmhouse where soldiers were stationed to ambush smugglers.

The next stretch of the Ouse is often lined with cormorants, though soon one's eyes are fastened on the castle dominating the sky line. No town is more aptly named than Lewes (*Hlaewes*, Anglo-Saxon for hills) since it is on a hill and surrounded by hills. Daniel Defoe was moved by the beauty of its setting. He writes, 'Lewes is in the most romatic situation I ever saw.'

The hill commanded both the Ouse and the path over the Downs from Beachy Head to Hampshire and was a natural inland trading centre. (Roman pottery has been found in 1990 at Cliffe, though no coins), but it only became a real settlement in the ninth century when King Alfred made Lewes a *burh*, fortifying it with a deep ditch on the west; in the tenth century, King Aethelstan established a mint, where later Aethelred the Unredy had gold pennies struck. It is clear from Domesday Book that sea-going vessels had long been putting in to Lewes so that its revenues were nearly twice those of Chichester. The town had expanded; the network of twittens (alleys) south of the castle is a rare example of Anglo-Saxon town-planning, while the suburb called Cliffe arose on the far side of the river.

At the Norman Conquest, Lewes was given to William de Warenne, the Conqueror's son-in-law, later Earl of Surrey. He built a stronghold on the hilltop to guard the estuary and the river route north, and to cow the rape. It consisted of an oval bailey with most unusually, *two* mottes – one of which was eventually replaced by a shell-keep. In the fourteenth century, his last descendant in the male line added a massive barbican of gleaming black flint and green sandstone. Below is the Gun Garden, once a moat. The castle dominates the little town, crouching over it. From the keep you see the Weald stretching north, the estuary south towards Newhaven; with Mount Caburn to the east – and further downland to the west.

When the navvies were digging the railway in 1846 they unearthed a huge charnel pit, out of which came a terrible stench, '*effluvium*' from those who had fallen at the battle of Lewes nearly six centuries before; thirteen waggon-loads of bones were taken away. On 14 May 1264, led by Simon de Montfort, the barons of England occupied a great hill outside the town, 'Black Harry'. They had marched through the darkness from Fletching, taking King Henry III by surprise. According to baronial supporters, the royalists had spent the night with '700 whores' whom they brought with them. After his enfeebled army was routed trying to storm Mount Harry, Henry fled to Lewes Priory while his son, the future Edward I, took refuge in the castle with the Warenne of the day but soon surrendered.

The Warennes held sway at Lewes until they died out in 1347, their lands and titles passing to the Fitzalans of Arundel who rarely visited the town. It was dominated by another magnate, the prior, richer and more powerful than many an earl, let alone a mitred abbot. William de Warenne and the Conqueror's step-daughter Gundrada had founded the priory of St Pancras in 1076 for Benedictines from Cluny in Burgundy. Among the richest monasteries in England its church was twenty-five feet longer than Chichester Cathedral. The monks played an important part in local life. They helped to organise coastal defence; during a fierce little battle at Rottingdean in 1377 the French captured Prior John de Cariloco who was leading a force against them. In 1450 the prior sent armed men to join Jack Cade's rebellion, protesting against misrule; afterwards he had to obtain a pardon. As late as 1537, the last prior, Robert Crowham, visited 'Flanders' to learn about Dutch methods of drainage and dyke maintenance, with a view to taming the Lewes Levels. It may well have been Prior Crowham's report which persuaded the gentry to divert the Ouse to Newhaven.

The priory had an annual income of over £900 when it was dissolved in 1539, Prior Crowham being made a prebendary of Lincoln Cathedral in recompense. The commissioner who provided 'evidence' for the dissolution, Richard Layton, alleged 'corruption in both sorts' – that some monks slept with women and some with men. The twenty-four brethren received small pensions, the magnificent monastery buildings being granted to Thomas Cromwell, who at once had most of them demolished – the worst architectural disaster in the entire history of Sussex. Only a few walls survive, apart from the monks' lavatory (or 'reredorter) and the guest-house. Standing next to a fragment of the Great Gate, the guest-house was rebuilt during the fourteenth century to provide a parish church for the Southover area of the town – on the boundary of the old borough. A chapel in the church contains the lead coffins which held the bones of William de Warenne and his wife Gundrada, together with Gundrada's superb tomb slab which was carved in black Tournai marble about the year 1145. The discovery of the coffins by navvies, when the railway was being built in 1846, aroused such interest that the Sussex Archaelogical Society was founded to protect what was left of Lewes Priory.

During Queen Mary's reign seventeen Protestants were burnt outside the Star Inn. (The Victorian Town Hall stands on the site, but a fourteenth-century staircase leads down to a vaulted undercroft in which ten of the martyrs are believed to have been confined before their execution.) All of them came from Sussex and at least two are known to have lived in Lewes.

Brutality did not end with the Reformation. Here is a gloating contemporary account of what was done with the corpse of the murderer Robert Blinkhurst in 1679 after he committed suicide. (When being interrogated, he had swallowed some of the arsenic with which he had poisoned a neighbour.) His relatives came with a coffin and grave clothes, offering to inter him decently in a proper burial plot, but the authorities insisted that Blinkhurst must suffer the traditional fate of suicides:

> On Monday afternoon, being the 8th of December, a dung cart was provided, which being littered with straw, the body in its wrap, without any coffin, was cast into it; thus with part of the face and the feet bare it was drawn through the town, a ghastly spectacle to the beholders. At a fair cross-way at the Spittle, a grave was ready digged lying north and south into which the body was put by two fellows; their hearts failing them for that other service, a third was prevailed with to drive a stake through his bowels . . . the earth being cast in on him, a fair bulk was raised over the grave and covered with green turf, the stake being left visible above it . . .

The cross-roads are where Spital Road meets the corner of the hospital, and presumably the bones of the miserable Blinkhurst still lie beneath, while his ghost is one of the many who haunt Lewes.

The town contained the court of the archdeacon of Lewes, which in effect made it the capital of East Sussex from very early times – as it became in name at the end of the last century. It was a rich little town, exporting grain and wool (usually illegally), together with cannon during the days of the wealden iron industry. There was a highly profitable barge trade up the Ouse, because roads were so bad; until the coming of the railways, anyone moving from London to Lewes – or indeed from anywhere else – found it easier to bring their furniture by sea. There were flourishing ship yards, and as late as 1866 an ocean-going schooner was built here.

The Pelham family dominated the town. Two Pelham brothers, prime ministers from 1743 to 1762, were the only English premiers born and bred Sussex men. The elder brother, Duke of Newcastle, made sure that his Pelham cousins represented Lewes and Seaford in Parliament, systematically patronising all the High Street shops and giving lavish dinners for voters at his Sussex seats – Halland and Bishopstone Place. He bought the Dog Alehouse in 1732, turning it into the Pelham Arms where his supporters might drink their fill at his expense, while at Newcastle House in the High Street (the present façade is a twentieth century pastiche) he installed a coffee room where the gentry could be his guests.

At the other end of the social scale, a failed corset-maker was appointed revenue officer at Lewes in 1768. He lodged with a tobacconist at Bull House (which is still there) and married his daughter. However, Mr Thomas Paine decamped in 1774, escaping from his debts and abandoning his wife. Otherwise, the author of *The Rights of Man* left precious little mark on the town, except perhaps on those who heard him ranting at the White Hart or on the Castle bowling-green.

A boom began in the 1780s, which lasted until the end of the Napoleonic Wars. Even at that late date the county still spoke of 'Proud Lewes, poor Brighthelmstone', letters to Brighton being addressed to 'Brighthelmstone near Lewes'. Many of the town's mansions were rebuilt. Others were simply given imposing façades so that some fine Elizabethan and Jacobean interiors survive, such as those of Barbican House beneath the castle, Shelley's Hotel in the High Street or Pelham House in St Andrew's Lane.

According to John Boys Ellman (born in the last years of George III's reign), 'Lewes was the place where each winter the good old families had their winter town houses'. They came here to avoid being cut off from each other by the season's vile roads. Ellman describes how ladies got into their sedan chairs in the hall of their own house and got out in the hall of the one they were visiting. There were assemblies and concerts at the Star Hotel, while a theatre was opened in 1789 – demolished long ago. In the summer, there were such well attended funtions as the Assizes, the Races, the Wool Show and the Fatstock Show. The Prince of Wales and his raffish little court began to ride over from Brighton in 1784, usually to attend the Races. On one occasion the prince drove a coach and four down the alarmingly steep Keere Street, presumably for a bet.

The geologist Gideon Mantell, author of *Thoughts on a Pebble*, was born at Lewes in 1792, later living at Castle Place – rebuilt by Amon Wilds in 1810. A shoemaker's son, Mantell became a doctor, and when a young man, saved a woman from being hanged; she was on trial for her life, accused of poisoning her husband with arsenic but Mantell proved that she could not have done so and was innocent. A keen antiquary, he opened many of the downland tumuli. However, his real claim to fame was discovering a fossilised monster in Tilgate Forest which he named the 'iguanodon'. He also found elephant tusks at Brighton, beneath the Steine.

Another Lewes antiquary was Mark Anthony Lower, born at Muddle's Green near Chiddingly in 1813, one of the founders of the Sussex Archaeological Society and the author of many books on the county; these include *The Worthies of Sussex* and *The Song of Solomon in the dialect of Sussex*. His lifelong friend was John Dudeney, the scholar shepherd. Lower quarrelled with the town's rowdy bonfire boys, describing what took place on 5 November as 'a saturnalia of the Roughs'. They only just failed to carry out their threat to throw him in the Ouse.

Bonfire Night was a real hazard in early Victorian Lewes. Drunken mobs rolled flaming tar-barrels through the streets, before tipping them into the river. In 1846 they tried to burn down the house of an unpopular magistrate, Sir Henry Blackman, piling three tar barrels, one on top of another, against it and then setting them alight; when Sir Henry emerged to remonstrate, he was knocked unconscious. Next year the Lord Lieutenant read the Riot Act from the steps of the County Hall, after which a hundred Metropolitan police specially brought down from London dispersed the mobs in a savage pitched battle. Some policemen carried cutlasses so a good deal of blood must have been shed before the bonfire boys were driven off the streets.

Although less rowdy, the celebrations continued. 'The procession containing Pope Pius IX, Guy Faux, and the homicidal Chinaman (the reputed murderer of Commodore Goodenough) started at half-past nine', a journalist reported in 1875. The main bonfire was in the middle of the road between County Hall and the White Hart, though there were many others, all being constantly stoked up with tar-barrels brought on waggons. 'There were people in long white bed gowns; in grotesque tunics ... other people wonderfully dressed as sages ... and yet others who simply wore masks and tinsel.' The three gigantic effigies, stuffed with fireworks, were burnt 'amid howls of execration'. Even today bonfire societies flourish at Lewes – only recently they burnt an effigy of Lady Thatcher.

This is one of the most attractive towns in England and, understandably, too many people want to live here, on the banks of the Ouse. In consequence, unsightly housing estates have been sprouting on the periphery ever since the Second World War. However, they have not destroyed Lewes's charm.

Continuing to walk up the Ouse, you are soon in unspoilt country again. So many of the little hamlets just north of Lewes have noble churches that it is impossible to describe all of them. Sometimes called 'lost church', that at Hamsey is approached through the yard of an old farmhouse and stands on a hillock overlooking the Ouse, which in past times became an island every winter; the field names round it are revealing: 'The Ox Brook' or 'The Fore-Right Cow Brook'. The loneliness of the Sussex Levels can be very bleak here, despite the lush landscape and the presence of Lewes Castle on the skyline. Hamsey church has a stout Perpendicular tower with weirdly beaming gargoyles. A deserted medieval village and the fortified manor house of the de Says lie somewhere under the fields nearby, once served by the church – which may account for an inescapable sense of desolation one feels here. According to a legend which could well be true, when the Black Death came to Hamsey its heroic inhabitants barricaded themselves off from the outside world so that they might not infect their neighbours – those of them who did not die of the plague perished from starvation.

The river winds on. Barcombe church, by a tranquil duckpond, has been over-restored. Barcombe Mills, further on, is a lovely spot, a group of millponds beside the Ouse which was mentioned in Domesday Book. Eventually the river brings you to Isfield.

Isfield church, in meadows at the end of a long, lonely lane (and, strictly speaking, in the Rape of Pevensey) contains the monuments of the Shurley family – a branch of the Shirleys of Wiston. There is John Shurley, clerk of the royal kitchens, who died in 1527; and 'Edward Shurley Esquyer ye sone of John Shurley of ye maner of Isfylde Esquyer & Cofferer to kynge Henry ye Eyght' who died in 1558. The most impressive tomb is that of Sir John who died in 1631, 'stovt in good cavses yea & good in all cavses'; he is shown with his two wives, the first a Shirley of Wiston. His second wife, Dorothy, was a Goring of Danny – 'Her pvrse open to a Prophet's name, her pity was ye clothing of ye poore . . .' Although the family died out in the male line in 1667, their pleasant old manor, Isfield House, remains. Partly Tudor, partly Jacobean, with a tower at each angle of the garden wall, it is the sort of mellow, red brick symphony beloved by Edwardian water-colourists.

The Ouse divides into three at Isfield. Chailey is on the western stream, with yet another over-restored church. Your time here is better spent in The Five Bells.

On the northern stream, Newick has a pretty church with a tower of about the same date as Hamsey's, decorated by four gargoyles who are mitred. This northern tributary ends in the beautiful lakes and gardens of Sheffield Park, originally laid out by Humphry Repton in the 1790s and considered by many to be the finest gardens in Sussex. There is an imposing mansion within them; built by James Wyatt in 1176–77 it is an early forerunner of neo-Gothic, and altogether different from the Strawberry Hill 'Gothick' of Horace Walpole.

The eastern stream goes to Uckfield, finally disappearing at Buxted Park.

Returning to Lewes and going west, you come to a remarkable survival at Kingston-by-Lewes. Under the Downs, a cosy hamlet with a Georgian manor house and a flint fourteenth-century church seem as if encapsulated in time, set apart from what is really a garden suburb of Lewes and said to be largely inhabited by dons from Sussex University. Kingston Down was W.H. Hudson's favourite hill in downland. The scholar shepherd, John Dudeney, was hired to tend sheep here in the year of Trafalgar at a wage of £6 per annum; he recalled days and nights in the open, sometimes in deep snow which he had to scrape away for his flock to graze. Even so, keeping his books in a hole in the chalk, he taught himself such languages as Hebrew, becoming a schoolmaster. There are two dewponds here where John must have watered his sheep. Nothing is more wonderful than sitting on Kingston Hill at dawn to watch the sun rise between Mount Caburn and Firle Beacon.

'Nan Kemp's Grave' is marked on the ordnance survey map as just outside Kingston village, but another tradition claims she was buried where the Juggs' Road crosses the lane from Kingston to the Lewes–Brighton motorway. Since she was a suicide, the latter seems more likely. No one knows who she was or when she lived – or died – though it was probably during the 1700s. Legend says she killed her husband and child, cooked them in the bread-oven, ate them, and then did away with herself, after which she was buried at the crossroads with a stake through her heart. An alternative version claims she was killed by horrified neighbours, who bricked her up in her own bread-oven to die, before staking her out. Until quite recently, locals believed that if you walked twelve times round Nan Kemp's grave at midnight, she would 'come out to get you'. There was also a charm for curing warts: rub a piece of meat against the warts and then bury it in Nan's grave after walking round three times – which sounds as though she must have been a witch.

Nearby are Iford and Swanborough Manor. Set amid pleasant farm buildings, the church at Iford (thatched until only 200 years ago) shows the impact of the Black Death; the Norman fabric survives, but one can see where an aisle added about 1200 was pulled down because of a smaller congregation. Parts of Swanborough Manor also date from 1200. Built by the Lewes monks, it now houses the Vice-Chancellor of Sussex University. Huddled round its church in a fold of the Downs, Telscombe has been miraculously saved from the bungalow sprawl along the cliffs a short way off. In past times it was as lawless as it was lonely, a haunt of smugglers; John Lulham from Telscombe was probably the last man to be hanged for sheep stealing, in 1819.

Further west, one comes to villages swallowed up by Brighton. An isolated downland community of farmers and shepherds, with a fair number of well-to-do 'traders' (smugglers) who built snug Georgian houses, Rottingdean was discovered by writers and artists in about 1870. Among those who settled here was Sir Edward Burne-Jones, whose wife found it while on a walk from Brighton. Their nephew Rudyard Kipling lived at the Elms, but left in 1902 because of the trippers who came by horse-bus to stare at him over his garden gate. Nowadays it is an outlying suburb of Brighton, if still very pretty, its barns and farm buildings converted into desirable residences.

They used to have a good bonfire procession here every 5 November, singing a fine anti-Papist song. One verse ran:

> A tuppeny loaf to feed old Pope
> And a penn'orth of cheese to choke him,
> A pint of beer to rinse it down
> And a faggot of bush to burn him

In his powerfully nostalgic book, *A Song for Every Season*, the folk-singer Bob Copper tells of the life led at the turn of the century by his own farming family at Rottingdean. He recalls the age-old way of life of Sussex country folk which vanished between the Wars. 'They ploughed their land with teams of oxen, sowed their seed by hand, reaped the corn with sickle and threshed the grain with flails as their Saxon ancestors had done', he says. 'Their lives were hard but uncomplicated, and through living and working close to nature, they had a clearly defined and well balanced sense of values. In the main, they were content and were aware when they sang, in the words of one of their old songs, "Peace and Plenty fill the year", that it was not so very far from the truth.'

Falmer and Stanmer have gone the way of Rottingdean. Flanked by a motorway and a teacher training college, around its duckpond Falmer somehow manages to keep the ghostly semblance of a hamlet. So does Stanmer amid its parkland, under the shadow of Sussex University, but the great Palladian mansion which was once the seat of the Earls of Chichester is sadly forlorn.

Northwards, on the far side of the Downs, are villages of undeniable charm, and a landscape which almost bears out Gilbert White's flattering use of the word 'mountains'. Ditchling Beacon makes the very finest sort of landmark, with a dramatic rounded outline despite the encroachment of scrub. Although it possesses a noble church and a pretty Tudor mansion supposedly associated with Anne of Cleves, to my mind the village of Ditchling is memorable for little save charm. That very odd fish the sculptor (and sex maniac) Eric Gill lived on Ditchling Common in a house called 'Hopkin's Crank' – somehow, one feels, a fitting name. It was Gill who said that there is beauty in electricity pylons, no doubt in return for a discreet backhander from the Electricity Generating Board.

A far more likeable Ditchling figure was Esther Meynell, latterly of Conds Cottage, whose *Sussex* (1947) ran to eight impressions. Born during the 1880s – she was coy about her age – she married a nephew of the poet Wilfrid Meynell and died in 1955. If occasionally her books may seem a bit dated, at once overblown and faded in style, she is often well worth reading, as when describing the vista from Ditchling Beacon or recalling ghosts. She understood downland: 'there is something about the Downs after the sun has set which says "Go away, you little human creatures, leave us to ourselves".'

Never lavish with his compliments, Ian Nairn unreservedly calls Plumpton Place 'enchanted'. Part Tudor and part Jacobean, it had sunk to being a mere farmhouse by the beginning of this century, but was rescued and transformed by Sir Edwin Lutyens. The house's most interesting occupant was the Tudor horticulturist, Leonard Mascall, 'who much delighted in Gardening, man's Original vocation' – according to Thomas Fuller in *The Worthies of England*. At Plumpton church next door, which is half Norman and half what used to be labelled 'Early English', there are pale fragments of medieval wall paintings in the same style as those of Hardham. They too may have been the work of the remarkably prolific monks of Lewes Priory.

A stretch of rail near Plumpton provides what must be the

most macabre train ride in England, for those who know what lies beneath them, though very few passengers can be aware that they are travelling over dead men's bones. Should you glance up from Plumpton Agricultural College, you will make out – much overgrown – a great grey cross, once white, on the green downs above. It was carved in the chalk by the Lewes monks after the battle of 1266 and is flanked by large pits into which the bodies of the fallen had been thrown by way of burial. When the railways were being built during the 1840s their skeletons were disinterred and sold to the railway contractors for imaginative use as ballast under the wooden sleepers which support the rails.

Murals even more complete than those at Hardham were found in Clayton church during 1956, painted like them by the remarkable monks from Lewes. There is a superb red and yellow Christ in Glory over the chancel. The tiny, very pretty, village of Clayton lies below a hill on which stand two famous windmills, Jack and Jill. Not far away, the entrance to the London to Brighton railway tunnel is guarded by two mock Gothic towers just like the gatehouse of a castle. Between them nestles Tunnel Cottage, which must surely be inhabited by the stone deaf.

Devil's Dyke, once one of the last haunts of the great bustard, is a traditional downland playground for Brighton, if not to such an extent today as formerly. It can certainly be lonely and bleak enough. There is a magnificent walk westward across the Downs, along Fulking Hill, Edburton Hill and Truleigh Hill, with glimpses of the sea on one side and the Weald on the other. Below Fulking lies the site of Perching Castle, abandoned long ago. On top of Edburton Hill there are what are known as the Castle Rings, traces of a tiny motte-and-bailey castle. No more than a stockaded wooden fort, it was erected by the Normans during the Conquest on the border of the rapes of Lewes and Bramber as a look-out post over the Weald – and no doubt as a signalling post too. Edburton church is worth a visit, not so much for itself as its dramatic setting; looking up at the Downs, you might think you were in the Lake District.

Poynings, just north of the Dyke, has a fine Perpendicular church, built with money left by Michael de Poynings in 1369. A poem of 1608 in the parish register commemorates Richard Weller, 'a man of much mercie and pittie towards the poore . . .' Before he left to take the waters, seeking a cure for ill health, he feasted the entire village:

> The morning that away he went,
>   They all came him to greete;
> Then for a barrell of beer he sent,
>   And set it in the streete.

Alas, he died at the baths though he left ten pounds for the indigent. Another poem comes from Poynings parsonage, written at the end of the eighteenth century, as an inscription for a hermitage in the rectory garden:

> Thou lov'st the quiet Hermitage;
> Where the eye may wander still
> Over dale and over hill,
> And see the lessening Downs arise,
> Melting soft into the skies.

Driving north, you should take care to let the eye wander as little as possible over the unlovely sprawl of Haywards Heath. It owes its origin to Cuckfield's refusal to let the railway pass through it in 1841; track and station were banished to a wild heath which then formed a distant part of the parish. (There is a local belief, quite without foundation, that 'Hayward' was a highwayman who terrorised the heath.)

The church at Twineham was built in Henry VIII's reign, entirely from red brick which has faded to a lovely pale rose colour. Though Tudor, it has the flat, depressed arches of late Perpendicular. Either the bricks were made by Flemish workers, many of whom settled in Sussex at the end of the fifteenth century, or else they were shipped from Flanders and up the Adur. The hamlet is between two branches of the River Adur (hence the name 'Betwyneham'), which were navigable up to here and even beyond — there used to be a harbour master's cottage.

You are deep into the Weald by now. Amid its woods,

Cuckfield, once a little market town, possesses enormous charm, even though threatened by absorption into the monster which it spawned. A bypass saves it from too much traffic. The noble church was built twenty years before the Black Death; the beams of its fifteenth-century roof have been gaily painted and gilded since Victorian times while one wall is covered by monuments to the Burrell family, here since Richard III's reign when Gerard Burrell bought Ockenden Manor, not far from the church.

Cuckfield Park lies in a valley below the village, an Elizabethan mansion altered by the Victorians. It keeps a turreted gatehouse from which the corpses of the Bowyers, who lived here till 1690, set out to their burial – at midnight, by the light of torches. (There is a brass of its builder, Henry Bowyer, in the church.) Until a hundred years ago, the house was haunted by a blue lady.

There was also a belief that should a bough fall in the owner's path as he rode down a great avenue of limes, it foretold his death. In *Rookwood*, a popular shocker of 1834, Harrison Ainsworth says that Cuckfield Park was the model for Rookwood Hall and he gives a lurid version of the legend; a witch, hunted to death in the park by bloodhounds, had had her heart impaled by a limewood stake out of which grew the avenue. The omen was still believed in Augustus Hare's day, when the Sergison family lived there.

At Slaugham (pronounced 'Slaffam') one really does have a sense of remoteness, of being in a forest. Deep in the High Weald, the village faces on to a triangular green, its houses being built of reddish-brown sandstone ('Tilgate Stone', from quarries near Crawley). The church is filled with brasses and reliefs, and monuments to the ancient family of Covert, who lived here from the fifteenth to the seventeenth centuries. Their lands were said to stretch from Southwark to the sea; in fact they ran from Crawley to Hangleton near Brighton, which is almost to the sea. Their seat, Slaugham Place, lies in a romantic valley behind the church and is among the most haunting ruins in Sussex. A Renaissance 'courtyard' house, it was built by Sir Robert Covert in 1612. Surrounded by a turreted wall and a moat, and staffed by seventy servants, it stood in a deerpark of 700 acres. Sir Robert was the most prominent of his family, twice High Sheriff of Sussex and several times a Member of Parliament. The last Covert to lie here was Sir John, a Cavalier made a baronet for his loyalty, who died in 1678. The house was soon abandoned, its magnificent oak staircase being removed and installed at Lewes Town Hall.

Ardingly is best known for its public school, built in red brick between 1867 and 1927. Glimpsed from a train passing over Balcombe viaduct, this looks like some medieval priory in a forest clearing. The viaduct is a triumph of Victorian engineering – to appreciate its full splendour one must stand beneath and listen to the wind sighing among the thirty-seven arches.

A brass at Ardingly commemorates Richard Wakehurst of Wakehurst Place who died in 1454. Member of Parliament for Sussex in Henry V's first Parliament, he wears the rich robes of a wealthy man. Here too are the brasses of Nicholas and Richard Culpeper, both in armour, who died in 1510 and 1516. They were a pair of ruthless fortune hunters. When old Richard Wakehurst died, his heiresses were two orphaned grand-daughters, Margaret and Elizabeth, whose guardian was his neighbour Sir John Culpeper. One day Sir John's brothers, Nicholas and Richard, came to Wakehurst Place 'arrayed in the manner of war' – in full armour – to abduct the girls and marry them despite 'great and piteous lamentation and weeping'. As soon as their wives' grandmother died, the brothers took possession of the Wakehurst estates. From Nicholas' brass we see that he fathered eighteen children on his unwilling bride.

The Culpepers (distant kinsmen of the herbalist) stayed here until 1694. Sir Edward Culpeper rebuilt Wakehurst Place in 1590, another courtyard house which, though much altered by the Victorians, remains a noble mansion. Today it is leased to Kew Gardens and the grounds are a horticultural paradise, with specialised habitats which include deciduous and coniferous woodland, meadowland, streamsides and rocky outcrops. There are also heath and bog gardens besides a wonderful collection of trees and shrubs. The latter was begun by Gerald Loder, Lord Wakehurst, who was one of the great Sussex gardeners.

The country round here is dense woodland with deep ghylls, some of them dammed not so long ago to make beautiful lakes. Local resentment at the creation of the largest of these, Balcombe reservoir, has been soothed to a certain extent by the new bird life; in the summer of 1993 nine great crested grebes adorned it. Amid the heavy mists of early morning the atmosphere can be oddly oppressive below the Balcombe Forest ridge and you realise why the Saxons called the place Balcombe – 'Evil Valley'.

At the edge of the Ashdown Forest, West Hoathly is another village where Tilgate stone is much in evidence. Once a tiny Norman building, its church was enlarged in the thirteenth century, to cater for the enlarged population which resulted from clearing the Weald. It contains cast-iron tomb slabs, commemorating members of the Infield family. The fifteenth century Priest's House was acquired by that splendid body, the Sussex Archaeological Society, and restored in 1906 as a museum of village life. It belonged to Lewes Priory and may have served as a vicarage or an estate office, even as a recruiting office during Jack Cade's rebellion in 1450.

In past times a rock called 'Big-on-Little' in a valley about half a mile from West Hoathly church, was said to be haunted by a black ghost hound.

Just over a mile from West Hoathly is Gravetye, a beautiful Elizabethan manor with great brick chimneys, built in 1598 by the ironmaster Richard Infield. Its glory is its gardens, created between the 1880s and his death in 1935 by William Robertson, the friend of Gertrude Jekyll and author of *The English Flower Garden*. One of the most imaginative of English landscape gardeners, his approach was romantic and naturalistic, never formal, a 'wild' garden – informal planting against a background of parkland, woods and rocky outcrops.

Crawley, on the Surrey border, was already ruined when E. V. Lucas revised his *Highways and Byways* after the Great War –

'Motor buses, charabancs, motor cars and bicycles pass through Crawley so numerously as almost to constitute one elongated vehicle.'

Then came Gatwick Airport and the New Town. Begun in 1947, the latter was intended to relieve the 'overspill' of London's population, employment being provided by a factory zone – the first large concentration of industry in Sussex. It has a certain interest for students of the unlovely architecture of the 'fifties, but its real significance is as a monument to the halcyon days of Social Control and the Ration Book.

Amazingly, there is unspoilt wealden country round about, with fine churches and houses. Crabbet Park, almost on the outskirts, was the home of Wilfrid Scawen Blunt, poet, explorer and (by adoption) Irish Nationalist. Hare calls it:

> a modern Georgian house, built from the admirable design of its mistress, Lady Anne Blunt, the African traveller and grand-daughter of the poet Byron. The place has become celebrated for its breed of Arab horses and their sales. The owner of the house, Mr Wilfrid Blunt, has insisted on a wild plot of land, covered with rubbish heaps and brushwood – 'the African desert' – being left in front of the house door, in curious contrast to the well-kept lawns and bleached alleys a little further off.

The prim old bachelor can have had little in common with the virile Blunt, a superb horseman and inveterate seducer of ladies.

Blunt was sufficiently fond of his native landscape to write a poem about it, 'Worth Forest'. No one reads his verse nowadays, save perhaps for 'The Old Squire':

> I like the hunting of the hare;
> New sports I hold in scorn.
> I like to be as my fathers were,
> In the days ere I was born.

So much has been written in praise of the eleventh-century Saxon church at Worth in Worth Forest that I expected a disappointment. I was wrong, even though Victorian restorers tried to ruin it. Hare laments 'all that vulgar tiles, revolting glass and coarse woodwork can do to spoil a church, has been liberally bestowed'. But in 1986 a fire made it possible to undo much of the damage. The effect is staggering. Outside, there are Saxon pilasters and, far rarer, a northern and a southern 'porticus' where private Masses were said. Entering through the west door, one is overwhelmed by massive simplicity and harmony, above all by a vast chancel arch; there are two very tall and very narrow doorways, with windows divided by a single balustrade, none of which can be Norman work. Worth is England before 1066.

There is a moving inscription here, on a monument to Mrs Mildred Whitfield who died in 1631:

A woman wth many sorrowes & mvch sicknes even from yvth till old age strongly & strangely afflicted, yet even by firme faithe & rare patience devinely supported. Job shee was in life, Simeon in death: God whom in sincerity shee served hath now wiped all teares from her eyes.

In my view, Worth church is the most beautiful thing in Sussex.

XI

The Civil War:
'The Crooked Rebel of Sussex'

Climb Mount Caburn and you look down over the Glynde
Reach, a tributary of the Ouse, dawdling through the Glynde
Levels, which at times seem to have more and noisier
moorhens than anywhere else in England. Two great houses
can be seen. That at Glynde, immediately below, belonged to a
man who virtually ruled Sussex on Parliament's behalf during
the Civil War and for a time under the Commonwealth. The
other, in the distance on the far side of the Reach is Firle, home
of a family from which came one of the most popular Cavalier
commanders.

In Sussex the Civil War was on a very small scale owing to
the county's isolation from the main campaigns. Yet if
undeniably on the periphery, it was important to both sides
because of its iron foundries, while money and munitions
could be shipped in all along the coast. No decisive battle was
fought here, no Naseby or Marston Moor, but there were
some fierce little engagements, together with the sieges of
Chichester and Arundel.

Sussex produced those fire-eating Cavaliers, Lord Goring
and Sir Thomas Lunsford, and also seven regicides who signed
King Charles's death-warrant. From the outset the county was
split, though not evenly. Superficially, it might seem that the
Puritan east was for Parliament, with the exception of
Hastings and a few Papist squires, and that save for Chichester
the west was for the King. In reality, loyalties were confused.
Few played so active a role as Colonel Harbert Morely of
Glynde, MP for Lewes, a Puritan who fought for good
government and a Presbyterian Church of England. Even if an
angry royalist called him 'the crooked rebel of Sussex', his

sheer decency places him among the most honourable of the Sussex men who took part, and in many ways he personifies the period.

In 1628, Chichester had been outraged by the king billeting his ruffianly soldiers on its citizens. In 1634, it was forced to contribute towards the cost of an 800-ton ship, while in the following year it had to pay £800 in 'ship-money'; there were riots against this tax in 1640. Most Chichester men were Puritans who bitterly resented the cathedral's dominance and its popish services. They had a leader in William Cawley, MP for Midhurst.

On 24 August 1642, two days after Charles I had raised his standard at Nottingham, Chichester declared for Parliament and a trained-band began drilling in Priory Park. The clergy retaliated by raising a troop of royalist horse which drilled in the Close.

The situation was more straightforward in East Sussex where Harbert Morley raised a company of 'dragoneers' (probably mounted musketeers on the French model) and declared for Parliament, fortifying Lewes. There was no open royalist opposition on his side of the county.

On 15 November, a Cavalier force recruited from local gentry forced the mayor of Chichester to surrender his keys, seizing the guns and the powder magazine. Next day, the royalist high sheriff of Sussex, Sir Edward Ford of Uppark, rode in with a hundred horsemen and a large trained-band. He did not trust the latter, disarming them as soon as possible.

On 21 November 1642, Parliament appointed Harbert Morley, Anthony Stapley, Sir Thomas Pelham and Sir Thomas Parker deputy lieutenants for Sussex, 'to disarme all such as shall refuse to joyne with them in securing the County'. It expelled the five Sussex MPs involved in the seizure of Chichester, ordering that 'all Papists and persons disaffected to the Parliament' should be made to contribute towards the maintenance of its army.

Early in December, Sir Edward Ford advanced on Lewes, forcing men to join him by threatening to hang them and burn their houses. However, at Haywards Heath he was intercepted by Parliamentary troops. After an hour's fierce fighting, during which they inflicted 200 casualties, these drove the Cavaliers back to Chichester in headlong confusion.

Meanwhile, Sir William Waller, who had just captured Portsmouth for Parliament, advanced on Chichester with 6,000 men and 600 guns. A hundred of his horse rode on to Arundel, defended by about the same number of Cavaliers; cowing the town, they then blew in the castle gates and overcame the garrison without losing a single man. Morely joined Waller at Chichester, with three troops of horse and two companies of 'dragoneers'. Mounting his cannon on Broyle Down, immediately north of the city, Sir William summoned Ford to surrender. The sheriff declined, though he offered to hand over any Papists. The guns opened fire but the range was too great. They were moved further in, to Cowley's hospital within 'half a musket shot of the North Gate'; the city was also invested at the South and East Gates while musketeers poured in volley after volley from the church of St Pancras just outside the walls. Considerable damage was done, more from thatched roofs catching fire than by the bombardment; a drought hindered attempts to extinguish the flames which destroyed numerous houses.

Clarendon says that the defenders were hampered by the citizens' hostility; the number of ordinary folk among the royalists was so small 'that the constant duty was performed by the officers and gentlemen of quality, who were absolutely tired out'. At ten o'clock on the evening of the seventh day, a trumpet sounded from the walls and the garrison requested a parley the following morning. By then Waller was preparing to assault simultaneously from the east and the west, and to blow in a back gate of the Close. Next day, he offered only 'Quarter and with it honourable usage.' The defenders refused indignantly, but they were exhausted. They surrendered at 7.00 am the day after.

Waller's troops marched in, taking over 800 prisoners. Nearly sixty of them were 'gentlemen of quality and officers of name', most being fined though not too severely. (Thomas

Shepherds like this tended sheep on the Sussex Downs from Neolithic times until the 1960s. *East Sussex County Library*

Since the Stone Age sheep have drunk from dew-ponds on the otherwise waterless Downs. *S & O Matthews Photography*

Falmer Bottom, archetypal Sussex downland. *Iain Roy*

Up Marden Church. '. . . one of the loveliest interiors of any church
in England.' *National Monuments Record/RCHME Crown Copyright*
Lazarus, Chichester Cathedral. Anglo-Saxon art, even if twelfth-
century. *Britain on View/Mirror Syndication International*
The Market in East Street in 1814. Chichester as the poet John
Keats knew it. *East Sussex County Record Office*

Fan-vaulting at Cowdray House. *Country Life*

Dewy Morning by J.M.W. Turner. A view of Petworth House from the lake in 1810. *Tate Gallery, London*

'Walking up the Cuckmere Valley is to walk into a nineteenth-century English watercolour.' *Peter Wakely, English Nature*

Fairlight Cove, near Hastings, used regularly for 'run-ins' by smugglers during the eighteenth century. *Iain Roy*

The Look Out, a print of 1824. Smuggling was once the major Sussex industry after agriculture. *Hastings Museum & Art Gallery*

Hurstmonceux Castle. Begun about 1440, a mansion instead of a fortress. *Britain on View/Mirror Syndication International*

Eighteenth-century wyverns guarding the Elizabethan Glynde Place beneath Mount Caburn. *Courtesy of the Viscount Hampden*

Firle Place, another ancient house beneath the Downs. The Gage family have lived here since 1477. *S & O Matthews Photography*

Jevington Church. Leonora Rochester summons her husband to join her in the grave, 1758. *S & O Matthews Photography*

The original Pavilion and the Steyne in 1796, by Cracklow. *Royal Pavilion, Art Gallery and Museums, Brighton*

Gounter, Colonel Gounter's cousin, had to pay £110.) Ford was sent to London but soon set at liberty – to fight for King Charles again. The clergy were treated more harshly, the dean being fined £120 and losing his house, as did the canons. A thousand captives were marched to London, including the poet-bishop, Dr Henry King, who was 'a proud Prelate, as all the rest are, and a most pragmaticall malignant against the Parliament'. His palace was sacked and then sold, together with his manor houses.

The cathedral was looted. The soldiers broke up the Holy Table and the organ, crying 'Hark how the organs go', as they smashed the pipes. Although the city escaped a full scale sack, it was to be many years before Chichester recovered from the siege. Colonel Anthony Stapley, MP for the County of Sussex, stayed as military govenor until 1646.

Colonel Morley was even more highly regarded than Stapley, becoming the most powerful man in Sussex. Born in 1616, he had been educated at Lewes free-school, where he made life-long friends with another pupil, the diarist John Evelyn who was living at Southover Grange. He had an extraordinary gift for friendship, even with those who differed from him in religion or politics, a gift well attested by Evelyn and others.

A devout Puritan, Harbert Morley was suspected of being an 'Independent', a man who today would be a Congregationalist or a Seventh Day Adventist. It is much more likely that he was a Presbyterian and wanted the Church of England to be governed on Scottish lines. The English Presbyterians of his day have had a bad press. In *Hudibras* Samuel Butler speaks of:

> A sect whose chief devotion lies
> In odd perverse antipathies . . .
> Still so perverse and opposite
> As if they worshipped God for spite

But though his zeal sometimes verged on the excessive, nobody ever accused Colonel Morley of spite.

Parliament recognised his worth early on. He was formally thanked by the House of Commons for his part in capturing Chichester, and by the spring of 1643 he was its principal representative in the county, recruiting troops, levying taxes, sequestrating estates. He arrested gentry suspected of royalist sympathies and kept an eye on prelatist clergy.

The Cavaliers did not despair of Sussex, especially when Waller marched off into the West Country. In September 1643, Morley wrote to the Speaker that the enemy were about to besiege Southampton, which was likely to fall: 'This approaching cloud may raise a storm in Sussex, which county is full of neuters and malignants; and I have ever observed neuters to turn malignants on such occasions.' He warned that if the southern counties were lost, London would be in very grave danger indeed.

Sussex's greatest defence, particularly in winter, was its appalling roads. But there were very sharp frosts that December and Sir Ralph Hopton, the royalist commander in the south, saw his chance. 'The exceeding hard frost made his march more easy through those deep and dirty ways than any better weather would have done, and he came to Arundel before there was any imagination that he had that place in prospect', Clarendon tells us. The Cavaliers reached Arundel on 6 December. Morley tried to relieve the castle but it surrendered three days later. Hopton installed a royalist garrison under Sir Edward Ford.

However, the same hard frost enabled Sir William Waller to move with equal speed. He arrived at Arundel on 19 December with 6,000 men and artillery which included leather guns. ('One horse may draw a piece, which will carry a bullet of a pound and half weight and do execution very far', reports a contemporary newspaper.) Next day he captured the town, storming the earthworks which defended it, and taking 140 prisoners. (He also survived an attempt to murder him, when the would-be assassin's musket misfired.) Colonel Morley and his regiment joined him on 21 December. But then the weather broke, with snow, rain and high winds. Most of the townspeople fled; all their windows were broken by gunfire while the shops and ground floors were used as stables. The garrison hoisted a red flag to show that it meant to fight to the end. Waller persevered grimly, mounting two light cannon on Arundel church tower, which fired down into the castle. He also cut off its water supply.

Hopton marched to relieve Arundel, with 2,000 horse and

1,500 foot. Leaving troops to continue the siege, Waller went to meet him and the two little armies confronted each other on the Downs between North Marden and West Dean. Hopton, who had a healthy respect for 'William the Conqueror', quickly realised that he was outnumbered. After exchanging a few shots, he ordered his men to retreat.

Waller now brought up heavy guns from Portsmouth to bombard the castle. Although the garrison had plenty of meat, it had no bread and water was running short. Sickness broke out. On 5 January 1644 its commander asked for a truce. Waller at once invited the ladies in the castle to dinner. The garrison surrendered at 9.00 o'clock the following morning, having been promised quarter – officers and gentlemen 'civil usage' as well.

Over a thousand men were taken prisoner. 'I never saw so many weak and feeble creatures together in my life, for almost all the common soldiers were half starved, and many of them hardly able to set one foot before another' wrote a Roundhead. Colonel Morley and Sir William Springett were appointed joint-governors. The latter died soon after and the colonel made Arundel his headquarters.

The First Civil War was over in Sussex. Morley was appointed to the committee for sequestrating the property of Sussex 'malignants'. This imposed massive fines on royalist landowners, though it was not unreasonable; when Colonel Gounter of Racton pleaded that his income was only £130, his fine was reduced. Recusants were treated with greater severity, Sir Garrett Kemp of Slindon being made to pay nearly £3,000.

Many clergy were ejected from their livings as 'Prelatists' or for using the Book of Common Prayer, harried by bigots like Dr Francis Cheynell who took over the church at Petworth. Some of the martyrs were not without stain, such as the rector at Ardingley, 'a common drunkard and alehouse haunter, and in his sermons hath wished that every knee might rot that would not bow at the name of Jesus'. The incumbent at East Grinstead was not only a swearer of bloody oaths, often drunk and a singer of bawdy songs, but 'keepeth company with papists and scandalous persons'.

Colonel Morley made a fool of himself in June 1644 over a picture found in a ship from Dunkirk. It depicted the wedding of two saints, whom he mistook for the Pope and the Virgin Mary, 'most gross idolatry'. At his suggestion, it was exhibited in London, whereupon royalist pamphleteers made him a laughing stock. He was more effective at the siege of Basing in Hampshire the same month, using cannon which fired 18lb shot and bringing the garrison within pistol range. However, he received a bullet in the shoulder, which spoilt his handwriting, while Basing was relieved by a royalist force under another Sussex man, Colonel Gage of the Firle family. (Although reputedly 'the most Jesuitical Papist alive', according to Clarendon Sir Henry Gage was 'among the very few soldiers who made himself to be universally loved and esteemed'.) Nevertheless, Morley was thanked by Parliament for his efforts at Basing.

If strict in enforcing loyalty to Parliament, the young colonel was also humane and courteous. 'Old acquaintance needes no apology', he wrote to the royalist Sir William Campion on 23 July 1645. 'All yr Sussex friendes in health continue their wonted affections towardes you, equally valewing yr welfare with their owne. I could imparte more, but ltrs are subiect to miscarriage . . .' He offered to obtain a pass for Lady Campion who was pregnant, to leave Oxford.

Ordinary folk grew resentful of soldiers billeting themselves where they wished, commandeering food and fodder, bullying and robbing. In September 1645, a thousand 'Clubmen', small farmers with clubs, assembled on Rooks Hill (the Trundle) not far from Chichester. Their object was to organise protection against further plundering. But at dawn on 21 September 50 soldiers sent by Morley attacked their camp at Walberton five miles from Arundel; the Clubmen gave no more trouble. Two 'malignant ministers' taken prisoner may have hoped to win them over to the king's side.

'The country is generally risen about Horsham, and protest that it will fight for the King and the country', it was reported in July 1648. A letter from Steyning the same month speaks of unrest among the 'countrymen . . . This is a very malignant county'. What had upset them was a new five per cent tax on food. A regiment arrived at Horsham and quickly crushed the rebels, a trooper and three townsmen being killed – including 'Edward Filder, one of the soldiers thrusting a sword through the window of his house in the back lane'.

In January 1649, Harbert Morley was one of ten Sussex men among a hundred and thirty who judged King Charles in Westminster Hall. He attended the trial on only three days, refusing to sign the death-warrant, as did his brother-in-law Colonel Fagge of Wiston. Their refusal needed considerable courage; in some cases force was used to obtain signatures. (The seven from Sussex who signed were General William Goffe, Peregrine Pelham, Captain James Temple, William Cawley, Colonel Anthony Stapley, Colonel John Downes and Sir Gregory Norton.) After the king's execution, Parliament brought in a new constitution; the monarchy and the House of Lords were abolished, the executive being a council of state of forty-five commissioners elected by the Commons from among its members – Morley himself being chosen in 1650.

There is a glimpse of Morley in October the following year through the eyes of none other than Charles II. During his escape from Worcester, the king and Colonel Gounter met Colonel Morley near Arundel, on his way to hunt. They dismounted, to avoid being noticed. Charles commented 'I did not much like his starched mouchates [moustaches]'.

As a declared opponent of General Cromwell, when the Long Parliament was expelled in 1653, Morley must have known that the new Protectorate regarded him as 'almost malcontent'. Elected MP for Rye and for the county next year, he wisely stayed away from London. Even so, he co-operated with Cromwell's spy-master, John Thurloe, in watching for royalist agents who might try to enter England through Sussex ports.

He showed his coolness towards the Protector when William Goffe was made 'Major-General of Sussex, Hampshire and Berkshire', a Cromwellian *gauleiter* (A major-general's duties included enforcing laws against drunkenness and blasphemy.) One of the regicides, Goffe was a Sussex man himself, a son of the rector of Stanmer; a captain in the New Model Army in 1645, he had commanded Oliver's own regiment during the battle of Dunbar in 1650 'and at the push of pike did repel the stoutest regiment the enemy had there'. He visited Morley at Glynde in November 1655 but the colonel declined to become one of his officers. So did Morley's brother-in-law who, according to Goffe, 'hath been for some time too gracious to disaffected persons, and besides will not stir a hair's breadth without Col. Morley'.

'You have vipers in your bosom, divers delinquents' Morley told the House in 1659 – meaning Cavalier MPs. Richard Cromwell had succeeded his father as Protector and England seethed with plots by the generals and by the royalists. When General Lambert tried to cow Parliament with his soldiers, Morley threatened to shoot him, but the general evicted the MPs. The colonel went down to Sussex where his brother-in-law had 2,000 militia at Arundel and Chichester, returning to London with them and reinstating the MPs. Parliament made him Lieutenant of the Tower with virtual control of London. He was also one of the Council of State, a commissioner for the army and colonel of a regiment of foot.

Harbert Morley believed in Parliament so long as men like himself could influence the destiny of their country – and their county. If a republic meant military dictatorship, then he preferred monarchy. Secretly, he contacted the exiled king. By December 1659 he was begging his old friend John Evelyn to intercede with Charles II on his account and on that of his brother-in-law Fagge. 'I treated privately with Col Morley, then lieutenant of the Tower, and in great trust and power, concerning delivering it to the King, and the bringing of him in, to the great hazard of my life' Evelyn recorded in his diary a few days later, 'but the Colonel had been my school fellow and I knew would not betray me.' Although the diarist tried several times to persuade him, Morley refused to launch a coup d'état. 'O the sottish omission of this gentleman', Evelyn complained bitterly after the Restoration. 'What did I not undergo of danger in this negotiation to have brought him over to His Majesty's interest, when it was entirely in his hands.' Yet by staying quietly at the Tower, Morley had been able to ensure General Monck's peaceful occupation of London and to play a key role in bringing back the monarch without bloodshed.

Charles II returned unopposed in May 1660. There was rejoicing throughout Sussex; the beacons were set alight in celebration while the Downs were ablaze with bonfires. As well as royalists, many of the county's leading Parliamentarians profited – John Fagge received not only a pardon but a baronetcy. However, Colonel Morley had been much too zealous a Roundhead throughout the Civil Wars, too fierce an enemy of Cavaliers, to hope for any such leniency. He had to sue for a pardon, being made to pay £1,000 for it, after which he was effectively barred from public office for the rest of his life.

There were no pardons for regicides. Three of the Sussex signatories were dead already. Captain Temple and Colonel Downe were tried and condemned to death but died in prison. Crawley escaped to Switzerland. Major-General Goffe had fled to America even before the Restoration; there had been a warrant for his arrest, apparently because of involvement in Lambert's abortive coup. He died about 1679 at Hadley, Massachusetts, where he had been active in fighting Red Indians.

Colonel Morley cannot have relished the downfall of the 'Good Old Cause', especially the changes in religion. There was such anger at Chichester in 1662 after the eviction of dissenting ministers from their livings – a quarter of the Sussex clergy – that troops were rushed in to forestall a rising. The Colonel took one of the dissenting ministers, Nathaniel Beaton, into his own house.

Harbert Morley died in 1667, in his bed. In his quiet way he had been something of a hero, fighting steadily and honourably against what he saw as royal misrule on the one hand and military tyranny on the other. Never once was he influenced by personal ambition. There was no stauncher Roundhead in Sussex. His mellow old house at Glynde still stands and belongs to his wife's descendants. Ironically, during the eighteenth century it was embellished by a proud prelate, a Bishop of Durham. Even so, Harbert Morley would still feel at home here, beneath Mount Caburn.

XII
Sussex Iron

In *Puck of Pook's Hill* Kipling makes a Tudor ghost say of the country around Burwash, 'The valley was full o' forges and fineries as a May shaw o' cuckoos'. Who ever saw a shaw filled with cuckoos? However, it is certainly true that in its day the Weald was the centre of the English iron industry.

Iron has been worked in Sussex since Celtic times, and the method of smelting it did not change for two thousand years. Alternative layers of iron ore and charcoal were stacked in mounds about three feet tall, coated with clay, on sandstone platforms nine feet in diameter. These were then set on fire, air being pumped in by primitive, hand worked bellows for several days until the charcoal was burnt up and the slag drawn off; a spongy lump (or 'bloom') of hot iron weighing about 10lbs was left at the bottom, to be hammered into shape. The Romans employed the same method but on a bigger scale, using slave labour; the slag surfaced their roads. The Saxons too had bloomeries. ('Bloom' derives from *bloma*, Anglo-Saxon for lump.) Iron went on being produced like this throughout the Middle Ages.

About 1500 a much more effective technique was introduced from France. Stone lined furnaces were built, sometimes 24 feet square and 28 feet high, with chimneys and 20 foot long water-operated bellows. They produced 'pigs' of iron of as much as 2,000lbs, the bigger ones being called 'sows'. This cast-iron was then remelted and beaten out at an adjoining forge by tilt hammers weighing half a ton. Streams were dammed, forming hammer ponds – some covering twenty acres – to work the machinery. The furnaces were kept burning for up to forty weeks, by adding further quantities of iron ore and burning vast quantities of charcoal (twenty-four loads a day might go in six days a week, each load weighing 2¾ cwt.) They made it possible to found cannon in one piece at Buxted in 1543, for the first time in English history; previous guns had been made of strips of wrought iron, held together by iron bands – now a solid core was bored out with a steel tipped drill. For two centuries the Weald enjoyed a monopoly of gun-casting. In a famous passage in his *Britannia* of 1586 the topographer William Camden speaks of 'hammer mill'.

Iron workers lived in a huddle of sheds around the forge, miners and charcoal burners in huts in the forest. An insatiable demand for Sussex timber soon caused alarm. 'In the rapes of Lewes, Pevensey and Hastings are iron mills and hammers to the number of fifty and upward' a commission reported in 1548-9, noting how 'every iron mill spendeth at the least nearly 1,500 loads of great wood made in to coals'. It warned that 'if the iron mills be suffered to continue there will not only be scant of timber to build in the parts near them either houses, water mills or windmills, bridges, sluices, ships . . .' Rye and Hastings would be unable to repair their jetties or find 'necessary wood for fuel for the relieving of the poor fishers after their arrival from their daily fishing to dry their clothes and warm their bodies'. 'Such a heat issueth out of the many Forges and Furnaces for the making of iron, and out of the glass kilns as hath devoured many famous woods within the wealds' observed John Norden in 1607. He feared that in only a few years not many good trees would be left standing. An Act of Parliament of 1616 forbade the glass-makers to burn wood, killing the Sussex glass industry.

Roads suffered from the constant passage of oxen drawing heavy loads of ore, charcoal and cast iron. An act of 1585 stipulated that for every six loads of charcoal, or every ton of iron, a cartload of slag, gravel, stones, sand or chalk must be laid down. But the foul highways and byeways of Sussex grew steadily fouler. All this heavy traffic smashed up what was left of the Roman roads.

However, the real worry continued to be the felling of timber. In 1612 Michael Drayton lamented:

Jove's Oke, the warlike Ash, veyn'd Elme, the softer Beech,
Short Hazell, Maple plain, light Asp, the bending Wych,
Tough Holly, and smooth Birch must altogether burn,
What should the Builder serve, supplies the Forger's turn.

In 1664 John Evelyn suggested 'Twere better to purchase all
our iron out of America, than thus to exhaust our woods at
home'.

Such fears were groundless. Evelyn had heard of an iron-
master who 'so ordered his works, that they were a means of
preserving even his woods'. In fact coppicing was general
practice, to ensure a dependable supply of timber for the
furnaces. 'As would maintaine iron workes soe doe iron
workes mutually maintaine them' a grand jury at Lewes,
looking into the decline of the iron industry, had declared
three years earlier. 'If the English iron works cease the coppices
will be grubbed up, which are the greater nurseries of timber.'

The majority of foundries were on the Forest Ridge. Water
was vital, the tributaries of the rivers Adur, Arun, Ouse and
Rother being harnessed, as well as those of the Brede and the
Cuckmere. Streams became triangular hammer ponds; sunken
lanes show where oxen dragged loads to and fro from
furnaces, the slag with which they were paved having proved
hopelessly inadequate. Sometimes the streams were dammed
where their banks were high, making finger-like ponds.
Today, when the foundries have long departed and the trees
have grown again, these lonely pools are among the most
beautiful stretches of water in the county.

Cannon were the most impressive product, but the
foundries also made firebacks, andirons (for holding fire-logs),
grave-slabs, railings, pots and pans, even stocks and
whipping-posts. There were ten wealden gun-founders in
1575. They included Ralph Hogge 'the quenes Maiesties
gonnestone maker of yron for the office of her Maiesties
ordinnances whin her Maties tower of of London'. The house
which he built at Buxted in 1581, Hogge House, may still be
seen, at the entrance to Buxted Place; it has a cast iron panel
with the figure of a hog and the date. A deed of 1588 is
endorsed: 'In this house lived ralf Hog who at the then furnace

at Buxted cast the first cannon that was cast in England.' However Holinshed's *Chronicle* records that in 1543 'Master Hugget and his man John/ They did make the first cannon'. Hugget's foundry was taken over by Parson William Levett, the entrepreneurial rector of Buxted (deprived in 1545 for denying Henry VIII's supremacy over the Church but restored under Queen Mary) and Hogge had been his servant.

The iron-masters prospered and were accounted gentry. In any case many were gentlemen born. They built fine houses such as Richard Infield's Gravetye Manor of 1598 at West Hoathly. Furnace-masters had smart enough dwellings too – Furnace Pond Cottage at Slaugham being a good example.

Many of the foundries were owned by local landowners. When Sir John Gage returned Ashburnham Forest to Queen Mary in 1555, he referred to 'my smithy (*fabricium*) and my hereditament called the Stele-Forge and the Iron Forge in the Forest of Aysshedown aforesaid' and to 'my furnace called the Stumblett'. The Morleys of Glynde owned a forge in Hawksden near Mayfield from before 1558 until 1662. The Carylls worked the furnace at Knepp (with the biggest hammer pond in Sussex) from 1568 to 1604; Edward Caryll seized a rival's ore in 1587, sending men armed with swords, daggers, mattocks and staves to do so. The Shirleys of Wiston had two foundries which they leased to iron-masters. However, they retained an interest, Sir Robert Shirley persuading the Shah of Persia to order Sussex cannon although their export was strictly forbidden by law.

The manufacture of cannon decreased during the period of peace which coincided with the reign of James I and the first years of Charles I, but increased dramatically when the Civil War began. Although the Crown had iron works in St Leonard's Forest the Cavaliers were unable to obtain artillery from them; in January 1644, while beseiging Arundel, Sir William Waller sent a troup of horse to destroy the royal foundries in St Leonard's Forest. By contrast John Browne of Brede, who had been the King's Gun-founder before the war, supplied Parliament with most of its artillery. He secured further orders for naval guns during the Commonwealth, casting cannon for three frigates. His grandson was nonetheless appointed Gun-founder to Charles II at the Restoration.

However a decline had set in by then. A report of 1664 speaks of 'half the ironworks heretofore imployed in ye sd County [Sussex] being already layd downe', of the imminent 'decay of our ironworks' because of foreign imports. By 1717 a mere two foundries were operating in Sussex – even if the railings for St Paul's Cathedral were made in the county.

Daniel Defoe made a point of visiting the furnaces of Kent and Sussex in 1724, during *A Tour thru' the whole Island of Great Britain*. Defoe tells us:

> I have seen one Tree on a Carriage which they call here a *Tug*, drawn by two and twenty Oxen; and even then 'tis carry'd so little a Way, and then thrown down and left for other *Tugs* to take up and carry on, that sometimes 'tis Two or Three Years before it gets to *Chatham*; for if the rains come in, it stirs no more that Year, and sometimes a whole Summer is not dry enough to make the roads passable. Here I had a Sight which indeed I never saw in any other part of *England*: Namely that going to Church at a Country Village not far from Lewes, I saw an antient Lady *and a Lady of very good Quality I assure you,* drawn to Church in her Coach with Six Oxen, nor was it done but out of mere Necessity, the Way being so stiff and deep, that no Horses could go in it.

The discovery during the first half of the eighteenth century of how to make coke from coal was to prove a mortal wound. Coke was much cheaper than charcoal which had grown increasingly dear, though not from shortage of wood (Defoe says there was enough timber to rebuild all the navies in Europe), but because the expanding hop industry had forced up production costs. Gradually the iron works moved to the Midlands or to the North where coal was plentiful, there being none in Sussex. Even so, three foundries – Fernhurst, Robertsbridge and Ashburnham – were still casting cannon for the Royal Navy during the American War of Independence. The loss of these naval contracts to the Carron works in Scotland proved a death blow.

The only foundry left by 1800 was Ashburnham Forge, in a beautiful wooded valley. The immediate cause of its closure in 1813 seems to have been a drunken party. The foundry was tended by two furnace men, with two men who stoked it and two boys; one of the boys drank a bottle of gin which killed him, while the others were so drunk that they forgot to mix chalk with the ore; the molten iron stopped flowing and spoilt the furnace. The forge's last surviving worker, a pensioner of Lord Ashburnham, died in 1883.

There is a wonderful passage in Kipling's *Something of Myself* which tells of faint traces left by the foundries:

> Just beyond the west fringe of our land, in a little valley running from Nowhere to Nothing-at-all, stood the long, overgrown slag-heap of a most ancient forge, supposed to have been worked by the Phoenicians and Romans and, since then, uninterruptedly till the middle of the eighteenth century. The bracken and rush-patches still hid stray pigs of iron, and if one scratched a few inches through the rabbit-shaven turf, one came on the narrow mule-tracks of peacock-hued furnace-slag laid down in Elizabeth's day. The ghost of a road climbed up out of this dead arena, and crossed our fields, where it was known as 'The Gunway', and popularly connected with Armada times. Every foot of that little corner was alive with ghosts and shadows.

Wealden iron is commemorated more substantially by the hammer ponds, which are certainly among the loveliest features of the Sussex landscape. There is a particularly fine example at Ebernoe, still called 'Furnace Pond'. Sometimes there is a chain of 'bayed-up' pools, as at Maresfield on the Ouse. It is difficult to imagine that these lonely and tranquil stretches of water once knew the noise, smoke and flames of furnaces and forges.

XIII
Pevensey and the Rape of Pevensey

For the year 491 the *Anglo-Saxon Chronicle* has an entry which is unusually grim, even by its own harsh standards: 'In this year Aelle and Cissa besieged Andredsceaster, and slew all the inhabitants there; there was not even one Briton left there.' It has been suggested that they were sacrificed to Woden.

The fort of Anderida, one of a chain commanded by the 'count of the Saxon Shore', had been built by the Romans in the third century to protect the coast from pirates. The Emperor Constans (son of Constantine the Great) probably visited it in AD 345 during a tour of inspection. On a peninsula covering nine acres, and surrounded by the sea on three sides, it overlooked a bay dotted with small islands. It had walls thirty feet high and ten bastions, mounting catapults which threw huge stone balls; they are built of flint and cement with red brick courses, faced by blocks of greensand stone, so sturdily that much of them survives, twenty feet high in some places. Yet archaeologists have been unable to find any trace of the Roman town which is known to have stood next to the fort.

There is no sign either of the fort having been occupied by the Saxons but undoubtedly they founded a town here, probably inside its walls. They gave it a new name, Peofn's ea – 'Peofa's River'. This may have been the burh called 'Heorepeburan'.

The Bayeux Tapestry specifically mentions 'Pevensae' and, as has been seen, William the Conqueror landed here in 1066. The twelfth-century *Roman de Rou* tells us that when he disembarked Duke William fell flat on his face on the sand. His companions were horrified by such an evil omen. 'My lords, by the splendour of God I have seized this land with my two hands', the Duke calmly reassured them as he rose to his feet. 'However much there may be, all of it belongs to us'.

Afterwards, William gave Pevensey to his half-brother Robert of Mortmain, who built an earthen ramp and a stockade across the south-eastern angle, the rest of the ruined walls serving as a bailey. Later, the south-eastern area was rebuilt in stone as a rectangular keep while the Roman walls were repaired. During the thirteenth century an inner bailey was added, a curtain wall with three D-shaped towers.

When its Norman lords rebelled, the castle was besieged by the Conqueror's successors, William Rufus and Henry I – events which inspired Kipling's tale 'Old Men at Pevensey' in *Puck of Pook's Hill*. It was besieged again by Simon de Montfort during the Barons' War against Henry III; some of the royalists whom Simon defeated at Lewes in 1265 took refuge here and succeeded in beating him off. There was a last siege in 1399, when Joan Pelham held it for her husband Sir John Pelham, the constable of the castle, who was a supporter of the future Henry IV. 'I am here laid by in a manner of a siege with the county of Sussex, Surrey and a great parcel of Kent, so that I may not [go] out nor no victuals get me' she wrote to her spouse, signing herself 'your own poor J Pelham'. But Richard II was soon deposed, and King Henry's men rescued Lady Pelham.

The castle was left to decay, though occasionally used as a prison for those of high rank during the fifteenth century. James I, the captive King of Scots, spent some time in confinement here. So did a queen dowager of England, Joan of Navarre, in 1419 after being charged with trying to bewitch her stepson Henry V – 'by sorcery and necromancy for to have destroyed the king'.

Over five hundred years later, it became a strategic strong-point again during the German invasion scare in the summer of 1940. The towers of the inner bailey were repaired and garrisoned while pillbox forts were added, in such a way as to blend with the masonry. Once more it barred the way to London, at any rate in theory.

The town of Pevensey flourished under the early

Plantagenets, and became one of the Cinque Ports. It was governed by a bailiff – styled mayor – and twelve jurats, who could try people for their lives. (A freeman of Pevensey condemned to death might choose drowning 'in the Haven' instead of hanging; he would be thrown from the harbour bridge at full-tide.) The minute Court House – 18 feet by 14 – formerly the Town Hall, which dates from before 1585, has two cells beneath the council chamber. During the 1780s the corporation found a man guilty of stealing a pair of buckskin breeches and were then dismayed to find that it was a capital offence; a judge visiting the neighbourhood advised them to change the verdict to manslaughter but this was a capital offence too, so presumably the man was hanged – drowning having gone out of fashion.

The town's decline never affected the corporation's pretensions. When, while thatching his pig-sty, a Georgian bailiff was brought a letter and held it upside down, he was told that it might be easier to read the other way up. 'Hold your tongue, Sir' he bellowed. 'While I am mayor of Pemsey, I'll hold a letter which way uppards I like.' Sadly, the town lost its borough status in 1883.

There is an imposing thirteenth-century church, reflecting the town's ancient prosperity. During the first years of the Reformation the vicar Dr Richard Borde – who also held the adjacent living of Westham – told his congregation that he would rather be torn in four by horses than recognise King Henry as 'Only Supreme Head in earth of the Church of England', and then prudently fled abroad.

Andrew Borde, who may have been the vicar's brother, lived at the Mint House. (Pevensey had a mint in Saxon and Norman times but the house is no earlier than the fifteenth century.) Born about 1490 at Cuckfield or Ditchling, he was freed from villeinage (serfdom) in 1511. After becoming a Carthusian monk he left his charterhouse and wandered through south-western Europe, visited North Africa, and then returned to England to practise as a physician, counselling the Duke of Norfolk. Later, like Rabelais, he studied what passed for medicine in those days at Montpelier.

He wrote many books, ranging from medicine to travel, from astronomy to farce. He could be acid, alleging of the Cornish that 'their ale is stark nought, looking white and thick as pigs have wrestled in it, smoky and ropy, and never a good sup'. 'Trust you no Scot' he wrote, while he thought the Irish ragged and barbarous. As for his fellow countrymen, they were hypocrites. But he was poetic about Sussex, even if he deplored its muddy roads: 'In the Forest of St Leonard's in Sussex there doth never sing nightingale, although the forest round about in time of the year is replenished with nightingales' he writes. 'They will sing round about the forest and never within the precinct of the forest, as divers keepers of the forest and other credible persons did show me.' In *The Merry Tales of the Wise Men of Gotham* he describes the attempted drowning of an eel for stealing salt fish. (A memory of what happened to criminal freemen at Pevensey?) 'To a considerable share of learning, professional and general, Dr Borde added the austerities of a monk with the low humour of a buffoon' says Lower. He had the courage to join his former Carthusian brethren in the Tower when they stayed loyal to the Pope, but his nerve broke after a few days. In his honesty, humanity and cheerful oddity, 'Merry Andrew' had a good deal in common with Rabelais. He is one of the most colourful figures in the county's history.

The Mint House is haunted by one of the most pitiful of the many phantoms in Sussex, a tongueless girl who tries vainly to speak. One night in 1586 the then owner of the house, a London merchant called Thomas Dight, arrived there unexpectedly to find his beautiful paramour Eleanor Fitzjohn in bed with a handsome young fisherman. Dight and his servants killed the fisherman slowly by hanging him from the ceiling and roasting him over a fire, while Eleanor was starved to death after her tongue had been cut out. Later both bodies were buried behind the house. Only on his deathbed in 1601 did Dight confess to their murder. Eleanor's ghost is said to have been seen in the house quite recently, certainly within the last ten years.

Gradually the sea destroyed Pevensey, as it did so many other ports in Sussex. Over the centuries shingle silted up the bay, allowing saltmarsh to spread inland (into the 'Honour of the Eagle', as the lordship was known) though even in King Stephen's reign the waves still lapped the castle walls at high tide. During the next hundred years the marshes were increasingly 'inned', converted into meadowland; much of this work was done by the monks of Battle, who had large estates here. But then the sea began to flood the land, turning it back to saltmarsh, despite such ambitious defences as the Crooked Ditch and the Mark Dyke, which were equipped with dams and sluices. Ironically, further inning ruined this system, causing more floods. By 1400, the Old Haven, Pevensey's main channel to the sea, had silted up. Attempts to dig further channels came to nothing though there was some access to the sea and the port continued to export goods, including cannon, until the seventeenth century. But it was reported in 1689 that no ship over 14 tons could reach the town, and the customs house was closed in 1714.

Westham, on the far side of the castle, began as a suburb but is now a separate village. When seen from the train, the Norman church with its massive Perpendicular tower, gives the impression that Pevensey actually has two churches – it has been suggested that its original function was serving a hospital just outside the castle.

If one takes the long, meandering road through the Pevensey Levels (marshland finally reclaimed) with their 'havens' (dykes) and rush-fringed ponds, one might think oneself in Norfolk but for the distant Downs on the skyline. Just north of the Levels, on 1 August 1100 as he was hunting in the Weald, Robert of Mortain, Lord of the Rape of Pevensey, saw a huge and terrible black goat bearing on its back the body of King William Rufus, who had been murdered by a mysterious arrow in the New Forest at the very same hour.

Eastward, a line of bungalows separates the Levels from what is now called Pevensey Bay. North is Hailsham, spoilt save for its church and manor house. According to Hare it was never very lovely: a 'dreary little market town'. He adds pleasantly, 'The rope-factory, which is the industry of the place, has the privilege of supplying the cords used in executions'.

Hellingly has an oval churchyard with five entrances, a Saxon 'ciric' or burial-ground which may be of pagan origin. A rector of Hellingly, John Milles, was burnt at Lewes in 1557 for his Protestant opinions. Sadly, the splendid timber manor of Horselunges, Tudor or even earlier, cannot be glimpsed from the road, while its iron gates appear to be electronically operated like those of a New York precinct. In former days it was haunted by the ghost of a gamekeeper murdered by Lord Dacre.

There are some fine Elizabethan and Jacobean monuments to the Jefferay family in Chiddingly church, which has a fifteenth century stone spire 130 feet tall. There is also an epitaph to a vicar, Thomas Eades, written by himself. He was a Non-Juror, a Jacobite, evicted for refusing to take the oath of allegiance to William and Mary in 1689:

> A faithful shepherd that did not pow'rs fear
> But kept Old Truth, and would not let her go,
> Nor turn out of the way for friend or foe.
> He was suspended in the Dutchman's days,
> Because he would not walk in their strange ways . . .

Like so many in Sussex, the churchyard has a wonderful vista behind it, over rolling oakwoods to the Downs. There is a much diminished mansion of faded red brick from the early years of Elizabeth's reign, now a mere farm but once a famous great house, Chiddingly Place, whose owners, the Jefferays, were supposed to be so proud that they used cheeses as stepping stones through the mud on their way to church. (On the monument of Sir John Jefferay, his daughter and son-in-law stand on shallow drums which are said to be cheeses.) A more recent legend is of Pablo Picasso, staying nearby with his painter friend Sir Roland Penrose, going into the village pub and, finding himself without money, trying to buy a drink with a sketch. 'I don't care if you're Michael Angelo!' roared the landlord as he threw him out.

The Pelham buckle can be seen on the Perpendicular tower

of East Hoathly church. This was where the diarist Thomas Turner worshipped in Georgian days. His diary is an eighteenth-century *Diary of a Nobody*, that of a rustic Mr Pooter. He was the village shopkeeper here – grocer, draper, haberdasher, hatter, clothier, druggist, ironmonger, stationer, glover and undertaker – besides dealing in hops and corn. His private life seems to have been a long and unsuccessful battle against alcohol – and tea. 'The too-frequent use of spirituous liquors, and the exorbitant practice of tea-drinking has corrupted the morals of people of almost every rank' he wrote during a wet, melancholy summer towards the end of George II's reign. (The weather could be just as bad in his time as it can be in ours: 'This is the twenty-ninth day on which we have had rain successively' he noted on 25 July 1757.) A deplorable victim of the demon drink was his neighbour Mr French, whose sad death in 1763 resulted from his potations, particularly gin. 'I should think he could not drink less on a moderate computation than twenty gallons a year.' Turner and his wife Margaret consumed a good deal themselves – on one occasion Mrs Turner had to be brought home on a neighbour's back. He was partial to 'bumboo', the Sussex word for a terrible concoction of beer and brandy. Less bibulous amusements included marital shopping expeditions to Lewes, the couple sitting on the same roan mare.

Waldron is another unspoilt village. The Roundheads who rolled downhill the round stone 'font', now in the churchyard, were justified in thinking it idolatrous; it began as the cauldron of a pagan temple and ritual horse-broth has been made in it. Opposite, there is a vineyard where one can sample the wine.

In Framfield church the brass to Edward Gage (who died in 1595) bears an inscription from the Catholic Office of the Dead, a piece of recusant effrontery. At Heathfield, almost in commuter territory, where again there are marvellous views from the churchyard, lies a vicar who was chaplain to the expedition which founded Jamestown, Virginia in 1607, Robert Hunt.

*

Fletching and Lindfield lie at the western edge of Pevensey Rape, amid the little tributaries of the upper Ouse. Fletching church is well worth a visit to see the fine, armoured brass of a member of the Dalyngrigge family who died at the end of the fourteenth century and is just possibly the builder of Bodiam. He wears plate, chainmail and *jupon* (tunic) of the sort which must have been worn by the Black Prince at Poitiers, and is flanked by his no less elegant wife beneath a Gothic canopy; he stands on a lion, she on a lap-dog. The mausoleum of the Holroyd family – the earls of Sheffield who built Sheffield Park and first created those lovely gardens – also holds the bones of Edward Gibbon, author of *The Decline and Fall of the Roman Empire*. However, the most memorable monument here is a tiny pair of brass gloves (like something out of Grimm's fairy tales) with a brief inscription in black-letter asking us to pray for the soul of 'Peter Denot, glouer'. We know a little about Mr Denot. In 1450 he joined that army of 'Silly Sussex' folk which together with the Kentishmen accompanied Jack Cade up to London and looted the City – he was among the lucky ones receiving a pardon from King Henry VI and escaping the terrible death of being hanged, drawn and quartered.

Lindfield has a long rambling village street with many pretty houses, ranging from the Medieval Wealden to the Victorian Fanciful, and a duck-infested, picture postcard village pond. E. V. Lucas quotes an epitaph in the churchyard, which I have been unable to locate despite much searching:

> Long was my pain, great was my grief,
> Surgeons I'd many, but no relief.
> I trust through Christ to rise with the just:
> My leg and thigh was buried fust.

It has been called the finest village street in the county, 'the long Street Beautiful', but it is on a main road which grows noisier every day – the tragedy of so many Sussex villages – and is being sucked into Haywards Heath.

Returning to the coast, Lucas thought that Edwardian Eastborne was 'always the most select, or least democratic, of the Sussex watering places'. There were less than 3,000 souls here when Horsefield published his history of the county in 1835. 'The SEA HOUSES, which are built to the very margin of old Neptune's domain, overlook the waters of "the dark blue sea" ' he writes, 'as the place becomes better known and more visited, the smaller buildings will doubtless disappear, and be superseded by costly marine mansions.' However, the town did not become fashionable until the 1860s. There are some splendid late Victorian hotels with an exuberant town hall from the same period.

Pre-resort Eastbourne was an agricultural rather than a fishing community and quietly prosperous. The 'Old Town' has a stately medieval church, with a majestic Norman arch over the chancel and a monument to Henry Lushington who survived the Black Hole of Calcutta only to be murdered. The church is flanked by a big Tudor parsonage. It has been claimed that the Lamb Inn next to them dates from 1180 and has been a hostelry since the fifteenth century. There is an astonishing rib-vaulted undercroft below the premises, with an armorial roof-boss, which can be no later than 1300, while records show that it has certainly been operating as an inn since Stuart times. As the Lamb was the main coaching stop between Eastbourne and Hastings from the mid-eighteenth century until the Victorian era it was a centre of social life, with assembly rooms where routs and hunt balls took place.

From here to Seaford the coast has been saved from developers. Beachy Head – so popular with suicides – is famous but the names of the Seven Sisters, white headlands which stretch from Birling Gap to Cuckmere Haven, are less familiar. (The Gap is the only way down to the beach before the Cuckmere.) The first Sister is Went Hill Brow, 146 feet high. Then comes Bailey's Brow, 194 feet, at the top of Crowlink Valley (during the Great War a German submarine ended up on the beach below), then Flagstaff Point, 150 feet, beneath which the *Nympha Americana*, a Spanish prize, went down in 1747 with one of the richest cargoes in the whole history of Sussex wrecking; she was built of cedar and a good deal of her timbers was made into furniture. The last four Sisters grow taller: Brass Point is 160 feet, Rough Brow 216 feet, Short Brow 214 and finally Haven Brow – overlooking the Cuckmere estuary – is 255.

Friston and Eastdean are spoilt by having expanded into each other. Looking over the sea through Birling Gap, the former has a Jacobean manor house, Friston Place, once the home of the ancient family of Selwyn, and a good, partly Norman church whose Selwyn monuments are worth seeing. (The last of the family, Edward who died in 1704, is described in dog Latin as *Ultimus Selwynorum*.) at Eastdean, not to be confused with East Dean in West Sussex, the church was viciously restored by maniacal Victorians; there is too much housing development. Its greatest charm is the prospect of Crowlink Valley, which only just escaped the developers.

Asser, the Welsh bishop who became King Alfred's tutor and friend, first met him at 'Dene' in Sussex. Whether it was in East or West Sussex is not known, but Alfred certainly owned manors at Seaford and Lullington. However the meeting may have been at West Dean in the Cuckmere valley.

From 1706 to 1728, Dr Jonathan Darby was vicar of Eastdean (and of Friston and Litlington). Saddened by all the corpses drowned at sea whom he had to bury, he dug a cave down through the cliffs near Beachy Head, coming out twenty feet over the beach – just above the high water mark. He is said to have spent many stormy nights here with a lanthorn to warn ships, lowering ropes to shipwrecked mariners. An irreverent version of the story says that he merely came to the cave to escape from Mrs Darby. The remote community of those days left no record other than folk memory. Most of his cave has been washed away but one can still see his parsonage at Friston.

A little further inland lies Jevington, an unspoilt hamlet hidden in a fold of the Downs, with a cheerful old smugglers' pub – *The Eight Bells*, once owned by Jevington Jig (see Ch. XV, 'Sussex Smugglers') – and a church which has a Saxon tower and a weird Saxon Christ. The church contains a monument which depicts a haunted man and the ghost who haunts him. A large oval medallion of white marble, it shows in half-relief a triple-chinned Georgian squire in a powdered wig. His face wears a strained, uneasy expression. An inscriptions tells us that the monument commemorates Charles Rochester, Esquire, of Filching Manor nearby, who died in 1758, and also his lamented wife Leonora who predeceased him. Then, looking closer, you see sketched in faint relief a very pretty, lady-like young phantom peering slyly over his shoulder – come to summon her husband to their grave. No wonder he seems uneasy. For me this marble medallion at Jevington has something of the horror of an M. R. James ghost story.

Not far away, Lullington claims to have 'the smallest church in England', but it is a fraud, being merely the chancel of a long demolished fourteenth-century building. However, it almost certainly stands on the site of a pagan temple. The area was one of the earliest in Sussex to be colonised by Saxons.

The Cuckmere valley must look much as it did when the first Saxons penetrated Sussex up the rivers. This may well have been where King Aelle 'fought against the Welsh near the bank of the *Mearcraedesburne*' in 485. From the haven it corkscrews beneath the Downs up to Alfriston, a triumph of conservation.

It has inspired many a purple passage. ('The river, a riband of royal blue, loosed as from a love-knot, lay on a carpet of tender green stretching from the bridge right away to the eastward cliff of Cuckmere' observes Arthur Stanley Cooke in *Off the Beaten Track in Sussex*.) If narrow, its mouth is wide enough, a true haven for ships running before a storm, in dread of being driven on the rocks – the first record of it as such being in the *Mariner's Mirror* of 1588. At Exceat, near the estuary, oxen were still in use during the 1920s, while even today walking up the Cuckmere valley is to walk into a nineteenth-century water colour – gentle green slopes with grazing sheep, majestic copses, little wooden bridges and, above all, the winding river with its cormorants and herons.

Westdean is a Cuckmere hamlet which remains quite unspoilt, hidden by trees, with a ruined medieval manor house and dovecote, a thirteenth-century rectory and a fourteenth-century church with an odd spire like a monk's hood. This has been called 'the most sequestred village in downland' and I can well believe that King Alfred met Asser here eleven hundred years ago.

Alfriston, futher up the Cuckmere, is the reverse of sequestred, the victim of its own beauty. There is an undeniably noble church of cathedral-like proportions, a pre-Reformation priest's house, and fine old smugglers' inns. But cream teas and the tourist industry have taken over.

North-east of Alfriston stands Windover Hill, brooding above Wilmington, with a heavily restored church and what is left of a small Benedictine priory. However, the village is best known for 'The Long Man of Wilmington', the outline of a giant 231 feet tall, which has been carved on the hill. A lot of ink has been spilt over his origins but, as I have said earlier, I am convinced that he is Woden.

If one goes back to the coast again, to Bishopstone, there is another Saxon relic, a Saxon doorway with a sundial bearing inscribed 'EADRIC'. One of the earliest Saxon cemeteries in Sussex was found on a hillside here. I wonder if it has anything to do with the oddly oppressive atmosphere which I always sense in this pretty village?

Seaford Head is another great white cliff once dreaded by storm-tossed mariners. St Lewinna, a Briton converted by St Wilfrid, was martyred at Seaford 'during the days when Theodore was Archbishop' [of Canterbury]; i.e. before 690. Some regard her as evidence of British survival in Sussex, but I suspect she is a medieval invention.

Seaford was a prosperous town during the Middle Ages when it was at the mouth of the Ouse, and a member of the Cinque Ports. Then, in about 1539, the landowners of the Ouse valley, eager to reclaim its marshes, dug a new channel to divert the river so that it emerged instead at Meeching – which was rechristened 'Newhaven'. It was not caused by a terrible storm in Elizabeth's reign, the traditional story, but by an act of ruthless greed which condemned Seaford to what one historian has called 'a state of living death'. There were only thirty-eight householders in the town in 1596, including seven fishermen with one boat between them – though it continued to elect an MP until 1832. A low area between the esplanade and the town was once filled by wharves and quays, but the only medieval building to survive is the church. During its decline, the Seaford men acquired a bad name as wreckers and were called 'Shags' after birds popularly believed to rob fishermen's nets. The town tried unsuccessfully to become a watering place during the Napoleonic Wars but towards the end of the Victorian era it grew popular with retired people, developing into the sedate little resort which it is today.

Like Eastbourne, Seaford's greatest charm is its access to the Downs. There is a fine walk north across them to Firle Beacon. It is only 700 feet high, yet seen from the Weald on the other side its steep slopes make it seem like a mountain. It is the most mysterious of the Downs, a peak when glimpsed from Lewes or Alfriston, but from the Weald to the north merely a slightly higher curve than the rest of the line. Its ridge has an unfriendly feel – there are over 50 Bronze Age 'bowl' barrows here. From the summit one can see Crowborough Beacon, almost on the Surrey border, while below are Glynde and Glyndebourne with, immediately beneath, West Firle.

West Firle is the least spoilt village in Sussex, its houses lived in by people who work nearby instead of weekenders or commuters. It has a flourishing village school and a perfect pub, the Ram. (Even in 1831 a visitor remarked on its neat cottages.) Firle has been saved from 'development' because it still belongs to a great Sussex family, the Gages, who have been here since the fifteenth century. Often at the cost of very real self-sacrifice, landowners like these do infinitely more to preserve the landscape than any county council. The sixth Viscount Gage, who died in 1984, should be carved in outline on the Downs like the Wilmington Giant in memory of all that he did to save the countryside of East Sussex.

During the reign of King Henry VIII the Captain of his Yeomen of the Guard, Sir John Gage, built a new house at Firle, using Caen stone for the sake of cheapness, which he had shipped across the Channel and then up the Ouse and along its tributary the Glynde Reach – a revealing comment on the Sussex roads of the period. His mansion was Palladianised during George II's time by a local architect, John Morris of Lewes, who gave it that rarity, an eighteenth century long gallery. No mellower, more soothing house can be imagined than Firle Place, yet there are rumours that it is badly haunted by alarming ghosts.

One night a hundred years ago a headless white horse was seen galloping through Firle Park, under which lies a lost village. This was Heighton St Clere or East Firle. Presumably it was abandoned after being stricken by the Black Death and the survivors took refuge in East Firle. No records are available, but the manor court rolls of Alciston not far away tell us that in 1349 seventy-six tenants at Alciston and the hamlets nearby died of the plague and that no-one came forward to claim their holdings – which means that all their families must have perished with them.

The Sir John Gage of Henry VII's day built a chapel in the village church to hold his tomb and those of his heirs. Among the latter was the Sir Edward who arrested Deryk Carver; the face on Edward's brass is a portrait of a very handsome man. There is a window in memory of the sixth Lord Gage, designed by John Piper; it shows the Tree of Life in the heavenly Jerusalem. The church also contains a helpful Table of Affinity, explaining that it is forbidden to marry one's grandfather.

The family produced some remarkable men during the seventeenth century. Four brothers are of particular note. George Gage was James I's agent at the Papal court. That famous soldier of fortune and 'Jesuitical' cavalier, Sir Henry Gage, military governor of Oxford for Charles I, was mortally wounded in a cavalry skirmish outside Abingdon in 1645 – 'who, having done His Majesty special service, was whilst living, generally beloved, and dead is still universally lamented' Clarendon tells us. Another brother was President of the English Catholic college at Douai. The strangest of the brothers was Thomas, a Dominican friar, who lived for some years among the Indians of Guatemala, 'learning the languages of Cacchiquel and Poconchi'. He renounced Catholicism in 1641, preaching a recantation sermon at St Paul's Cathedral in which he declared: 'I was like a foule and ugly monkey'. He became a rabid Parliamentarian, was appointed vicar of Deal, published *The English-American: his Travail by Sea and Land*, and died in Jamaica as chaplain of an expedition sent by Cromwell to conquer Hispaniola.

The eighteenth-century Gages, who conformed to the Church of England in 1730, were no less colourful. The first Viscount Gage, Master of the Household to Frederick, Prince of Wales and a scandalously venal politician, prospered so much that he was able to rebuild Firle Place. His younger brother, Count Joseph Gage, who stayed a Papist, made a huge fortune in Paris from investing in Mississippi stock and offered the Poles £3,000,000 to make him their king. General Thomas Gage was commander-in-chief, North America, and lost 1,100 men out of 2,500 when he stormed Bunker's Hill in 1776.

Gage women were just as lively. In 1611 the seventeen-year-old Lady Penelope Darcy, daughter of Earl Rivers, was fought over by three suitors – Sir George Trenchard, Sir John Gage and Sir William Hervey. She promised to be wife of all three, if they were patient. First she married Trenchard, who died after a few months; then Gage, by whom she had nine children; and at his death thirty years later, Hervey, who outlived her. Judging from a striking portrait at Firle by David Martin, Thomas Gage's American wife, Margaret Kemble, was another formidable personality.

In the church there is a brass of an earlier owner of Firle, wearing full Yorkist armour with elbow pieces like giant steel butterflies, as befits a gentleman who died in 1477. Beside him is his wasp-waisted little wife. Bartholomew Bolney was born about 1405 into a family of prosperous yeomen from Bolney near Cuckfield. Educated at Winchester and at one of the Inns of Court, during the 1420s he became Seneschal of Battle Abbey – the monks' business manager and legal adviser. He bought an estate of nearly 900 acres, which he described in

The Book of Bartholomew Bolne [sic]. He was unwise enough to join Jack Cade's rebellion, no doubt because the Abbot of Battle supported it, but was pardoned, and sat as MP for Sussex in the first parliament of Edward IV. Appointed a JP in 1460, Mr Bolney dealt with cases of piracy and smuggling, levying money to hire competent watchmen; coastal folk were complaining that 'watch is kept by old men and boys, and the king's enemies have descended and taken prisoners'. He was also commissioned to arrest 'certain persons of Sussex wandering about in the country, spoiling, beating, maiming and slaying'. When he died his little estate was divided among his children, 'Westfirlez' being the dowry of Alice Bolney, spouse of William Gage.

Near Firle, at Alciston under Bo-peep Hill (one of the steeper slopes of the Downs' northern escarpment), there is a group of farm buildings which Bartholomew would still recognise. Unrestored, they are among the most beautiful in Sussex; they should have been painted by Constable. Once a grange of Battle Abbey, the monks stored tithes here, besides using the farm as a rest-home for sick brethren. Their 'stews' remain, a chain of fish-ponds along the spring which runs behind Old Clergy House, while a crumbling medieval dovecote and cottage are in the farmyard. Inside the tithe barn, 170 feet long, rugged beams and posts cast strange shadows when the sun shines through holes in its red roof. At the dissolution of the monasteries Alciston was acquired by the Gages who own it today.

Across the valley from Firle, Glynde – best known as the station for Glyndebourne – is a lovely village, still 'feudal' and unsuburbanised. Glynde Place is among the most romantic houses in the entire county and with Firle is one of the two great mansions in East Sussex to have passed always by descent, the present owner being descended from a cousin of the family who built it. The setting is superb, at the foot of Mount Caburn and with wonderful views over the Ouse Valley to Firle Beacon. E. V. Lucas thought it 'a little sombre, the very place for a clandestine interview or midnight elopement'. There is a most elegant church next to the house, a Palladian temple which would be equally at home in Italy, with a prince-bishop's mitre and coronet carved over the door. Yet the little church is very Sussex in using knapped flint, each stone being a square diamond as though cut by a jeweller, and set in hard white chalk.

The Morleys, who acquired the Glynde estate during the Wars of the Roses, had a long standing feud with the Gages across the valley. When Thomas Morley came of age in 1531, Sir John Gage did his best to obtain possession of Glynde, harrying the tenants. Thomas petitioned Henry VIII, accusing Sir John of 'intending with continual suit in the law so to weary your said subject that he shall be driven to relinquish his lawful title', and Gage was forced to desist. After the Reformation, there was little love between the Puritan Morleys and the Papist Gages. William Morley, one of the first gentlemen in Sussex to embrace the Protestant faith, built a courtyard house here in 1569 of Sussex flint and Caen stone, the latter being shipped along the Glynde Reach – a tributary of the Ouse. (The tiny courtyard with its Tudor doorways is like something from an Oxford College.)

When the last Morley died in 1679, he bequeathed Glynde to a cousin, John Trevor. Unhinged by the death of a young wife, the third John Trevor committed suicide in 1743 and left the property to a cousin – in preference to his nine sisters. The cousin, the most interesting of the Trevors, was a bachelor, Richard Trevor (1707–71), who became Bishop of Durham in 1752. Nicknamed 'The Beauty of Holiness' by George II and 'St Durham' by Horace Walpole, at one time he was regarded as a future Archbishop of Canterbury. He was the first Englishman to collect the paintings of Zurbarán, acquiring twelve Old Testament scenes for his palace at Bishops Auckland. It was he who built the Palladian church and transformed Glynde Place by adding a new great hall, long gallery and stable block; his architect for the house was the same John Morris of Lewes who had been employed at Firle. The bishop set two magnificent heraldic beasts on top of the gate piers, lead wyverns, who still rule Glynde. He bequeathed the house to his elder brother, Lord Hampden.

Glynde passed to the Brands in 1824. They found the house sadly neglected, while almost the entire parish was organised as one farm and was farmed on his own account by the much respected steward, Mr John Ellman. However it became a home again under Henry Brand who entered Parliament in 1852 as Whig MP for Lewes, serving as Palmerston's Chief Whip and then as Speaker of the House of Commons from 1872–84, before being created Viscount Hampden – a title born by the last of his Trevor cousins. (Later he inherited the barony of Dacre, once that of the owners of Hurstmonceux.) His descendant, the present Lord Hampden, has published the correspondence of Mr Speaker Brand and his wife, *Henry and Eliza*, which brings to life again their idyllically happy Victorian marriage.

Glynde Place, hitherto surprisingly little known, is now being made more accessible to the public. A room devoted to the life and career of Mr Speaker Brand was opened in 1994 and two others will illustrate those of Colonel Morley the Roundhead and Bishop Trevor. One particular chamber remains to be found. Some years ago a great iron key, from the eighteenth century if not earlier, came to light; a tattered label was tied to it, labelled in faded brown ink 'Ghost Room'. The key has since been lost while the room was never discovered. Yet the house has a soothing happy atmosphere. It has some good portraits by Alan Ramsay, Zoffany and Lawrence. However, for me the most memorable picture here is a conversation piece depicting the seventeenth-century Sir John Trevor and his family – nowhere else will you see such comically Puritan children.

A famous Georgian agriculturist, John Ellman grazed his flocks on the Downs round Glynde. Brought by his father, a well-to-do yeoman from Hartfield in the north of the county, he settled here in 1764 when he was eleven years old. As soon as he grew up, he set about creating a new breed of sheep, specially suited to downland grazing, crossing the East and West Sussex varieties to produce the South Down. Now a rare animal, in his time it was widely admired for both its mutton and its wool; a leg from one of Ellman's sheep was noticeably rounder and shorter than those of other breeds. In 1784, with the Earl of Sheffield he founded the annual South Down sheep-fair at Lewes. (A fine flock of South Downs may still be seen at Courthouse Farm near Offham.)

Until the day he died in 1832, Mr Ellman lived in patriarchal style at Trevor House next to Glynde Place, housing his young farmhands under his own roof and eating with them; when they married, he gave them a plot of land for growing vegetables and on which to keep the cow and pig he supplied. He gave harvest suppers for over eighty men, women and children at a time, providing 'fifteen or sixteen stone of beef, six or eight stone of mutton, besides more than one cwt. of plum-pudding, forty or fifty gallons of strong beer, and bread &c. in proportion'.

Above Glynde towers the Caburn or 'Mount Caburn'. On top, there is a deep hollow which gives complete shelter from the sharp downland winds; perhaps this is why one of the very last Sussex shepherds went on working here right up to the mid-1960s. Caburn was the site of an Iron Age fort, erected in about 500. It was defended by a single ditch on three sides and by a double on the north where approach is easy, all topped by palisades. There were perhaps seventy houses of wattle and daub, whose inhabitants kept horses and dogs, ate beef, mutton and pork, hunted deer and boar, and shaved with iron razors. It is likely that they were grouped around a single great hall, the seat of a nobleman who ruled for twenty miles around. In time of war it may have served as a refuge for men and their flocks; there are 140 pits for grain storage and a well. After the arrival of the Belgae, it must have been very like a frontier town. When Roman rule ended, it was re-fortified, though whether by Britons or Saxons is unknown. Caburn is Celtic for 'fortified hill', *caer bryn* and one romantic suggestion is that Britons made a last stand here. Excavation has shown that it was fortified once more during the 'Nineteen Long Winters' of King Stephen's reign, becoming a robber baron's castle.

Caburn is another magic hill. In July at least one of the paths up it is fringed by vipers' bugloss, as if by sentinels; tall and stately, like coarse hollyhocks, with blue and red flowers they are among downland's most attractive plants. One often sees wild orchids – bee, pyramid, burnt-tip, early purple and the occasional late spotted. There is a wonderful view of the Ouse.

'At about half a mile distant from Glynde Place, and at the foot of the north-eastern point of the Downs, stands Glynde Bourne, a neat but unpretending edifice, once a fashionable abode of the Muses', wrote the Revd Mr Horsefield in 1835. He was referring to some long (and deservedly) forgotten poets, yet was undeniably prophetic. Glyndebourne is now a place of happy memories, where audiences learn to love insufficiently appreciated operas. (In my case it was Richard Strauss's *Capriccio*, with Felicity Lott singing the Countess, while a friend tells me she will never forget Janet Baker's farewell in Monteverdi's *L'Incoronazione di Poppea*.) The predecessor of the part Tudor, part Victorian, manor house here was the Morleys' home before they built Glynde Place, the Christies inheriting it during William IV's reign. With its atmosphere of fête champêtre, Glyndebourne Opera – the creation of John Christie (1882–1963) – has been a cherished feature of English musical life ever since the first production in 1934. The little 'thirties opera house blended with the landscape – since John Christie built with weathered brick and tiles – and I do not like the vast new opera house which has replaced it, a horseshoe of red brick and metal plating, but the auditorium is magnificent. I am grateful for the ugly monster as it means that at last I shall be able to obtain tickets – whose rarity was a source of much local grumbling.

Northward lies Ringmer with an unusually large and handsome village green. Among its church's monuments is that of a Roundhead, Sir William Springett, clean shaven but with long, flowing hair. 'He (being a Collonel in ye service of ye Parliament at ye taking in of Arvndell Castle in Svssex there) contracted a sickness whereof hee died Febvruary ye 3th Ano Dni: 1643: being 23 yeares of age . . .' Only a fragment of Sir William's house, Broyle Place, survives; one would never suspect that Broyle Farm had once been part of an imposing mansion, surrounded by a great park with fine stands of timber. His daughter Gulielma Maria Springett was brought up a Quaker by her stepfather and became William Penn's first wife – his beloved 'Guli', a girl of notable beauty and saintly character.

In a letter from Ringmer of December 1773 Gilbert White of Selborne – who came here often to stay with his aunt Rebecca Snooke – mentions seeing kites, yet very soon they were gone. 'An old gamekeeper of my grandfather's, who died in 1855, at the age of 73, has often told me that in his younger days the "forky-tailed Kites" were not uncommon in Sussex, and that they gave a great deal of trouble by taking young ducks and chickens from the farm-yard' says William Borrer, who had seen this bird in the county only once – on the shore near Eastbourne in 1881.

Berwick is in flat, characterless land below the Downs. The church, spoilt by 'restoration', contains murals painted by Duncan Grant and Vanessa Bell, which were commissioned during the 1939–45 War by the saintly Bishop Bell of Chichester – even the artists' admirers admit they are disappointing. However, the churchyard is delightful. For many years the rector here was Edward Boys Ellman, Farmer John's grandson and author of *Recollections of a Sussex Parson*, who remembered a time when salmon-trout came up the Cuckmere and polecats raided hen-roosts. [During the last seventy years] 'the alterations that have occured are so great that I doubt whether any like period of the world's history can show as great changes' he wrote in 1889.

At first glance, St Pancras at Arlington is uninspiring, yet it is a very ancient church. The nave is Saxon and there are Roman tiles in the masonry, from some long lost villa. There is a deserted medieval village not far away, abandoned at the time of the Black Death.

One may walk up the Cuckmere, from near Arlington, to Michelham Priory. The best preserved medieval religious house in Sussex, even if its church was pulled down at the Dissolution, it is a rare example in England of a fortified monastery. A magic place when there are not too many visitors, in summertime its moat is bordered by yellow flags. The Sussex Archaeological Society has cleaned out the moat and done as much as possible to restore the buildings; the water-mill has been rebuilt and its wheel, turned by a leet, grinds corn once more. Founded in 1229, the priory contained up to a dozen Austin canons, in white habits with black cloaks and hoods. The gatehouse, sixty feet high and with flint walls four feet thick, was built about 1395 by Prior John Leeming, no doubt with memories of the Peasants' Revolt and French raids in mind, and had a wooden drawbridge.

Sometimes it was an unhappy community; in 1478 it was reported that three canons had left, that one was still wandering 'apostate' while another who had returned after fifteen years was 'poisoning the whole house with his strange and evil arguments'. The prior was an important figure in local life; in 1533 the Prior of Michelham, the Abbot of Bayham, the Prior of Lewes and Lord Dacre decided to stop all illegal fishing in the Levels – an incident lampooned by Andrew Borde in his *Merry Tales of Gotham*.

After the canons' departure, Michelham became a farm. Even when secularised it was not always happy. In 1973 a 'witch-jar' was unearthed here, a seventeenth-century Bellarine flask containing the wax model of a heart pierced by pins – this was a counter-spell, to throw a spell back at the witch.

Turning west again, at Laughton there is a moated, redbrick farmhouse in the fields, Laughton Place, built in 1534 as a great mansion at the top of Glynde Reach; the river made it easier to bring the red and black bricks with which it was constructed. This was a home of the Pelhams, whose badge of a buckle is seen on many buildings in the area; the badge commemorates a Pelham receiving the surrender of King John II of France at Poitiers in 1356. Here lived Sir Nicholas Pelham, High Sheriff of Sussex in 1549. His monument in St Michael's church at Lewes tells how he drove off would-be French raiders:

> What time the French sought to have sack't Sea-Foord,
> This Pelham did Re-pel-em back aboord.

Only a single tower remains at Laughton Place, which the family abandoned in favour of nearby Halland in 1595. (They left Halland for Stanmer in 1769). When the miasma of the sea mist comes in along the Levels, the lonely tower seems peculiarly bleak and one can well understand Sir Nicholas having a town house in Lewes. His descendants included the Duke of Newcastle and the Earls of Chichester who, with forty other Pelhams, lie buried in the church at Laughton village.

The hilly, wooded country of the High Weald is in striking contrast to these flat meadows. Mayfield is unquestionably its most beautiful village. On a high hilltop, it has weather-board houses and the remains of a palace of the Archbishops of Canterbury; the latter is now a convent, the nuns using the fourteenth-century hall as their chapel. Around Mayfield 'the rural ground plan with its thickly timbered shaws, wayside hazel coppice, greenways bordered by marl pits, and small fields sloping away to the humble, unregarded farmhouses almost lost to sight amid trees in the hollows is, in essence, the work of the Age of Clearing', wrote Peter Brandon in 1974; he marvelled that such traditional countryside should survive unspoilt within forty-five miles of central London. It is still unspoilt in the nineties.

Rotherfield, also in the High Weald, is a nice enough village. It has a good church with fine thirteenth-century murals of Christ, the Archangel Michael and Doom, but like so many Sussex villages it is ruined by being on a main road.

Crowborough is commuter land. Nevertheless, it is worth climbing Crowborough Beacon, over 800 feet, from where one can see the sea twenty-five miles away. Beacons were lit here to warn of enemy warships in the Channel, notably in 1588 – pitch burning in an iron basket on top of a wooden pole.

Sprawled along its ridge, East Grinstead seems unpromising when one drives into it. Yet the centre is impressive, that of a former Assize town, with a fine High Street; the Judge's Lodging is suitably dignified. The church is magnificent, not medieval as it seems at first glance, but built at the end of the eighteenth century by James Wyatt. Sackville College, founded in 1609 by Robert Sackville, Earl of Dorset as a combined almshouse and feudal pied-à-terre, still shelters eighteen old folk. (An inscription in the hall reminds them to be grateful: 'I pray God bles my Lord of Dorset and my Ladie and al their posterities.') One nineteenth-century warden was the hymn writer John Mason Neale, responsible for *Hymns Ancient and Modern.*

You meet the Sackvilles again, in rolling country some miles east of East Grinstead, at Withyam, even if only a Tudor gatehouse remains from Old Buckhurst, their family seat. Struck by lightning in 1663 and rebuilt in Gothic style even at this late date, the church (like many dedicated to the Archangel Michael) stands on a low hill within sight of the house. It contains some marvellous monuments to the Sackvilles. In Cibbers' group commemorating the thirteen-year-old Thomas Sackville who died in 1677, a beaming, long haired boy holds a skull while a ringleted lady and a moustachioed nobleman in armour mourn him. ((The nobleman looks rather like Charles II.) Though Thomas was a mere younger son, the inscription tells us:

> He whose sacred ashes here doth lie
> Was the great hope of all our family.

Nollekens's dancing cherubs, who lament the cricketing Duke of Dorset, are almost gleeful in their exuberance. Flaxman's bewhiskered fourth Duke has a doleful charm only surpassed by Chantrey's portrayal of his bereaved mother. The tiny hamlet in the hollow below the church is very pretty and unspoilt, with a nice and no less unspoilt pub, the Dorset Arms. In the woods to the south there is a fine hammer pond.

Eridge Castle, built as a seat for the Nevills in 1787, replaced a medieval stronghold which had stood on the edge of the long forgotten Waterdown Forest. (First as Lords 'Burgavenny', then as Marquesses of Abergavenny, the Nevills have been great Sussex landowners since the fifteenth century, their crest of a bull's head being on countless farms and cottages.)

Augustus Hare thought it 'an ugly ginger-bread gothic building'. Demolished in 1938–9, it is now regretted as a fine example of the eighteenth-century 'Gothick' taste.

Frant – which should be pronounced with a long 'a' – was described by Augustus Hare as 'a village possessing an ugly church in a lofty situation, with wide woodland views of great beauty'. In fact the church built in 1819 in the 'Gothick' style is quite pretty, and remarkable for its cast iron columns. These were not made here, though Frant had once been a centre of the iron industry. A little book by a local historian, Patricia Wright, *Frant: The Story of a Wealden Parish*, contains a vivid evocation of the village in about 1580:

> It must have been an impressive sight to stand outside the Bull Inn at night and look down on a crimson glow lighting the Eridge valley below, because once a furnace was fired it was force-blasted for three months or more, until the fuel was used up. The power to drive the bellows and forge hammers came from water wheels and water supplies were erratic, when the streams were flowing the hammer and bellows worked non-stop under the light of flares, pine-knot plaits, animal fat burners and glowing charcoal ... [When molten iron was tapped off] The flare of these tappings would light up the sky for miles around, so watchers in the village above would see black figures outlined against white-scarlet heat, scurrying about with rods, hammers and moulds ...

Wadhurst, another village in the High Weald, has over thirty iron tomb-slabs in its church, one as late as 1799 – some may have been cast in Frant. The graceful, airy church is part Norman, part thirteenth-century. There are cheerful twittens round it, while from the churchyard one can see the reservoir which drowns the site of several houses in the Wealden museum. The high street is long, thin and straggling. Wadhurst Castle is an ordinary house built at the beginning of Victoria's reign but with four octagonal towers. (Seventy years ago a friend of mine, then a small boy, saw a ghost here, a man in a blue light.)

In a marshy park at the north-eastern corner of the rape, the ruins of Bayham Abbey are entrancing. A house of White Canons founded in 1208, its impressive church of about that date has a polygonal apse. In 1448 brethren were rebuked for wearing smart clothes; three years later they were in trouble for 'wandering abroad' and what sounds like poaching. In 1525, Cardinal Wolsey dissolved the abbey whereupon the locals, dressed in skins as goats or donkeys, broke in and re-instated the canons, after which several Frant men were arrested. Hare, lyrical for once, quotes a description of Bayham in the 1890s – 'with its emerald lawns and grey ivied arches reflected in the bosom of its own sweet lake'.

XIV

Sussex Palaces: Petworth, Goodwood, Uppark

'Sussex, upon the whole, is a healthy pleasant county, on which account there are so many of the nobility and gentry who have their seats there' reported George Walpole in 1784. However, he had to admit that 'the roads, in the winter season, are the worst in England'. Some of these country houses are among the most beautiful in the British Isles. Once they were as much communities as dwelling places, each centred around its master and mistress. Three in particular were built in the great ages of English architecture and, unlike Arundel, have nothing of the fortress about them. They are not castles but palaces.

Although the old manor house at Petworth is known to have been fortified in 1309, it is unlikely to have been on the same scale as Arundel or Lewes because it possessed little strategic importance. Nevertheless, the great Baroque house which succeeded it dominates the little town like some feudal *palazzo* in Southern Italy. It is still inhabited by descendants of the family who acquired the estate during the twelfth century. Created Earls of Northumberland in 1377, they were an unlucky race, proud and quarrelsome; seven of the eleven earls died in battle, on the scaffold or in prison. Yet if in the North they fought savagely with their neighbours, in Sussex they seem to have kept on sufficiently good terms with their fellow grandees.

Any violent streak was bred out by the time of Henry Percy, the ninth earl, who was born in 1564. As a Papist he was suspected of complicity in the Gun Powder Plot and spent sixteen years in the Tower, released only in 1621 after paying the enormous fine of £11,000. He passed the remaining years of his life at Petworth, conducting experiments in alchemy which earned him the name of 'The Wizard Earl'. Presumably he hoped to find the philosopher's stone and the secret of making gold; no doubt he intended, if successful, to rebuild Petworth – as it was, he added a 'stable court'. He amassed a superb library and, with his son, began the marvellous collection of pictures.

The last earl of Northumberland died in 1670 leaving an only daughter, Elizabeth. At the age of thirteen she was married to Lord Ogle, who died within the year. At fifteen, her second husband, Thomas Thynne, was murdered by her lover, Count Koenigsmark, whereupon she married Charles Seymour, Duke of Somerset. Obsessed with his rank and lineage, he was called the 'Proud Duke'; when travelling, outriders went ahead of his coach to clear everybody else off the road. He insisted that his children remain standing in his presence; falling asleep, he awoke to find that a daughter had sat down and so he disinherited her on the spot. Yet he was also a man of learning and generosity; at Cambridge he endowed Trinity College and Catharine Hall richly, and he helped to found the University Press. Both his pride and his good taste are commemorated by Petworth.

As soon as the duchess reached the age of twenty-one and her fortune became available, he began rebuilding the house. The architect is unknown but the Huguenot, Daniel Marot, has been suggested. Work was completed in 1696. The result resembles a great French château of the age of Louis XIV. During the eighteenth century the park was landscaped by Capability Brown. One can only agree with Ian Nairn about the overall effect: '. . . proud and patrician, scorning false ostentation but not afraid of extreme richness when richness is needed . . . the impression is overwhelming and ennobling.' Pride has its virtues.

Petworth House was soon celebrated as one of the finest mansions in the kingdom, fit for royalty. In 1708 'Charles III' – the Habsburg pretender to the throne of Spain who later became the Holy Roman Emperor Charles VI – stayed here after landing at Portsmouth. Prince George of Denmark,

Queen Anne's consort, paid him a visit. An anonymous courtier has left an account of Prince George's journey from Godalming, which gives some idea of Sussex roads in those days:

> We set out by torchlight, and did not get out of the coaches (save only when we were overturned or stuck fast in the mud) till we arrived at our journey's end. 'Twas hard for the Prince to sit 14 hours in the coach that day without eating anything, and passing through the worst ways that ever I saw in my life. We were thrown but once indeed in going, but both our coach, which was the leading, and his Highness's body-coach, would have suffered very often if the nimble boors of Sussex had not frequently poised or supported it with their shoulders from Godalming almost to Petworth; and the nearer we approached the Duke's house the more inaccessible it seemed to be. The last nine miles of the way cost us six hours time to conquer them; and indeed we had never done it, if our good master had not several times lent us a pair of horses out of his own coach, whereby we were able to trace out the way for him.

No wonder the county was considered remote.

The proud duke's only son and successor died in 1750. The Northumberland title with half the northern estates went to the husband of this last duke's daughter, Sir Hugh Smithson, who changed his name to Percy. Petworth, together with the Cumberland and Yorkshire estates, passed to the last duke's nephew, Charles Wyndham, who became Earl of Egremont. (The Egremont title had been borne by a junior branch of the Percys during the Wars of the Roses.)

The third Earl of Egremont, who succeeded in 1763 at the age of twelve, was a great Whig nobleman who much preferred the country to the capital. Despite spending some years in London he was famous for his shyness and retired to Petworth for the second half of his life. 'The very animals at Petworth seemed happier than in any other spot on earth', the artist Benjamin Haydon recalled nostalgically. 'His charities were unbounded, and the liberal encouragement which he extended to art and agriculture will hand his name down to posterity as a great benefactor', the Sussex historian Mark Anthony Lower recorded reverentially yet without exaggeration. When in

1814 the Tsar and the King of Prussia wanted to see how an English noble lived, the Prince Regent took them down to Petworth, where they were duly impressed by the majestic house with its staff of 160 servants and air of being an all but independent principality. Turner spent so much time there that he has even been called its painter in residence; the earl himself would never enter Turner's studio without a special knock. Other artists who came to stay included Constable, Blake, Haydon and the sculptor, Flaxman.

Lord Egremont's second passion was farming. In 1810 he introduced one of the first threshing machines, while he took a keen interest in South Down sheep. He built several roads, financed and encouraged West Sussex canals, and spent the staggering sum of £1,250,000 on improving the town of Petworth. Genuinely benevolent, he gave parties for the poor, inviting 6,000 at a time, and helped paupers to emigrate to Canada. He was largely responsible for abolishing the sports of bull-baiting and cock-shying. Even the diarist Charles Greville, not prone to paying compliments, called him 'a fine old fellow'. The earl died in the year Queen Victoria came to the throne of England, after his own reign of sixty-five years – truly the golden age of Petworth. One of his monuments is that delicious Sussex apple, the russet Egremont (named in his honour) which has an aftertaste well brought out by a glass of port.

Lord Egremont had loved the house just as it was when he inherited it. His only addition was a large north gallery to house his father's collection of antique statuary. And he expanded immeasurably its wonderful collection of pictures.

One of the best rooms is the Carved Room, worked by Grinling Gibbons into a perfect cornucopia of lime wood fruit and flowers. Yet the contents of the Turner Room, with Turner's views of Petworth, make even this pale into insignificance. The picture collection is one of the finest ever assembled in a private house, the paintings by Titian, Hieronymus Bosch, Claude, Van Dyck, Cuyp, Reynolds, Gainsborough, Zoffany, Romney, Hopner, Blake and many other masters. (Among them are Van Dyck's portraits of

Robert Shirley of Wiston and his Circassian wife, in their Persian dress.) However, it is those stupendous Turners which stay in a visitor's memory.

'The prospect from this seat is beautiful beyond description' was how George Walpole reacted in the 1780s. Forty years later, William Cobbett – of all people – waxed lyrical: 'The Park is very fine, and consists of a parcel of those hills and dells, which Nature formed here when she was in one of her most sportive moods. I have never seen the earth flung about in such a wild way . . .' It remains just as beautiful today.

During the 1890s, no doubt in reprisal for never having been invited to stay, Augustus Hare made one of the testiest and most unjustified of all his pronouncements when describing Petworth House in his guide to Sussex: 'Magnificently uninteresting in itself'. Nevertheless, he had to concede that its pictures were superb, especially the family portraits of the Percys and the Seymours. In particular, Mr Hare took angry exception to the conducted tours of the house, 'a very rapid walk' through the rooms which lasted precisely an hour. 'There is no time or possibility of examining or enjoying any special picture, but, with the crowds – chiefly uninterested and uneducated – who have to be herded along, no other system is possible. No casual visitor can carry away more than a confused jumble of beautiful impressions.' Today's tours of the house are less shepherded and more leisurely than they seem to have been in Hare's time.

Petworth's survival was due to the late Lord Egremont (John Wyndham). One of the wittiest men of his generation, he was also one of its most effective, in public as well as in private life. For many years Harold Macmillan's close friend and confidant, he acted as his private secretary during the War and later when Macmillan was foreign secretary and prime minister. (When he died in 1972, *The Times* commented that 'Their friendship and collaboration, that of statesman and private secretary, had no counterpart in modern history.') During the early 1950s, faced by ruinous death duties in a climate aggressively hostile to inherited wealth, after lengthy and complex negotiations he reached an agreement by which pictures were accepted in lieu of death duties – the first agreement of its kind. Although the terms were heavily in favour of the National Trust, which obtained over twenty Turners of literally fabulous value, they at least ensured that future generations of the Wyndham family would continue to live here. In consequence, Petworth has remained a home – the function for which it was built – and has escaped the fate of becoming a soulless institution like so many less fortunate great houses.

Goodwood has shown amazing adaptability, developing businesses which have included air taxis and a test circuit for cars. It is altogether different from Petworth, partly because of its setting on the Downs below the Trundle, and partly from being built of that most characteristic of Sussex materials: downland flint. Unlike Petworth it is unmistakeably English.

Modern Goodwood is the home of the Gordon-Lennox family who descend from Charles II and his Breton mistress Louise de Kerouaille. The first Duke of Richmond bought Goodwood in 1697, to use as a hunting lodge. (The local pack, the Charlton, was the first to hunt foxes in England and was famous throughout the eighteenth century; in January 1738 one gallant old vixen gave the second duke, who was master, a run of ten hours from East Dean to the Arun, the duke being in at the death.) This duke, Charles, was married in Holland at the age of eighteen, to the Earl of Cadogan's daugher, Sarah, to settle a gambling debt between their fathers. Sent on the Grand Tour for three years, on returning to London he went to the play where he saw a charming young woman among the audience; asking her name he discovered she was his wife, after which they had twelve children during a notably happy marriage. His principal interest was hunting, but he kept a menagerie at Goodwood which included a lion and a tiger. He also found time to fight at Dettingen, and at Culloden under 'Butcher' Cumberland against his cousin, Bonny Prince Charlie.

The third duke, another Charles, was to Goodwood what Lord Egremont was to Petworth. Still more, he rebuilt the house. During the 1760s Sir William Chambers, who had already built an imposing stable-block, enlarged it. Then the duke employed James Wyatt to design an enormous new mansion with an unusual plan – a great octagon, with a round tower at each angle. One stipulation was that flint be employed as the main material. 'The duke is adding other improvements, under that excellent artist, Mr Wyatt, which, when completed, will render it a very noble and magnificent edifice' George Walpole told his readers in 1784. However, by 1800 when only three sides of the octagon had been completed, funds ran out. Architectural historians generally think it odd or dull (like Nairn) but personally I find it very attractive, especially the side with the pillared front portico flanked by towers with green copper domes. The house is filled with French furniture and tapestries, and a collection of paintings to rival Petworth.

This Duke Charles had several distinguished careers: as a general at twenty-six, as an ambassador to Louis XV (when he acquired the furniture) and as Master of the Ordnance. A true Whig, he introduced a private Bill which would have given every Englishman the vote. He founded the Goodwood race-meeting on the Downs, planted a vast forest and saw that every labourer on the estate was given a comfortable cottage which had a garden with a pig in it.

The fourth duke's duchess gave the famous ball at Brussels before the battle of Waterloo. The fifth duke, who had been Wellington's A.D.C. during much of the Peninsular War, fought at the battle. From his mother's brother he inherited the additional dukedom of Gordon – hence the name Gordon-Lennox – while he perfected Goodwood racecourse.

I cannot help wondering if Anthony Trollope went to Goodwood. Gatherum Castle, the seat of the Dukes of Omnium and the social centre of Trollope's Barsetshire, is often thought to be Badminton. But just as Chichester has been suggested as the model for Barset instead of Winchester, Goodwood may be the model for Gatherum. The celebrations for the coming of age of Lord March, the future sixth duke, in 1839 were considered 'one of the most magnificent entertainments ever known in West Sussex'. They started on

Wednesday 27 February, with a stag hunt in the morning, dinner for 300 gentlemen, and then a ball and supper for 700; on Friday there was a dinner for 200 farmers with their families; while on Sunday a party was held in the park for 700 estate workers, who were all given a cash present. The Dukes of Richmond were much richer than the Dukes of Beaufort at Badminton – during the 1870s their rent-roll was £79,000 as opposed to £56,000.

When he succeeded as duke, Lord March became a great improver of the estate, building 400 new cottages (of flint) for his employees. Goodwood continued to flourish despite the agricultural depression at the end of the century and after the Great War, but incurred enormous death-duties when the eighth duke died in 1935. However, his successor ensured its survival. He sold his Scottish estates, sold 70,000 trees in Sussex, and established an efficient forestry business and a race track. Because of this realistic approach, the house was able to survive as a family home during the difficult years after the Second World War. Between 1966 and 1970 it was completely renovated, including the state appartments.

The family portraits here are outstanding. There is one of the finest of all Van Dyck's paintings of Charles I and Henrietta Maria. The dukes and their duchesses had them-selves immortalised by the greatest artists of their time; Kneller, Reynolds, Hopner and Lawrence – the latter thought his painting of the lovely fifth duchess the best he had ever done. For E. V. Lucas, 'the most beautiful thing at Goodwood' was one of Canaletto's views of the Thames. I myself admire most a breathtaking Stubbs, of the third duke watching his horses being trained on the Downs. There is also a sinister, haunting painting, the *Cenotaph of Lord Darnley* – a murdered ancestor, the husband of Mary, Queen of Scots – which stays uncomfortably in the mind.

South of the Hartings, in a valley in the Downs, stands Uppark, once the most beautiful mansion in Sussex. It was until recently a charred ruin. But now, like Phoebus, it is rising from the ashes.

Ironically, this loveliest of houses was built by one of the most unpleasant men in the county's history. Born in 1655, Ford, Lord Grey was referred to contemptuously by Dryden as 'cold Caleb', while a modern historian calls him 'this cowardly and incestuous traitor'. He was involved in the Rye House Plot to murder Charles II, seduced his eighteen-year-old sister-in-law, contributed to the Duke of Monmouth's destruction at Sedgmoor in 1685 by mishandling his cavalry, and then saved himself by turning King's Evidence, grovelling before James II; 'I lie, Sir, at Your Majesty's feet, where, though I cannot expect, yet it is a pleasure to beg for mercy' he pleaded, ending 'may all those perish that ever lift up a thought against yr Majesty's life or for disturbing the peace of your Government'. He went over to William of Orange in 1689, being made Earl of Tankerville and a Privy Counsellor before his death in 1701.

Sometime during the 1690s he rebuilt the old house of his maternal grandfather, the Sussex Cavalier Sir Edward Ford. The architect William Talman, William III's Comptroller of the King's Works, was also responsible for much of Chatsworth. Talman's Uppark is a Wren-style house with a fine carved centre-piece on its south front; it charms by simplicity, enhanced by its setting. 'I went to Chichester through a very fine Parke of the Lord Tankervaille's stately woods and shady tall trees at least 2 mile', wrote the diarist Celia Fiennes in 1695, 'in the middle stands his house which is new built, square, 9 windows in the front and seven in the sides, brickwork with free stone coynes and windows, itts in the midst of fine gardens, gravell and grass walks and bowling green . . .'

In 1747, Lord Grey's grandson sold Uppark to a Northumbrian, Sir Matthew Fetherstonhaugh, who was said to be worth £400,000. He loved the house, beautifying it with furniture, carpets and pictures. He was a close friend of the historian Edward Gibbon who informed him that Trajan's Column was carved 'with as much delicacy as any chimney-piece at Up-park'.

Sir Matthew died in 1774. His heir, the twenty-year-old Sir Harry, was immortalised when on the Grand Tour in a portrait by Pompeo Batoni. He was rich enough to indulge himself and became something of a rake. In 1780 he acquired the seventeen-year-old Emma Hart, a Cheshire girl of wonderful beauty – one day to be Admiral Nelson's great love. She had been working in London at the Temple of Aesculapius in the Adelphi, as what would today be called a 'hostess'. Installed in a cottage on the estate, she spent a lively year at Uppark, on one occasion dancing naked on the dining-room table (if rumour can be believed) before being sent back to Cheshire six months pregnant – presumably by Sir Harry. However, a sparkling career awaited the future Lady Hamilton.

After the Prince of Wales established himself at Brighton he made firm friends with Harry Fetherstonhaugh, frequently driving over to Uppark in his yellow phaeton and staying for the races on West Harting Downs. In 1785, he brought with him the Duc de Chartres, Philippe Egalité, who would one day vote for Louis XVI's execution. The Prince wrote, 'I beg of you to give me my old Bed at Up Park'. But when he became Regent, the Prince dropped Sir Harry.

By that time Harry had become a confirmed countryman, busy embellishing the house with French furniture and redecorating it on Humphrey Repton's advice, though his main amusement was shooting pheasants. He had no heirs. One day he went into the dairy and proposed to his head dairy maid, Mary Anne Bullock, whom he sent to Paris to be educated. They were married in 1823; he was seventy-one, she was twenty. Shortly after, he told his gamekeeper, 'I've made a fool of myself, Legge', but Mary Anne cared for him devotedly until his death aged ninety-two in 1846. He bequeathed Uppark to his wife, who at her own death in 1875 left it to her sister and lifelong companion, Frances, who lived on until 1895.

There is a monument to Sir Harry in Harting church from his 'devoted and grateful widow'. Although snubbed by many of the local gentry and their ladies, the two sisters entertained lavishly. Their half-sister lived with them, Miss Sutherland, one of Sir Harry's bastards. Frances Bullock took the name

Fetherstonhaugh when Mary Anne died. She bequeathed the house for life to a childless neighbour, Lord Winterton's brother, Colonel Turner who also took the name Fetherstonhaugh, and then to a young friend who eventually became Admiral Sir Herbert Meade-Fetherstonhaugh. Finally, the house passed to the National Trust.

The great charm of Uppark was that it remained just as it was in Sir Harry's day, subtly renovated with the utmost sympathy by the Meade-Featherstonhaughs, who altered nothing. There was an extraordinary atmosphere, as if time had stood still. Sadly, in August 1989 it was gutted by fire, though many of its moveable treasures were saved from the flames. However, the basic structure remained intact and the decision was taken to restore it, using the latest scientific techniques. Soon it will return to life and people will be able to visit Uppark again.

Among the housekeepers here in the last days of Miss Fetherstonhaugh (Frances Bullock) was the mother of H. G. Wells. Normally an iconoclast, he wrote in an often quoted passage how he was profoundly convinced that modern civilisation had been begotten and nursed in such houses as Uppark. 'Within these households, behind their screen of deer park and park wall and sheltered service, men could talk, think and write at their leisure.' There is no finer tribute to the palaces of Sussex.

XV
Sussex Smugglers

Sussex has always had a name for smuggling. Everyone knows Kipling's poem about Sussex 'Gentlemen':

> Five and twenty ponies;
> Trotting through the dark —
> Brandy for the Parson,
> 'Baccy for the Clerk:
> Laces for a lady, letters for a spy . . .

For centuries it was the county's main industry after agriculture.

For hundreds of years 'owling', or wool-running out of Sussex, was the main form of contraband. The export of wool was taxed from very early on, wool-packs having to be registered at Lewes or Chichester, with all the additional expense of transport. This meant real hardship for downland farmers, who, to avoid it, often rushed their wool to the coast as soon as the sheep had been sheared; merchants bought the untaxed wool and shipped it over the Channel. As early as 1274 a Shoreham merchant is known to have been in trouble with the law for owling. In 1698, an Act of Parliament imposed strict controls on the sale of wool within fifteen miles of the sea, and a force of 'riding officers' was set up, which could call on the Army for help in emergencies. Twenty years later, Daniel Defoe watched dragoons searching the marshes near Rye as though beating for game. The Act had no effect. Defoe says that the revenue men were attacked and sometimes killed, 'obliged as it were to stand still and see the wool carried off before their very faces, not daring to meddle, the boats taking it from the very horses' backs'. Some ships crossed the Channel once a week, returning to Sussex with brandy and lace — convoys of wagons left the beaches every night.

Owling continued until well into the eighteenth century. In 1731, it was alleged that not less than 150,000 wool-packs were being shipped out of Sussex every year and that the squirearchy was heavily involved: 'Some gentlemen of no mean rank, whose estates bordered on the sea-coast, were too much influenced by a near but false prospect of gain.'

However, by that date the smugglers were switching to other types of contraband. Smuggling *into* Sussex as opposed to owling, had begun on a large scale during the Civil War, when Royalist agents brought in arms and money for King Charles. During the Commonwealth, Cromwell imposed import duties on many household goods, duties which were increased after the Restoration. They continued to rise, steadily and steeply. In the same year that the Act against owling was passed, 1698, smuggled brandy is known to have been stored in cellars at Seaford from where it was sold to tavern keepers at Lewes.

During the early eighteenth century the rise in import duties accelerated. Most foreign goods such as wine, spirits, tea, lace, silks or porcelain became much more expensive. Claret grew so dear that many drinkers switched to port. Meanwhile, the collapse of the iron industry and a decline in weaving caused widespread poverty. The result was a smuggling boom when the war with France ended in 1713.

Some contraband was human. French spies had been caught landing in Sussex during the recent war, while others must have got through. Jacobites, supporters of the exiled house of Stuart, also used smuggling routes to enter and leave England undetected, on behalf of the 'King over the Water'. Among them was Colonel Sir Harry Goring, MP for Horsham and the head of an old Sussex family, who in 1721 was reported to be involved with an owling gang in an obscure plot to put James III on the throne.

Secret backers, often leading figures in the City of London, put up large sums of money to finance formidable gangs, who were recruited from poachers and deer stealers as well as from owlers. One of the most notorious was based on Mayfield, with depots at Horsham and West Chiltington. At night it sent scores of men with blackened faces down to the Sussex beaches to unload contraband cargoes; others armed with pistols, blunderbusses, cutlasses or 'bats' (long bludgeons) stood guard on the cliffs, ready to flash a warning from spout lanterns. The gang's landing grounds were between Seaford and Hastings, where it loaded wool and ran in brandy and tea. There were high rewards for the apprehension of such gangs, but the excisemen were hopelessly outnumbered while an experienced team of smugglers could run in 500 barrels in twenty minutes.

The leader of the Mayfield Gang was a former bricklayer called Gabriel Tomkins, nicknamed 'Uncle' though he often went under such aliases as 'Kitt Jarvis' or 'Joseph Rawlins'. In 1717, he was tried for the murder of a riding officer, Gerard Reeves, at Langney Bridge near Eastbourne but there was insufficient evidence to convict him. After several brushes with the revenue men, during one of which he received a bullet in the arm, Tomkins and most of his gang were caught in Ashdown Forest in September 1721 after being chased from Burwash. He escaped but was recaptured; sentenced to seven years transportation, he turned King's Evidence, destroying his own gang, and was pardoned. His subsequent career sounds like something from *The Beggars' Opera*. After many more run-ins, during which £100 was offered for his capture, he was caught at Battle in 1729 having just landed a cargo of brandy. He proved so co-operative that the authorities made him a riding officer. However, in 1741 he fell into debt and returned to smuggling. He then became a highwayman, and was hanged four years later for robbing the Chester Mail.

In March 1735, the commissioners of customs received a secret report on 'the late battle between the smuglers [sic] and officers at Bulverhide'. Writing under the assumed name of 'Goring', their informant says that twenty-six smugglers had taken part, each with a musket, two being killed and several wounded. 'There were no foreign persons at this business, but all Sussex men and may be easily spoke with [identified].' Informants like this risked their lives.

The government grew increasingly alarmed since, in the days before income tax, customs duties formed the bulk of the nation's revenue. At one time a third of the tea and spirits consumed in England was contraband; tea bought abroad which had escaped paying duty could be re-sold at eight times the cost price. In 1736, smuggling became an offence punishable by transportation; ten years later the penalty ws increased to hanging. Under the Act of 1736 a smuggler who turned King's Evidence received a full pardon if he named his accomplices; under that of 1746 the names of smugglers who had been identified were published in the *Gazette*; if they did not surrender within forty days they were sentenced to death and a price of £500 was put on their heads. Savage though it was, the legislation had little effect.

The first appearance of the most violent and ruthless of all Sussex smugglers, the Hawkhurst Gang, was in autumn 1735 when they and their pack horses were ambushed by soldiers near Hastings but escaped. Although they took their name from a Kentish village, most were Sussex men and operated mainly in Sussex. The outbreak of the War of Jenkins' Ear in 1739 made the trade still more profitable, the gang specialising in tea and brandy. Their leader, Arthur Gray, and his brother William built themselves fine houses from the profits; the former was credited with being worth £10,000. They had no difficulty in recruiting; a man could earn more from a night's work running contraband than he could from a whole week on a farm. In 1740 a large consignment of tea which had been hidden in a barn at Etchingham was found by riding officers and loaded onto a wagon to be taken to Hastings; on Silver Hill, outside Robertsbridge, thirty members of the gang attacked the escort, killing the chief customs officer, wounding a dragoon and taking the rest prisoner. The gang's operations began to be conducted on a far bigger scale. When three cutters sailed into Pevensey Beach in November 1744, the cargo was taken inland by 500 pack horses; during the previous day sixty armed men had smashed up the house of the nearest riding officer at Bexhill, terrorising his family. The gang enjoyed its reputation for brutality, firing pistols in the air when they visited taverns at Rye. They fought with other gangs, menaced entire villages, ran in cargoes in broad daylight, and insulted and beat up revenue men.

Arthur Gray was arrested as a highwayman in 1747. An even more vicious figure took over as the gang's leader, a twenty-six-year-old Kentishman called Thomas Kingsmill, later reckoned to be one of 'the most audacious, wicked fellows among the smugglers'. In October that year a cutter bringing the gang a cargo of tea, brandy and rum was intercepted by a revenue sloop and taken to Poole Harbour in Dorset. The cutter's crew, led by Richard Perin — once a carpenter at Chichester until a stroke crippled his hand — escaped in the ship's boat. Kingsmill gathered thirty men and rode to Poole where they broke into the customs house with axes to recover their 'property'. On their way back, a shoe-maker named Daniel Chater recognised one of them as John Diamond, an old friend who threw him a bag of tea.

By now the Hawkhurst Gang had become a public nuisance, menacing rich and poor alike. As long ago as 1735 the Duke of Richmond had received a letter at Goodwood demanding that he invest 250 guineas in a smuggling venture; if he did not 'we will destroy all you have and we will shoot his Grace whearever we sees him.' Later, his servants were found to be selling contraband while his huntsman was accused of smuggling.

The raid on Poole customs house infuriated the authorities and, as a result of his shoemaker friend's gossip, Diamond was arrested. To obtain a conviction it was essential that Chater should identify him; an elderly exciseman, William Galley, was sent to bring Chater to a magistrate. The entire gang was in danger. En route, Chater and Galley stopped at an inn whose landlady found out where they were going and warned the smugglers. A group led by two Chichester men who worked with the Hawkhurst Gang hurried to the inn and began to ply the pair with rum till they fell asleep. They were then tied on a horse, their legs bound beneath its belly. As they rode both were beaten so hard with horsewhips that twice they fell under the horse's belly, their tormentors shouting 'Lick them, Damn them, Cut them, Slash them, Whip them'. Galley was flogged until he appeared to be dead and was buried in a sandpit on the Downs; he may have been still alive. Chater was taken to Trotton where, after his eyes had been gouged out with a knife, he was hanged in a well, rocks being thrown down to finish him off. (We know all this from *A Full & Genuine History of the Inhuman Unparalleled Murders of Mr William Galley . . . and Mr Daniel Chater*, published in 1749 by 'A Gentleman of Chichester' – probably the Duke of Richmond.)

Although the murders took place in February 1748, nothing happened until November when the names of many of the gang were published in the *Gazette*. One of them, Jacob Pring, turned King's Evidence. In consequence, over thirty men were hanged; some were gibbeted, their corpses hung in chains till they rotted, among them being Kingsmill and the murderers of Galley and Chater. It was the end of the Hawkhurst Gang, which had once boasted that it could raise 500 armed men in thirty minutes, and which in the past three years had beaten or wounded 250 excisemen and killed six.

The executions coincided with the end of the war with France and with lower import duties, after which smuggling became less profitable. 'Free-trading' continued, though on a smaller scale. While disliking such brutes as the Hawkhurst Gang, on the whole Sussex people sympathised with traders; in 1741, electors told the Duke of Richmond they would vote for his candidate if he released a smuggler from gaol, but otherwise would vote against him. There were some fine men among them, like Thomas Burrow, master of the sloop *Two Brothers* and a well known free-trader, who was drowned at sea on 13 October 1759. His tombstone in Bosham churchyard tells us:

> Though Boreas's storms and Neptune'swaves have tos'd
> me to and fro
> Now I at length by God's decree am harbourd here below
> Where at Anchor here I lay with many of our Fleet
> Yet once again I shall set Sail my Saviour Christ to meet
> It also shows him falling into the sea after a rope had snapped.

Not everyone approved of them. John Wesley, who often visited Rye and Winchelsea between 1758 and 1790, deplored that 'accursed thing smuggling'. In his view 'open smugglers are worse than common pick-pockets'. Among the guilty he included 'those who buy Tea, Liquors, Linen Handkerchiefs [and] everything else which has not paid duty'. He had reason to detest the free-traders, who shot and killed his would-be son-in-law Henry Haddock, a revenue captain.

Smuggling revived when the Seven Years War broke out in 1756, when Horace Walpole commented that the only news from France was 'run' by free-traders. They were encouraged by a steep rise in the duty on tea in 1759, which eventually reached 20 shillings a pound. A 'black economy' based on smuggling gradually emerged, employing thousands, its centres being Kent and Sussex. Generally, the free-traders used three-masted luggers of about 80 to 130 tons, built for speed, with crews of up to fifty men; many of these vessels came from a shipyard in Hastings. Often they were armed with only a single cannon on a swivel called a 'Long Tom' though sometimes they mounted twenty heavy guns. Other craft employed in the trade were sailing barges, oared galleys rowed by twenty men, or the tubby little fishing-boats known as 'Brighton Hogs' which could be beached quickly and were handy for picking up weighted barrels sunk off shore. Alternatively, the contraband was concealed on board Channel packets, merchantmen or fishing smacks. Cargoes included not just tea and spirits, but everything from the latest French fashions to wig-powder.

In 1779 a new Act introduced extra penalties for contraband found in vessels of less than 200 tons. Five years later the prime minister, William Pitt, slashed the duty and increased the number of revenue cutters to forty-four. It made no difference. It was estimated during the 1780s that in three years Kent and Sussex free-traders had landed nearly two million gallons of Dutch gin and over half a million gallons of brandy. Their rewards were enormous, a profit being made if only one run in three was successful.

On a single day in 1782 300 pack horses trotted through

Lindfield in broad daylight. During the summer of the following year a dozen or more luggers could be seen unloading at the same time in Cuckmere Haven, surrounded by hundreds of men. At Newhaven a revenue man was seized and tried by a court of 200 traders, for 'aiding and abetting in the murder of a smuggler'; he was acquitted, though only by ten votes. The savagery of the confrontations between revenue men and free-traders was evident in August 1783 when the customs sloop *Scourge*, commander Henry Haddock of Rye (betrothed to John Wesley's daughter), engaged a lugger off Dungeness Point. He was killed by its first broadside, the ball passing through his left thigh, body and right arm. A few years later the same lugger was boarded by a party from a revenue cutter whose captain cut the skipper down with his cutlass.

The still unspoilt hamlet of Jevington, at the foot of the Downs between Eastdean and Polegate, saw plenty of smuggling in the 1780s. The ring-leader James Pettit – known as Jevington Jigg – kept a public house here, the landing places being on the small stretch of coastline between Cuckmere Haven and Birling Gap. There were depots in the rectory's huge cellars and in those of Filching Manor not far away, which had an escape tunnel, and probably one in the Tiger Inn at Eastdean. Jigg had a very bad name. Early in 1789 he was arrested, accused of being involved with his friend 'Cream Pot Tom' in the theft of Major Gage's valuable blood mare from West Firle; he bribed the gaoler at Horsham into giving him a saw for his chains, but was caught when he tried to escape. However, he was then released without trial and the general opinion was that he had informed on Cream Pot Tom who was hanged. Undoubtedly he was a 'ten-shilling man', ten shillings being the sum which the Customs paid for information. In 1799, Jevington Jigg was himself sentenced to death for horse-stealing, though his sentence was commuted to seventeen years transportation to Botany Bay.

Another ten-shilling man was James Dean, who built the pretty house known as The Dipperays near the Tiger Inn. Nothing was known of his finances yet he died a rich man, leaving large sums to his gardener and to his gardener's son. It seems that he succeeded in being both free-trader and informer.

Saltdean Gap near Rottingdean was the lowest point in the cliffs between Brighton and Newhaven, with good paths down to the beaches where contraband could be landed. In those days (and until the 1920s) the area was lonely downland to the very edge of the cliffs; with some justice, it has been described as a smugglers' paradise. Rottingdean, then an isolated village on the Downs, was ideally suited for the trade, the entire community – farmers, shepherds and shopkeepers – being involved as early as the seventeenth century. After a run-in, goods would be hidden in caves along the cliffs or in the thick clumps of gorse on the Downs before removal to depots in Saltdean Vale or at the abandoned hamlet of Balsdean, though there were cellars and tunnels in the village.

Rottingdean traders first began to suffer from the attentions of revenue men in October 1770, when 133 tubs of brandy were seized at Saltdean Gap. Harassment increased steadily, a big cargo being confiscated at Balsdean in 1793. In August of the following year the *Sussex Weekly Advertiser* told its readers how:

> Last Wednesday morning Messrs Lindsey and Geere, riding officers at Rottingdene, seized 51 tubs of Geneva which they found concealed in a cavern at Telscombe, made by the smugglers for that purpose. The officers plugged one tub and invited all the old women of the parish to partake of it, which they helped to drink out, and some of them sipped so largely of the enlivening extract that they found themselves stimulated, as if under the provoking influence of some powerful diuretick, and if one might judge from appearances, the liquor had suffered no diminution in its double distillation; it is however but fair to say that the good dames of Telscombe conducted the process with as much modesty and decorum as the situation would admit of.

Every family in Telscombe was involved in the trade. Riding officer and ten-shilling men were not the only danger. In the autumn of 1798, a lugger with contraband on board was driven on to the rocks at Saltdean Gap, all her crew of five being drowned. Many other traders died in this way.

At Rottingdean, smugglers met to plan their operations at the public houses now known as *The Black Horse* and *The White Horse*, regardless of riding officers or ten-shilling men. The anonymous author of *A Summer of Rottingdean – Illustrated by Sketches – taken in the Year* 1814 noted 'Smuggling is the chief support of the inhabitants at which they are very Dextrous – a great deal being carried on at a Gap called Salt Dean Gap about ¾ of a Mile to the East, the goods being hid in the furze about there until they can be conveniently carried away, in which trade the leading man is Captain Dunk the butcher, a well-known character along the coast'. During the same year of 1814, Dunk – of Whipping Post House – was fined £500 at Horsham Assizes for smuggling, ten of his friends being sent to prison.

The sails of Rottingdean Mill, built on Beacon Hill outside the village in 1802 (when the skeleton of a warrior with a bronze sword was found while digging its foundations), were used to signal to luggers waiting off shore. The mill's cellars served as a depot for Lot Elphic, a local fisherman who owned several boats. Presumably much of Mr Elphic's prosperity came from free-trading as did that of the Rottingdean men who built such smart houses round the village green. Not all millers were so obliging as the one on Beacon Hill – in 1815 Windover Mill was burnt to the ground because its owner refused to signal with the sails.

Dr Hooker, a much respected vicar of Rottingdean from 1792 to 1838, owned a fast grey mare and often acted as look-out when there was a run-in at the Gap. His dignified and benevolent bust may be seen in the parish church, over the pulpit, while his rectory is the public library. Among neighbouring clerics who shared Dr Hooker's weakness for smuggling was the Pelhams' chaplain at Stanmer, wounded in a fight with the revenue men who chased him after he had helped with a run-in at Salt Dean. The parson of Hove and Preston preached at each church on alternate Sundays; on one occasion he confused the days, to find the nave at Hove filled with tubs of brandy. The church at West Blatchington was another depot. At Broadwater, tombs were designed to hold contraband, four feet high and with sliding panels; the vicar conducted mock services, tubs being hidden in the coffins. Church towers and vaults were often used without the incumbents' knowledge.

Unlike John Wesley, most clergymen seem to have thought smuggling a very minor peccadillo, as appears from the tombstone at Hastings of Thomas Noakes, a free-trader shot by an exciseman on the high seas in 1783. (His epitaph must have been approved by the parson):

> May it be known, tho' I am clay,
> A base man took my life away;
> But freely him I do forgive
> And hope in Heaven we shall live

A stone at Patcham near Brighton commemorated the passing of another Christian smuggler, Daniel Skayles:

> Who was unfortunately shot, on Tuesday evening,
> Nov. 7, 1790
> Alas. swift flew the fatal lead,
> Which pierced the young man's head.
> He instant fell, resigned his breath,
> And closed his languid eyes in death.

His widow's memorial is still more affecting:

> She in affliction bore a son,
> The milk foresook her breast,
> Her legs they mortified and run,
> But hope she's now at rest

Mr Skayles had been one of the most villainous members of a noted gang which had been overtaken by excisemen and soldiers when going heavy laden over the hill to Patcham. The riding officer who chased Daniel knew the speed of his horse and, taking no chances, shot him through the back of the head.

One reason why smugglers were so successful was the authorities' half-hearted approach. Only four revenue cutters patrolled the entire Kent and Sussex coast. In 1790, the government saw fit to disband an armed force which had been raised ten years before by the chief exciseman at Horsham, Mr

Walter, with the specific task of combating smugglers; it had fought some fierce battles, as at Lancing in the spring of 1784, when six of its members were wounded, besides capturing a significant amount of contraband. But it had incurred the disapproval of the MP for Horsham, who may have had private grounds for his dislike. Many a Justice of the Peace was a secret sympathiser with the trade, which often made it difficult to obtain a conviction. 'In the old free-trade days the smuggler was regarded, if not as the most respectable, certainly as one of the most useful members of society, and we have seen with what a delightful simplicity of method he plied his vocation' wrote Lieut. the Hon Henry Shore, RN (later Lord Teignmouth), a hundred years ago, in *Smuggling Days and Smuggling Ways, the Story of a Lost Art*.

During the Revolutionary and Napoleonic Wars, aristocratic refugees from France, and then spies, crossed the Channel to Sussex in large numbers. It was a two-way traffic; the London newspapers were shipped regularly to Bonaparte from Bexhill. The Navy's blockade made Dutch gin and French wines and brandy even more saleable; for convenience the spirits in the tubs were very high proof, as much as 180 per cent, to be adulterated after landing – some traders died from sampling them. Precautions against a French invasion, whether naval patrols or Martello towers, were a serious obstacle to smugglers. So too was the Preventive Waterguard, established in 1809, whose boatmen patrolled the coast nightly, and which recruited men from outside Sussex to man new watch towers on the cliffs. Yet the traders persevered since it was still possible to make enormous profits.

In 'Poor Honest Men' – which is how many traders saw themselves – Kipling portrays a smugglers' lugger escaping from a revenue cutter

> With no heart to fight,
> We take refuge in flight,
> But fire as we run, our retreat to defend,
> Until our stern-chasers
> Cut up her fore-braces,
> And she flies off the wind from us poor honest men . . .

To be drowned or be shot
Is our natural lot,
Why should we, moreover, be hanged in the end –
After all our great pains
For to dangle in chains,
As though we were smugglers, not poor honest men?

These were the reflections of traders who sometimes sailed as far afield as Virginia to bring back tobacco. However, the bulk of the smuggled goods came from across the Channel.

The flat beaches of West Sussex were ideal for landing cargoes, as were the gaps in the cliffs further east. Longboats from the luggers came in close to shore. 'Everything being ready, the man in charge of the party would be all eyes and ears, so to speak, to detect not only the approach of the boat but the presence of the patrols' says Lieutenant Shore, who had spoken to many of the old free traders:

> At length a dark object looms dimly through the gloom, the word is passed along the carriers to be ready, and almost before the boat keel grates on the beach, the party surround her, seize and sling the tubs, every man a pair, and make off with all dispatch inland. The whole affair is over in from three to five minutes . . . It was customary on reaching what was considered safe distance inland, to call a halt, when a flagon or small cask of spirits – which always found a place in a run cargo – would be broached and passed around. It was on these occasions, that by the indiscreet libations of the younger hands, and the resultant exaltation of spirits, the whereabouts of the party would sometimes be revealed to the coastguard . . .

If discovered, the smock-frocked labourers who were the tub carriers bolted into the night. More often, however, they went undetected.

From Chichester armed convoys set off almost every night, bound for London by way of Horsham or Petersfield, a journey of several days. The route from Brighton was through Lindfield, from Rye and Hastings via Sevenoaks. There were depots in every village as well as on the Downs. Shepherds grazed their sheep over the downland tracks after the pack horses or wagons had gone by, obliterating wheel and hoof marks. They also acted as look-outs, signalling with their crooks if there was danger.

At Brighton, cargoes were run in directly on to the beach at night, then rushed to such hiding places in the Lanes as The Spread Eagle (now The Sussex Tavern) or The Old Ship Hotel. Brighton men were famous for their cunning in outwitting the revenue officers, with whom they were often on ludicrously amiable terms; in 1803 strollers in the Steyne were diverted by the spectacle of fishermen dividing a cargo of tubs with excisemen. Goods also came in on the packet boats. One depot was Southdown House at Patcham, with its cellars and escape tunnels, and its doors and shutters reinforced by steel grilles.

Everything changed at the end of the Napoleonic Wars in 1814. A quarter of a million soldiers and sailors were discharged, which enormously increased the number of smugglers. The authorities responded in 1816 with a 'Coastal Blockade' along the Kentish coast to Beachy Head, to be extended in 1824 as far west as Chichester. The blockade was supplemented in 1831 by a coastguard, stationed in purpose built cottages; its members patrolled the shore instead of the sea, hunting smuggler rather than contraband. The blockade had its successes, as in February 1820 when the revenue cutter *Linnet* captured a Brighton lugger off Rottingdean, after a spirited attempt at escape during which she threw 200 tubs of brandy into the sea – most of them being retrieved. The crew of four received twelve months imprisonment each, while a boy with them was pressed into the Navy.

The revenue cutter *Hound*, Captain Butler commander, was permanently stationed at Brighton and to watch her chasing a smuggling lugger was a far from infrequent and most exciting entertainment for those watching from the front. The last successful run-in at Brighton in broad daylight was on 19 July 1821, when all the excisemen were at the sports being held on the Level to celebrate George IV's coronation. At 3.00 p.m. a lugger suddenly dashed in to the beach opposite The Old Ship Hotel, where a party of traders was waiting in the yard; within moments 300 kegs of Dutch gin had been landed and the tub-carriers had vanished inland.

The free-traders retaliated vigorously against harassment. A 'forced run' was a run made in spite of coastguards, employing a 'fighting gang' to protect the tub-carriers. The batmen, with long ash bludgeons and sometimes firearms, blackened their faces; paid twenty shillings as opposed to the tub-carriers' five, they considered themselves to be a superior class although most of them were on parish relief. More than one coastguard fell to his death from the cliffs in the dark because marker-stones had been deliberately misplaced. Pack horses were prefered to wagons since they made less noise, and downland tracks to roads. Rudyard Kipling's *Smugglers' Song* almost certainly reflects conversations with aged free-traders who remembered the final era of the run-ins:

> If you wake at midnight, and hear a horse's feet,
> Don't go drawing back the blind, or looking in the street,
> Them that asks no questions isn't told a lie.
> Watch the wall, my darling, while the Gentlemen go by! . . .
> If you meet King George's men, dressed in blue and red,
> You be careful what you say, and mindful what is said . . .

However, the 'Gentlemen' fought some very vicious battles with King George's men.

The great smuggling days of Alfriston were during this last period. The ringleader here was Stanton Collins, a butcher who lived at Market Cross House (now the Smugglers' Inn) which he acquired in 1823. His gang operated discreetly and probably on a very small scale; a few of their tubs were found by the excisemen but nothing significant. No doubt they brought their cargoes up the Cuckmere – it is unlikely that they tunnelled through the marsh ground around Alfriston to the sea, as has been suggested rather wildly. In 1831, Collins was sentenced to seven years transportation at Lewes Assizes, not for smuggling but for stealing sacks of barley. He returned from Botany Bay to spend his last days in Sussex, as a footman.

By 1825 nearly 3,000 men were patrolling the Kent and Sussex coast. There were twenty-nine coastguard stations between Chichester and Beachy Head, each one within signalling distance of its neighbour, to keep watch on inshore waters and the cliff paths. In 1835 the revenue service introduced steam cutters.

One reason why free-trading went on for so long in the face of such determined efforts to suppress it, was that anyone might join in for a very modest outlay. It was not just rich men – like the Brighton shopkeeper Mr Weston, fined £10,000 – who provided the financial backing. 'Each person would "venture" so many [tubs], paying down to me on the spot, £1 for each tub ventured' an old smuggler told Lieutenant Shore. 'Another £1 per tub would be lodged in the bank to pay expenses.' A tub (or 'half-anker') held four gallons of brandy and cost about £1 in France as opposed to £9 in England after duty had been charged, so that a successful run meant a substantial profit. The wages paid to the humble tub-carriers and batmen saved them from the workhouse; in 1833 it was reported that many more were asking for parish relief because of the decline in smuggling – hitherto Sussex farm labourers had depended on free-trading to see them through the winter when work was scarce. Despite the ten-shilling men, smugglers were renowned for their loyalty to each other – there are very few records of betrayal.

The traders made more use of 'crop-sewing' – sinking weighted tubs just off shore. They also attached the tubs to boat keels or brought them in under fishermen's catches. False trails were laid, with mysterious lamps and empty tubs, while boats were given secret bottoms. Land smugglers were no less ingenious; barrels were hidden in the walls of public houses, with pipes to take spirits down to the cellars – as at the Hastings Arms in Hastings. Tubs were also concealed in rivers and ponds. When revenue men caught a certain shepherd trying to retrieve a tub from a pond at Piddinghoe he convinced them he was a lunatic trying to catch the moon.

Violence became the norm. In 1824 a blockademan named Walsh jumped into a boat off Bexhill which had just landed a hundred tubs of spirits; the crew pulled off with him, to leave his battered corpse on a nearby sandbank. During an ambush near Fairlight in 1827, the traders wrested the blockademen's guns from them, beat them with the butt-ends and ran one through with a bayonet; three smugglers were killed, the rest carrying their wounded off on their backs – one being taken to his home at Udimore six miles away. In 1828, after a landing between Bexhill and Bo-peep and a running fight, the blockademen caught up with the traders at Sidley Green. There were sixteen batmen, armed with their six-foot long ash staves, and they fought like fury against the bayonets and cutlasses. Although they killed the blockademen's quarter-master, three of them fell dead; the body of one old smuggler, Smithhurst, was discovered in a barn next day, his hand still clutching a bat which had been hacked to pieces by cutlass blows. In 1833 there was another combat of this sort at Eastbourne when, after shooting their enemies' leader, the traders formed two lines so that the cargo could be run in between them.

Throughout the 1820s and the early 1830s free-trading remained profitable. A cargo destined for a draper in North Street, Brighton, which was impounded at Newhaven in 1822, contained 950 yards of silk, 200 pairs of soft leather gloves and an assortment of such items as opera glasses and bracelets of human hair. However, most contraband was brandy, like the 300 tubs landed, with much blood letting, on the sea-front at Worthing on a February night in 1832.

The odds grew too heavy. Old smugglers told Shore that informers destroyed the trade, but the real reason was a drastic reduction in import duties during the 1840s. Ironically, 'free trade' killed its namesake. Profits bore no proportion to the risk.

Yet there were a few isolated runs, as at Shoreham in August 1855. A travelling circus and wild beast show gave a performance near the Customs House (later Town Hall), all coastguards being presented with tickets. During the performance, fourteen tons of tobacco were transferred from a ship moored next to the Custom House into a barge, which sailed up the Adur to Beeding where four vans were waiting; one van was traced as far as Horsham, but there the trail ended. A large consignment of tubs was seized at Arundel in 1860, after what was probably the very last of the big runs.

Survivors of the trade lingered on almost into the present century. The last member of the Collins Gang at Alfriston died in Eastbourne workhouse in 1890. Trunky Thomas, a famous old smuggler who owned Rottingdean's four bathing machines besides several fishing boats, seems to have outlived him, hale and hearty to the end.

Smuggling has never quite died out in Sussex. Worthing trawlers, fishing for scallops in Caen Bay, are known to have run in a fair amount of brandy during the 1920s – if a customs officer appeared, they used boiling tar to disguise the smell. Two men were caught with a large quantity of expensive cognac at Cuckmere Haven in 1923. Illegal immigrants were landed in the Haven during the 1960s. The East Sussex police captured two and a half million pounds worth of heroin in 1982 which, it has been suggested, was landed at Rye Harbour. But many of the old free-traders were fine men in their own way, very different from modern drug-runners.

XVI
Hastings and the Rape of Hastings

The easternmost rape has always been different from the other rapes. Admittedly, it has 'Downs' of a sort and is crossed by the Forest Ridge. Yet there is no real downland. Once, cut off by woods and marshes, the coastal area was very much a separate region. Some historians believe the '*Haestingas*' were Franks, the Germanic tribe who gave their name to France and whose weapon was a throwing axe or *francisca*, others that they were Jutes. Whatever their origins, they retained a separate identity until the eleventh century. The *Anglo-Saxon Chronicle* refers to the Vikings ravaging 'all Kent and Sussex, and the region around Hastings'. Even so, as everyone who reads Kipling knows, many think of the area as the heartland of Sussex.

One difference is the number of oast-houses, relics from the Sussex hop-gardens of Richard Jefferies' time:

> In this district, far from the great historic hop-fields of Kent, the hops are really grown in gardens, little pieces of land often not more than half an acre or even less . . . always on a slope, if possible in the angle of a field and under the shelter of a copse, for the wind is the terror, and a great gale breaks them to pieces; the bines are bruised, bunches are torn off, and poles laid prostrate. The gardens being so small, from five to forty acres in a farm, of course but few pickers are required, and the hop-picking becomes a 'close' business, entirely confined to home families, to the cottagers working on the farm and their immediate friends. Instead of a scarcity of labour, it is a matter of privilege to get a bin allotted to you. There are no rough folk down from Bermondsey or Mile End way. All staid, stay-at-home, labouring people – no riots; a little romping no doubt on the sly, else the maids would not enjoy the season so much as they do. But there are none of those wild hordes which collect about the greater fields of Kent. Farmers' wives and daughters and many very respectable girls go out hopping, not so much for the money as the pleasant out-of-door enjoyment, which has an astonishing effect on the health. Pale cheeks begin to glow again in the hop-fields.

*

The town of Hastings is unlike other Sussex towns in being built on sandstone instead of the usual chalk. From its great cliff, the castle looks down on to the coastal plain, dominating the Old and the New Towns. Unlike Pevensey, it once stood further away from the sea, on a promontory lapped by tidal waters. A Saxon *burh* with a mint arose and by the end of the twelfth century it was a rich and powerful town, first among the Cinque Ports. However, in the thirteenth century the waves overwhelmed its harbour, drowning many streets and a priory while half the castle fell into the sea. Attempts to build a new harbour with breakwaters were washed away. French privateers completed the ruin, burning the town to the ground in 1377. The fortress-like towers of the remaining medieval churches, St Clement's and All Saints, bear witness to the inhabitants' fear of raiders from the sea. Although St Clement's was rebuilt in 1390 and All Souls in 1436 (it has a mural of Domesday, with Christ enthroned on two rainbows), inexorably the town declined into a poor little fishing village.

During the eighteenth century, like Brighton but on a much smaller scale, Hastings became a watering place. By 1794, a stage coach was coming down from London three times a week; there were circulating libraries and a bank. Turner painted here in 1810, while Byron visited it four years later: 'I have been swimming and eating turbot, and smuggling neat brandies and silk handkerchiefs' the wicked lord wrote happily, 'and walking on the cliffs, and tumbling down hills, and making the most of the *dolce far niente*.' On the sea front, Pelham Crescent, built in the 1820s, is as good as anything in Brighton.

In 1828, much as Kemp did in Brighton, the architect James Burton (father of Decimus) bought land to the west of the Old Town, on which to build 'New Hastings' – St Leonards. The fifteen-year-old Princess Victoria stayed here with her mother, the Duchess of Kent, in 1834 – at Burton's house, 57 Marina, still there. She became patron of the St Leonard's Archers.

Hastings arouses strong likes and dislikes. 'I love town, or country, but this detestable Cinque Port is neither', wrote

Charles Lamb in 1823. 'It is a place of fugitive resort, an heterogeneous assemblage of sea-mews and stockbrokers, Amphrites of the town, and Misses that coquet with the ocean.' Augustus Hare loathed it. 'The monotony of its wearisome line of featureless parades and terraces is some-what redeemed by the view eastwards of the cliff and the ragged ruins of the castle' he sniffed, but 'the so-called country roads are lined for miles in every direction by miserable, shabby, stucco villas, each more piteously ugly than the last.' Ian Nairn liked it no better in the 1960s, even if he admitted there were some good buildings. Understandably, he lamented the new road to the front made through the Old Town – 'the Rape of Hastings' indeed!

Just as many have doted on the place, including Henry James, who called it 'a quiet Brighton'. Coventry Patmore lived here, after he left Heron's Ghyll, at Old Hastings House in the High Street; near it, in 1882, he commissioned Basil Champneys to build the neo-gothic church of St Mary Star of the Sea – in Patmore's opinion, 'The only Catholic church with no bad taste in it'. Yet it is a town for painters rather than novelists or poets. 'Indeed, under certain conditions of light, Hastings is magnificent, with the craggy Castle Hill in its midst surmounted by its imposing ruin', commented E. V. Lucas, who understood this very well. 'The smoke of the town, rising and spreading, shrouds the modernity of the sea-front, and the castle on its commanding height seems to be brooding over the shores of old romance. Brighton has no such effect as this.' Many painters have agreed with him, besides Turner – among them Samuel Prout, David Cox and Edward Burrah.

Personally, I think that on a fine day in late autumn when the holiday season is over, the Old Town is one of the pleasantest places on the South Coast. Whatever Nairn may say, it is far from ruined, despite that unsightly new road through the centre, and is much more attractive than the Brighton Lanes. Although the last lugger built here was the *Enterprise* in 1909 (to be seen at the Fishermen's Museum), it is still a fishing port, twenty boats going out to trawl. Since there is no harbour, when not at sea they are run up on the beach, just as ships were in the Middle Ages. Their gear is still stored in tall, wooden sheds, known as 'net-shops' because in the old days nets were dried in them; something seen nowhere else in England; tall, black and windowless, they have a slightly sinister air. Sadly, fishermen are no longer called by the Dickensian nicknames in use till the end of the last century: Tipper, Wintry, Podger, Weasel, Penny Dog, Yellow Legs.

At first sight, whether from Trecherie Marsh or the railway station below – trains seldom stop here – Winchelsea looks no more than a high green hill, uninhabited. Then one sees a grey tower straddling the road, the fourteenth-century Strand Gate. But this is new Winchelsea.

Old Winchelsea lies under the beach at Rye Bay, three and a half miles away, first destroyed and then abandoned by the sea. It was on an island of shingle in the salt marshes, not far from Rye golf-course, protected by sand dunes and embankments. Known to have flourished as early as 1130, it was prosperous enough sixty years later to join the Cinque Ports as an 'Antient Town'. There was a royal dockyard here in King John's reign, while it provided Edward I with more ships than any other Cinque Port. Despite its prosperity, by the mid-thirteenth century the town's very existence was in jeopardy. During a dreadful storm in 1250 much of it was submerged by a freak high tide, the sea roaring in 'with a glint of fire on the waves', perhaps in response to an earthquake; 300 houses were lost. Two years later there was another freak tide, houses and mills disappearing beneath the water and many people drowning. Soon even the parish church had all but vanished; by 1280 almost the entire town was water-logged. In 1287, most of what was left was swept away in another terrible storm, the sea swallowing up the surrounding marshland, so that the Rother changed course.

However, King Edward I had already drawn up plans for a new 'Wynchelse'. It was to be on the hill of Iham, about three miles west of the old site, and a hill-top promontory above the harbour of the River Brede – in those days surrounded on all sides by the sea at high tide, save for a neck of land along which went the road from Hastings, today's Panell Lane. Anticipating danger from the French, the king employed an architect who had built fortified towns (*bastides*) for him in Gascony, Itier Bachard; it was to be 'a key, refuge and guard for those parts against the tempestuousness of the seas and the insults of our enemies' – and a vital link in the wine trade with Bordeaux. New Winchelsea was laid out on a grid of thirty-nine squares; five long streets running north to south, crossed by eight others running east to west, defended by walls and gates.

Although only half the squares were built on, at first the new town prospered. Magnificent vaulted cellars survive under some of the houses; once they held claret destined for London (over 700,000 gallons in 1306–7). Unusually, there was a good road to the capital and fish was supplied direct to the royal household, arriving in twenty-four hours. Among exports were wool, cheese and salt, together with iron and wood from the Weald. In 1292, the population included goldsmiths, jewellers and embroiderers in gold and silver. The most solid testimony to wealth, however, is the vast church of St Thomas.

Winchelsea seamen had a fearsome name for piracy, preying on English and foreign shipping alike. The crew of a captured vessel were thrown overboard or locked in the hold before it was scuttled. But the Winchelsea men would be repaid in their own coin.

On Sunday, 15 March 1359, 3,000 Frenchmen stormed the walls while the inhabitants were at Mass, and killed forty townsmen and raped many women. (A path next to the vanished church of St Giles where these were buried is still known as Deadman's Lane, and is haunted; no birds will sing there.) After spending a day and a night at the town, during which they looted and burnt, they sailed away in thirteen ships laden with booty and taking with them any pretty woman who had caught their fancy. Exactly a year later, on 15 March 1360, they returned and put Winchelsea to the torch for a second time. They came yet again in 1380 and in 1449.

The sea proved an even deadlier foe. Gradually the harbour silted up. Although used by ships of 200 tons in 1433, early in the sixteenth century the port had to be abandoned.

Marooned, Winchelsea entered an irreversible decline; by 1577 it had no more than 120 able-bodied men, and in the year of the Armada no ships, captains or mariners but only one sailor named William Bucston. 'This place being now all in rubbish, and a few despicable hovels and cottages only standing, hath yett a Mayor', wrote John Evelyn in 1652. Having preached there, John Wesley pitied 'that poor skeleton of ancient Winchelsea' in 1790. Yet in his day substantial houses were being built, for the huge cellars had come into their own again as smugglers' depots.

At the end of the nineteenth century, writers and painters discovered this medieval ghost town in the marshes, with less than 500 inhabitants but with a mayor and corporation. 'The place is full of a quiet melancholy beauty, very dear to the artist, with its ivied walls and venerable gateways, and streets so green with grass' was how Hare saw it. He thought the New Inn 'clean and commendable' as did Ralph Caldecott. Other admirers of Winchelsea included Coventry Patmore, Henry James and Ford Madox Ford.

Today it is still almost too beautiful, and the New Inn is still clean and commendable. The vast, half-ruined church is the best thing, but the medieval court house, what is left of the Franciscan friary, and many pretty houses – some Edwardian though none later – are all worth seeing. The outline of the town walls can still be traced and three of their gates remain. Some of the squares they enclose are green fields.

Inland towards Rye, one comes to Udimore. When the church here was being built on the far side of a pool, it always disappeared during the night. Then, one night the locals heard angels carrying the stones away, chanting 'Over the mere, over the mere.' So they built the church on the other side of the pool, over the mere – 'Udimore'. It is a handsome Norman edifice, outside at least. The village had a bad name for peculiarly vicious smugglers, always fighting with the revenue men; three of them, the Miller brothers and Spencer Whitman were sentenced to death at the Old Bailey but then transported to Tasmania instead. A polecat was trapped at Udimore as late as 1848. Near here, I can remember seeing otters hunted on the

River Brede, less than thirty years ago.

The village of Brede also has its legend, that of Sir Goddard Oxenbridge, a giant seven foot tall who ate a child for supper every night. Eventually the children of Sussex made him drunk with strong beer and then laid a huge wooden saw across his throat, see-sawing until they had cut his head off. Sir Goddard really existed; he was knighted by Henry VIII in 1509, while his tomb is in Brede church, erected when he died a natural death in 1537. Brede had a flourishing iron works, suppliers of cannon to the Parliament during the Civil War, which later became a powder mill. In 1808 it blew up, scattering debris over an area twelve miles wide.

Sir Goddard's ghost haunts his house, which still stands, Brede Place, a small fifteenth-century manor house of brick and stone, altered in Elizabethan times. (Sir Goddard's daughter, Lady Tyrwhit, was governess to the future Queen Elizabeth.) Sir Edward Lutyens thought it 'the most interesting inhabited house in England'. One especially bizarre inhabitant was the American novelist, Stephen Crane, best remembered for *The Red Badge of Courage*, who lived a Bohemian existence here from 1899 till 1900 with 'Mrs Crane' – Cora, formerly the madam of a Jacksonville brothel. They were frequently visited by Henry James, a loyal friend.

Camber Castle is on the road through the marshes to Rye, built by Henry VIII to defend the seaward approaches to Rye and Winchelsea. Originally called 'Winchelsea Castle', it consists of a central tower with five D-shaped bastions which form an octagon. They were gun-emplacements rather than towers, only twenty feet high but eleven feet thick, capable of standing up to the heaviest sixteenth-century cannon; inside they resembled the gun-turrets on Dreadnought battleships, gun chambers linked by vaulted passageways, loopholed so as to facilitate fire at any enemy who reached the courtyard. Constructed between 1539 and 1544, out of stones from the dissolved friaries at Winchester, it cost £23,000 – paid for by monastic loot. The Captain of Camber was responsible to the Constable of Dover Castle, with a garrison of six gunners and eight soldiers. Although it stood close to the sea when built, the inning of the marshes pushed it further away every year. At the outbreak of the Civil War in 1642 it was already a mile inland and its cannon were transferred to Rye, never having fired a shot in anger.

Rye is a hill town, on a sandstone bluff rising sharply out of the marshes, which is joined to the firm ground northward by a narrow neck of land. The Brede, Rother and Tillingham – once substantial rivers – border it south, east, and west. In earlier times their estuaries combined to form a land-locked lagoon known as the Camber, while at high tide the ground beneath the town was flooded. ('Rye' is an Anglo-Saxon word for 'island'.)

During the twelfth century, Rye joined the Cinque Ports. (See ch. XVII, 'Sussex and the Sea'.) For many years it prospered, building town walls to protect its wealth. However, these were not proof against French privateers, who burnt most of the town to the ground in 1377, destroying the church and stealing its bells. The townsmen's spirit remained unbroken – a year later they raided Normandy to recover their bells. But the French returned in 1448 and again set fire to the town. The townsmen complained to King Henry VI that Rye 'had fallen into devastation, destruction, waste and impoverishment, not only of lands and tenements, but also of inhabitants'. It could no longer muster an annual fleet to bring back claret from Bordeaux.

Decline set in, though the real cause was not so much French pirates as the marshes silting up. To some extent this was alleviated by the Brede and the Rother forming a new estuary west of the town, but at the end of the sixteenth century Camden reported that Rye was lamenting how 'the sea abandoneth it'.

Rye could only watch as the Armada sailed past in 1588. In *Rewards and Fairies* (in 'Simple Simon') Kipling recreates the spectacle of the running battle between the English and Spanish fleets as seen from the little port:

> 'Twas the noise of the gun-fire tarrified us. The wind favoured it our way from off behind the Isle of Wight. It made a mutter like, which growed and growed, and by the end of a week women was shruckin' in the streets.

Then *they* come slidderin' past Fairlight in a great smoky pat vambrished with red gun-fire, and our ships flyin' forth and duckin' in again. The smoke-pat sliddered over the French shore . . .

During the 1590s outbreaks of plague decimated the population. Until then it had stayed prosperous enough, helped by Huguenot refugees who established weaving and paper-making. (There were no less than 1,500 of them in 1572, many having fled from the St Bartholomew's Day massacres across the Channel.) However, by Charles II's time the harbour was choked with sand and Rye had sunk to being a minor market town whose main industry was fishing. Some of the inhabitants turned to smuggling, making fortunes which paid for fine Queen Anne or Georgian houses. 'I set out for Sussex and found abundance of people willing to hear the good word, at Rye in particular' wrote John Wesley in 1773. 'And they do many things gladly but they will not part with the accursed thing smuggling.'

During these years Rye was threatened with other dangers from the sea besides storms and revenue cutters. In the 1630s Algerian corsairs lay in wait outside the harbour; a few unlucky Sussex folk may even have found themselves up for sale in the slave markets of North Africa. In the Civil War the fishing fleets were at constant risk from Cavalier privateers, and then came the Dutch pickaroons that 'lurk under Beachy and thereabouts annoying poor fishermen'. As late as 1743 Rye was living in fear of raiders, this time French warships, though they fled on sighting British frigates – 'terryfied by the Approach of your Royal Navy and only night and tempest gave them opportunity of escape', the relieved jurats informed George II.

It is difficult to exaggerate the little town's isolation in Stuart and Georgian days. Until the late eighteenth century its only communications with the outside world were by sea. Before 1770 there was just one road along which carts might reach it, and no stage-coach till eight years later – a coach taking fifteen or sixteen hours to make the wearisome journey from London. The community remained isolated and in some ways barbarous; the bull-baiting at the St Bartholomew's Day Fair was only stopped about 1807. Yet staying anchored firmly in the past ensured that Rye retained its good looks, so that today it can claim to be 'the prettiest town in Sussex'.

'This ancient Town is as compact as a little City, stored with Buildings, and consisting of several Streets' an inhabitant boasted in the seventeenth century. 'The Town is of beautiful prospect . . .' In consequence the fortunes of Rye were restored by late Victorian sightseers in search of the 'picturesque'. It remains undeniably beautiful and wonderfully preserved. Esther Meynell – never at her best where history is concerned – likens it to a vignette from a medieval book of hours.

However, modern Rye can scarcely be described as 'a bit of the old world living pleasantly on, in ignorance of the new' as it was in Coventry Patmore's time. If it has not been ruined architecturally, it appears to be visited by more tourists than any other town in Sussex except seaside resorts. At night it regains something of its old character, which it keeps until early the next morning. A wet and windy day in winter, just before dusk, is the best time for a visit.

The pleasantly named little streets which lead off Church Square – such as Mermaid Street and Watchbell Street – are well aware of their prettiness. In summer the cobbles are bordered by a mass of roses, clematis, honeysuckle and stocks, augmented by a legion of flower-tubs; a rose bush even grows over the lavatory in the yard of the Mermaid Inn ('Rebuilt 1420').

The Mermaid epitomises Rye. There was an alehouse here in the eleventh century, it is claimed, and certainly there is a vault of the thirteenth beneath the present black-and-white building which dates from about 1530. By the eighteenth it had sunk, seeing very low company indeed. An old gentleman told a local antiquary how 'he remembered, when the Hawkhurst gang of smugglers were at the height of their pride and insolence, to have seen them (after having successfully run a cargo of goods on the sea shore) seated at the windows of this house, carousing and smoking their pipes, with their loaded pistols lying on the tables before them, no magistrate daring to interfere with them'. But since the nineteenth century the

Mermaid has risen in the world, and today is positively luxurious.

I do not agree with the old scholar that Rye church is 'the goodliest edifice of that kind in the Counties of Kent and Sussex, the Cathedrals excepted', but it is undeniably a noble building. Lucas considered the square round it the quietest and quaintest church square in England, and it can have changed little since Edwardian times save for the crowds. The church's fabric is basically Norman with Perpendicular features, such as the flying buttresses at the east end, apparently added after the French raid of 1377.

There are other medieval buildings in Rye, notably the Land Gate (sole survivor of the town's three gates, dating from about 1381) and the Ypres Tower, a small thirteenth-century castle which served as the town gaol from 1518 to 1865. (Patmore was ecstatic about the vista: 'The beauty of these views is beyond all description, and has never been expressed even in painting.') In Church Square there is also a fragment of what was once the house of the Friars of the Sack, an obscure order of French origin whose brethren wore sackcloth habits, dissolved in 1307. The chapel of the Austin friars on Conduit Hill was built in 1378 after the original friary had disappeared beneath the waves with the eastern side of Rye. During the late sixteenth century it served as a refuge for Huguenot refugees.

A ghost story, odd even by Sussex standards, is told about the friary. One of the brethren, Friar Cantator, fell in love with a young lady named Amanda who lived in a lane off Conduit Hill. Their affair was discovered and they were walled up alive together. The friar haunted the lane, gobbling like a turkey, so that the lane was renamed Turkey Cock Lane, while a white faced girl in white was sometimes glimpsed at a window. About 1850, the tale runs, two skeletons, locked in each other's arms, were discovered when a wall was demolished and, after their reburial in hallowed ground, the hauntings ceased.

The best known house in Rye is almost certainly Lamb House in West Street, built in the early eighteenth century by a Mr Lamb. Henry James lived here from 1897 until 1916 – to be followed by E. F. Benson, who wrote the Mapp and Lucia stories. Both worked in the 'Garden Room', an eighteenth-century gazebo which was destroyed by a Nazi bomb. (Curiously enough, despite its name, to judge from photographs it seems to have looked out on to West Street.) James was besotted with Rye, calling it a 'russet Arcadia'.

For over a century the Lambs were the great family of Rye, members of the family being elected mayor in no less than seventy-nine years between 1723 and 1832. On one occasion they played host to George I at Lamb House when a storm blew him into Rye Bay while returning from Hanover, on another to the Duke of Cumberland (the 'Butcher') when he came to inspect the defences – Rye being still seen as one of the 'principal gates of England' as in medieval times. Besides their house, the Lambs are remembered on account of the town's most celebrated crime.

Late on the evening of 17 March 1743 Mr Allen Grebell, a former mayor, returned to his home opposite the Lambs after attending a dinner on board a revenue sloop in honour of his nephew. As the then mayor, his brother-in-law James Lamb, was unwell he had deputised for him, wearing the red mayoral cloak. He told his servant that while walking back through the churchyard a drunken man had fallen against him and, since he was feeling a little shaken, he would sit by the fire before going up to bed. During the night Mr Lamb dreamt that his dead wife came to him three times, saying 'James, I am very alarmed about Allen. Get up and see if he is alright'. Twice he woke and went back to sleep. However, at dawn he walked across to Grebell's house, to find him dead in his chair amid a pool of blood, having bled to death from a stab-wound. At first the servant was suspected, but then it was learnt that John Breads, a proprietor of the Flushing Inn in Market Street and a butcher, had been seen dancing through the streets, very drunk, and bellowing 'Butchers should kill lambs'. A butcher's knife covered in blood was found in the churchyard; on its handle was the name 'Breads'. Six years previously, Mr Lamb had fined him for selling short-weight meat.

Cinque Port towns had the right to try and execute those

accused of capital crimes, and the mayor presided over the trial. The jury took ten hours to reach a verdict – on one occasion Lamb had sent Breads to prison for 'feigned madness' and he was probably insane. Finally Breads was found guilty. Before sentencing him, the mayor asked if he had anything to say. 'I did not mean to kill Mr Grebell. It was you I meant it for, and I would murder you now if I could' was the answer.

On 8 June Breads was led from the Ypres Tower, given a final drink at his own inn, then hanged from a gallows just outside Rye on what is now the town recreation ground. When cut down, his body was tarred (to preserve it) and cased in an iron cage by a blacksmith. For fifty years the corpse hung from the gallows on Gibbetts Marsh, the bones which fell to the ground as it rotted being much sought after by witches. The cage and Breads' skull may still be seen at the Town Hall. More than once, E. F. Benson glimpsed Mr Grebell's ghost at Lamb House, swathed in the red cloak.

In 1827, workmen employed by Sir Godfrey Webster, a profligate young gambler but proud of his heritage, cleared away rubble and discovered what was left of the high altar of Battle Abbey. It marks the spot where Harold Godwinson, last Saxon King of the English fell in 1066. William the Conqueror founded this abbey of Benedictine monks in thanksgiving, hence the name. In 1094, his son William Rufus (reputedly an atheist) presided over the dedication of the 'mynster' by Archbishop Anselm of Canterbury. The abbey was endowed with estates all over Sussex, while its mitred abbot became one of the realm's great magnates and sat in the House of Lords. A town arose beside it, with a population which was at one time larger than that of any other town in East Sussex save Lewes.

This was one of the richest monasteries in England. Most of it has been destroyed, including an abbey church longer than Canterbury Cathedral. The most impressive part to survive, the battlemented gatehouse which still dominates the town, was begun in 1338 by Abbot Alan of Ketling; ironically, it was built to guard against the French. At the Dissolution, the then abbot, John Hammond, was accused of 'unnatural crimes' –

no doubt homosexuality, a standard smear. 'The black sort of devilish monks, I am sorry to know, are past amendment' a commissioner reported. 'So beggary [sic] a house I never see, nor so filthy stuff' wrote another, Sir John Gage. Nevertheless, Abbot Hammond secured the enormous pension of £100, moving into a house in the town.

Henry VIII gave the abbey and most of its lands to his Master of the Horse, Sir Anthony Browne. Sir Anthony (who later inherited Cowdray) converted the buildings into a noble mansion. The Brownes sold it in 1719. Among the owners was the seventh Duke of Cleveland, who bought the abbey in 1858. A descendant of Charles II and the owner of over a hundred thousand acres, he was the last of his line. His duchess often rode through Battle side-saddle on a donkey – when the town's urchins saw her coming, they shouted 'Here comes the Duchess riding on her ass'.

Although attractive enough, with pleasant Georgian houses, there is not very much to see in Battle besides the abbey. A fine twelfth-century parish church, built by the monks for the townsmen, contains a monument to Sir Anthony Browne attributed to Torrigiano, who designed Henry VII's tomb in Westminster Abbey – and who, when a young man, broke Michelangelo's nose. It also contains a copy of the 'Roll of Battle Abbey', a hoary genealogical fraud claiming to be a list of the Norman knights who fought at Hastings. The Deanery, a seventeenth-century house, is the former rectory. (The rector was called 'dean', a survival from monastic times; in Augustus Hare's day the patron of the living was still styled 'abbot'.) A fifteenth-century building outside the gatehouse, now a restaurant, is known as the Pilgrim's Rest though some believe it was the cellarer's office. The Gothic station of 1852 is a delightful piece of Victoriana.

Not far from Battle is Ninfield. Here, according to legend, the Conqueror set up his banner on Standard Hill after his victory at Hastings. The church has been spoilt by Victorian restorers, but the village stocks and whipping post by the green deserve a look – they were cast in a Sussex foundry.

What is left of Ashburnham House is hidden in a wonderful

park designed by Capability Brown, a sad place of deep and sombre woods, of mournful lakes. A pitiful remnant is left of the house which was demolished in 1953. The Ashburnhams were said to descend from Saxon thanes, and in his *Worthies* Fuller called them 'a family of stupendous antiquity'. But the last Earl of Ashburnham died in 1924; he had been one of eight brothers, strong and gifted, who between them sired only a single daughter. In the church a marble knight, helmeted and in full armour, lies between his two wives, not some veteran of Poitiers of Agincourt but Jack Ashburnham, Charles I's groom of the chambers and loyal friend. (He kept Charles's shirt and winding sheet here, and as late as 1828 they were used to 'touch for the King's Evil' – to heal scrofula.)

Jack's brother William is here too, with his wife, the former Countess of Marlborough, who had been 'a young beautifull and rich widow'. William 'comeing from beyond Sea, where he was bred a Souldier, married her, and after Liued almost fiue and forty years most happily with her. She was a great louer and (through God's mercy) a great blessing to the Family...' An MP who was expelled from the House of Commons because of his fidelity to King Charles, he became a major general in the Cavalier army and Colonel General of Dorset. Yet William 'gloried in nothing in this World But his wife, and the almost unparalled loue & intire friendship that for Aboue fifty yeares was betweene his Deare Elder Brother John Ashburnham and himself'.

It is easy to lose one's way in this lonely part of the High Weald, with steep wooded valleys and winding lines. Yet it is worth persevering to find Penhurst, a hamlet which has been called 'a rare and exquisite manorial group'. It has an unspoilt church and an Elizabethan iron-master's house. The wooden screen in the former may be as early as 1330 while the latter has one of the last firebacks from Ashburnham Furnace nearby – marked with a coronet over an 'A' and the date 1813.

Brightling is best known for a nineteenth-century squire, Mad Jack Fuller, MP for East Sussex from 1801-12. A rich man, with estates bought by his iron-master ancestors and sugar-plantations in Jamaica, he purchased his seat for

£50,000 but always referred to himself as 'Honest Jack'. Others called him 'Hippopotamus' because of his twenty-two-stone body while a contemporary labelled him 'one of the pompous nobodies of Sussex' – rude, blunt and blatant. Yet he had enough taste to ask Turner to paint Sussex, saved Bodiam and founded two 'Fullerian' fellowships, one of which was held by Faraday. He built numerous follies here, including an observatory to celebrate Trafalgar. Perhaps the last man to powder his hair and wear a pigtail, when he died in 1834 he was buried under a massive pyramid next to the church – the locals believed he had been interred sitting at a table with a bottle of claret. There is a bust of him in the church, heavy jowled, by Henry Rouw.

Some say that Robertsbridge – where so many fine cricket bats are made from the local willows – is a corruption of 'Rotherbridge'. The bats date from about 1870 when a keen local cricketer L. J. Nicolls, began to make his own; they were so good that he founded an industry – Dr W. G. Grace invariably used a Nicolls bat during the later years of his triumphant career. Another explanation is that the name commemorates Robert de St Martin who built the first bridge and founded the Cistercian monastery here about 1176. One of those little Sussex towns which consist of a single street, Robertsbridge grew up around the abbey. The fact that the White Monks chose the Rother Valley shows how wild it must have been, for they always settled in a wilderness. Lay brethren and granges – barns with an oratory and rudimentary sleeping accommodation for two or three brethren – enabled them to clear vast areas of woodland and marsh. 'Give the Cistercians a desert or a forest and in a few years you will find a dignified abbey in the midst of smiling plenty' wrote Gerald of Wales before 1220. This was one of Sussex's three great religious houses, the other being Lewes and Battle; significantly, Sir Edward Dalyngrydge, the builder of Bodiam, was buried here. However, Robertsbridge abbey fell into a decline and though it survived the first dissolution in 1536, when it was dissolved two years later there were only eight monks, waited on by a troop of servants. All that survives today are a few fragments by the river round Abbey Farm, though the farmhouse was probably the abbot's lodging.

The Seven Stars inn at Robertsbridge may have been built by the monks. It claims to have been an inn since 1380, in Chaucer's lifetime. The ghost of a Cistercian, Dom Andrew, is supposed to haunt the corridors. According to his book *The Four Men*, in 1902 Hilaire Belloc obviously thought well of the port at another inn here, the George.

The eighteenth-century view of Sussex as a place of desperate men and vile roads emerges from a letter written by Horace Walpole during his expedition to Herstmonceux in 1752. When he arrived at 'a wretched village called Robertsbridge', at one inn he found all the beds occupied by smugglers – another was 'crammed with excise officers, one of whom had just shot a smuggler'.

Walpole describes the roads as 'bad beyond all badness' and refers to 'a famous precipice called Silver Hill'. Below this hill stands Stalehurst, where the people of Robertsbridge worship. The 'village' here is a hamlet of a few pretty houses clustered round the church – and what a church! Long and high, mainly from the fourteenth century, with an imposing tower, it has a charming little Virgin over the porch. Inside, it is less impressive but there is some good stained-glass of local manufacture, from the end of the century, with birds – among them a peacock and a hawk.

Further north, at the eastern edge of the rape, Burwash (properly pronounced 'Burrosh') is famous as the home of Rudyard Kipling, who praised Sussex more extravagantly than anyone:

> I'm just in love with all these three,
> The Weald and the Marsh and the Down countrie;
> Nor I don't know which I love the most,
> The Weald or the Marsh or the white chalk coast.

The background of his house, a rolling valley with wooded slopes, helps one understand why he was so proud of his county, and also that he was a man of the Weald rather than the Downs like Belloc. His house, 'Bateman's', a manor of honey-coloured stone with tall brick chimneys, was built by an iron-master in 1634. If nowadays people sneer at his 're-discovery of Old England', no can deny that he found it. Thurston Hopkins showed that *Puck of Pook's Hill* was based on the countryside around Burwash; Pook Hill was the name of an old farm not far away, Weland's Ford was Willingford Bridge, while the mill in 'Hal o' the Draft' was probably Dudwell Mill.

The village of Burwash has a spectacularly pretty high street, built with rose brick and white weatherboard, but the over-restored Norman church is disappointing. It contains the earliest known tomb slab in cast-iron, that of 'Jhone Coline' and dates from the fourteenth century. There is also a bronze tablet to Kipling's only son, John, killed at Loos when he was eighteen – although so short-sighted as to be almost blind, he had insisted on going to the front.

'It is all too easy when piecing together the past and present, opinion and observation, to rely over heavily on the parish churches' says Barbara Willard, one of the more graceful writers on modern Sussex. There is some truth in this, but it is impossible for any church-crawler not to be enthralled by Etchingham. The brass of the founder, Sir William de Echyngham, who died in 1387, lies in the chancel; wearing the armour of Poitiers, he has been headless for two hundred years. The Echynghams were great landowners in Sussex from Henry III's reign to Elizabeth's, their estates stretching as far south as Friston on the coast. Sir William built this church in the 1360s; it was served by a college of priests, which explains why the chancel is so long and contains stalls with misericords. There are fine brasses of fifteenth-century Echynghams, and a porch made from oak trees. This is a good example of a fortified church – once it had a moat.

Northiam on the Kent border is one of Sussex's most handsome villages, full of weather-boarded houses whose white paint sets off the faded red brick of Georgian dwellings. There are some famous black-and-white houses, such as Great Dixter from about 1450, or the Jacobean Brickwall where the Frewens, the great family of Northiam, lived. If attractive externally, with a noble stone spire, the church has been ruined

by unsymphathetic Victorian restorers who added a mausoleum for the Frewens. (In 1786 the entrance to their family
vault had had to be bricked up to stop smugglers storing
contraband among the coffins.) The puritan John Frewen
became rector here in 1583 and his descendants provided
incumbents until Victoria's reign. One was John's son,
Thankful Frewen. Thankful's brother, Accepted Frewen, was
tutor to Charles I; when President of Magdalen he sent the
college silver to the king's war chest and later had a price put
on his head by Cromwell, but he ended his life as Archbishop
of York. In the windows there are fragments of medieval
stained glass from the chapel at Brede; one is of the royal arms
of Edward IV or Richard III, flanked by two Yorkist white
roses. Queen Elizabeth dined on the village green here in the
summer of 1573, under an oak tree which still exists – she left
her green shoes behind and they may still be seen at Brickwall.

The rape of Hastings was the part of Sussex Kipling loved
best. Undoubtedly he preferred the easternmost part of the
county, and not just because he lived there:

> And east till dawdling Rother crawls
> To find the fickle tide,
> By dry and sea-forgotten walls,
> Our ports of stranded pride

As with other rapes, the river is the key.

XVII
Sussex and the Sea

In 1587 it was reported to the Privy Council that Sussex 'bordereth south on the sea and north on the wyld; in which towe places cumminly the people be geven mutch to rwedness and wyllfulness'. Undeniably, the Sussex men by the sea were a colourful, violent lot. If many were smugglers, others were fishermen and fine sailors – though some were wreckers and pirates too. They could all be heroes when it came to saving lives.

Ships played an important part in everyday life here from very early times. The races who settled here during the Bronze and Iron Ages came from mainland Europe, and Caesar tells us that the British Belgae frequently re-crossed the Channel to fight at the side of their Gaulish cousins – their vessels must have had sails of thin leather like those of the Gauls. Aelle and the Saxon invaders arrived in long, shallow-draughted rowing boats, but King Alfred's warships had sails. Sussex ports went on building wooden sailing ships down to the present century.

According to tradition, the Cinque Ports of Kent and Sussex first banded together during Edward the Confessor's reign. After the Norman Conquest they dominated the direct route to Normandy. Hastings, one of the five original members, became capital of this maritime federation of forty-two towns and villages grouped around the 'Five Ports and Two Antient Towns'; among its ports in Sussex, Rye and Winchelsea were the 'Antient Towns', while Pevensey, Seaford, Bulverhythe, Northeye, Petit Iham and Hydneye were associate members. Their great period was the thirteenth century when they ruled the Channel where it was narrowest, controlling every haven and inlet on both sides. Among the portsmen's obligations were providing the king with fifty-seven vessels for a fortnight each year, shipping the royal armies to France, and fighting pirates. In return they had the right to execute malefactors and were exempted from paying certain taxes. They exported wool or timber in their broad beamed 'cogs', bringing home wine, though fishing was always more important than trading. They also indulged in more than a little piracy.

However, during the mid-thirteenth century all Cinque Ports entered a decline from which they never emerged. Harbours silted up or disappeared beneath the sea, calamities compounded by plague and French raids. By the end of the Middle Ages the smaller Cinque Ports had been abandoned while even Hastings and Rye had lost their importance.

Nevertheless, ships continued to be built all along the coast until the end of the days of sail. In Charles I's reign a Shoreham shipyard produced craft as big as 300 tons. In 1628 it built a pinnace, *The Tenth Lion's Whelp*, of about 185 tons; she was three-masted, with oars as well as sails, mounting ten guns on two decks. During the eighteenth century Hastings specialised in luggers of up to 200 tons, three-masted and with long bowsprits which enabled them to carry a heavy spread of canvas. Popular with smugglers, they were designed for speed and often carvel-built of fir instead of oak. Smaller craft included 'hovellers' – fast sloop-rigged coasters.

From St Wilfrid's time onward, fishing centred around the herring because it could be salted for the winter. Boats sailed to the North Sea from every Sussex port, even from what are now inland villages in the Ouse Valley such as Rodmell or Piddinghoe which switched to farming when the marshes were reclaimed. The Cinque Ports established a right to send bailiffs to Yarmouth, governing the town jointly with the local bailiffs during the herring-fishing season from Michaelmas to Martinmas (29 September to 11 November). It was a sore blow to Sussex when Yarmouth regained full control in Charles II's reign, enacting byelaws which forebade any save Yarmouth men to sell herrings within fourteen miles of their town.

In their day the Sussex fisheries were famous. At Brighton 'hogboats' were used, tubby, shallow-draughted little luggers of from ten to fifteen tons, clinker-built, half-decked with a hold amidships for fish; difficult to capsize because of their wide beam, they were easy to beach; though they had to have lee-boards to stop them drifting. The last 'hoggie' was burnt on Brighton beach during the 1880s but there is a good model of one in the town museum. They were crewed by three or four men and a boy, fishing at night and resting on shore by day, after a single hearty meal washed down by a tot of gin or brandy; in 1798 they were said to be 'a hardy race and very healthy'. Their nets were in sections, sometimes as much as fifty yards long and fifty deep, kept afloat by cork blocks. Fish taken were mainly sole and mackerel in spring and summer, herring in autumn. Bigger boats trawled out to sea, but the smaller worked just off shore when trawling for mackerel; on sighting a shoal two would close in, each craft letting down a net between them, the crews jumping into the sea to drag the catch on to the beach.

Brighton fishermen were known as 'Jugs' and the path over the Downs along which their wives walked to Lewes to sell fish is still called the 'Jugs' Road'. At Hastings, fishermen were known as 'Chopbacks', at Seaford as 'Shags', at Eastbourne as 'Willickers' (guillemots) and at Worthing as 'Pork-Boilers'.

At Brighton the ceremony of 'Bending-on', derived from a benediction by pre-Reformation clergy, took place at the start of the mackerel season until 1896. It began with a party on the fish-market beach and the Bedford Street beach. First, nets were carefully folded and piled (a memory of being made ready for blessing), after which Dutch cheese and bread hot from the oven were eaten, accompanied by plenty of beer. When the boats had put to sea and were in position, the cork-floated nets were dropped overboard. Once, small barrels had been used as floats, which explains the prayer said line by line after they had been let down, alternately by skipper and crew with bared heads:

> Watch, barrel! Watch!
> Mackerel for to catch.
> White may they be like blossom on a tree.
> God sends thousands, one, two, three.
> Some by their heads, some by their tails.
> God sends thousands and never fails.

Then the skipper would say:

> There they goes then, God Almighty
> Send us a blessing, it is to be hoped.

From 162 boats in 1862, the Brighton fishing fleet sank to 88 in 1902, to 48 in 1948. Today a tiny handful of craft operate from the Marina; one or two sometimes sell fish on the shore. Yet up to the 1930s Brighton still saw blue jerseyed, sea-booted, sou'westered fishermen mending their nets on the beach beside all the bathers and paddlers.

However, Hastings still has a proper fishing fleet. In the Old Town, east of the castle, the net shops still house fishermen's gear. (The old nets had colourful names; hanns, tramells and bosinets.) Luggers were beached here, on the Stade – Saxon for landing-place – hauled up over the shingle. In the Fishing Museum one can see from the *Enterprise* – the last of the sailing luggers laid down in 1909 – how four men ate and slept in wretchedly cramped quarters below on their often nightmarish voyages to the North Sea.

As late as the eighteenth century Hastings was a pirates' lair. Dutch merchantmen were their favourite quarry. One gang would put to sea in stormy weather, to find a ship in distress. They ran alongside offering help, boarded her and locked the crew below; then, taking what they wanted from her cargo, they scuttled the ship leaving no survivors. Not all were so thorough, and some victims lived to tell the tale. In August 1758 the crews of two Hastings cutters boarded a Danish ship *Den Reisende Jacob* which was taking the Spanish ambassador, the Marquis Pignatelli, from Madrid to Denmark. They beat her master, Jurgen Muller, and stole twenty casks of butter but spared the sailors' lives. The Admiralty at once offered a reward of £500 for information and the skippers of both cutters, Adam Hyde and Nicholas Wingfield, were arrested. Found guilty of piracy on the high seas, they were hanged at Execution Dock in March 1759.

Other Hastings pirates were in no way cowed by their fate. On the night of 14 August 1768, a gang of thirty known as 'Ruxey's Crew' sailed out in a cutter and four hovellers, the cutter's skipper being their leader Stephen Ruxey alias Bourner. The *Sussex Weekly Advertiser* of 6 November 1769 tells us they had 'infested' the south coast for several years. 'Most of them were settled at Hastings, in Sussex, and under the appearance of fishermen, carried on the most attrocious practices, robbing and plundering every vessel they were able to overpower.' Three leagues off Beachy Head they boarded a Dutch ship carrying a cargo of glass. Disappointed, they fired a shot from the cutter's swivel gun across the bows of another Dutch craft, the dogger *De Drie Sustures*, making her heave to. On boarding they found her crew too strong for them and jumped back overboard, leaving behind a man whom the Dutch master promptly hanged at his yard-arm. Two more cutters joining them, they again boarded the dogger. They shut the crew in the cookhouse after wounding several of them, and killed the master by chopping through his backbone with an axe. Having cut down their still living comrade from the yard-arm they stole a consignment of sixty men's hats worth about £30 and sailed for home, some landing at Eastbourne and others at Birling Gap to avoid suspicion.

The Admiralty was so concerned that a force of 200 dragoons was sent to Hastings, while a man o'war and a Navy cutter lay off shore. The pirates asked the mayor why soldiers were coming to Hastings, attacking him when he gave an unsatisfactory answer, but fled when they arrived. Most were caught, the man cut down from the Dutchman's yard-arm turning King's Evidence. Thirteen were convicted of piracy and strung up at Execution Yard. For years afterwards Hastings fishermen were called 'Chop Backs'.

Just as one associates piracy with the Caribbean rather than Sussex, so one thinks of wreckers as Cornishmen. Yet in 1697 the playwright Congreve wrote of Sussex men praying devoutly in stormy weather for a ship to run ashore so that they could plunder her. Clearly they had a fearsome reputation. The county's two most famous wrecks during the eighteenth century were the *Nympha Americana* and the *Amsterdam*. The first was a Spanish prize ship of 800 tons and thirty-six guns, which had been captured by English privateers off Cadiz, with a cargo of mercury valued at £30,000 together with 'Superfine Velvets, Cloths, Gold and Silver Laces. And almost every other kind of Merchandise' including wines and spirits. On her way from Portsmouth to London, she was caught by the great storm of 29 November 1748, running aground off Beachy Head, below Crowlink and near the Birling Gap. When she struck, she split in two amidships, thirty of the 150 men on board being drowned, the rest trying desperately to reach the shore. As if by magic, a crowd appeared, growing to several thousand. Besides stripping the dead and robbing the survivors, they dragged as much of the cargo as they could into a cave. Many 'drinking too plentifully from a cask of very strong brandy, became intoxicated and perished in the snow, while others loaded themselves and their horses with the goods of the *Nympha* that were thrown up by the tide' reported the *Sussex Advertiser*. The plundering went on throughout the following morning, although the gale was fiercer than ever and soldiers tried to stop it, shooting two men before joining in themselves. At least sixty wreckers died from drink, on the beach or on the Downs.

Undoubtedly there were professional wreckers on the beach, even if they were not responsible for the *Nympha* going aground. Their brutality is described in a clumsy play written a year before by a Sussex farmer, William Hyland, who had obviously seen plenty of wrecks. He makes one 'sea-poacher' boast how he has thrown a half-drowned sailor back into the sea 'as he said nothing to the contrary'. Another jokes 'I once found a bulky fellow alongst sea, and the dog had nothing good about him but a pair of new boots, which I could not get off; and rather than spoil the boots by cutting, I lopt off both his legs and brought them home altogether and hung them up in the chimney until the legs dried and dropt out'. A gang of this sort, smugglers from Hooe, were seen carrying bales of velvet away – perhaps under their leader, James Blackman of the Red Lion.

Hyland makes his 'sea-poachers' speak of Dutch merchant-men coming ashore, which is what happened on Sunday 26

January 1749. The Dutch East Indiaman *Amsterdam* of 700 tons, on her maiden voyage and bound for Batavia, ran aground three miles west of Hastings, off Bulverhythe. Her crew had gone down with fever, dying at the rate of five a day, and were in no condition to ride out the terrible gale in which the ship found herself, and which had left her rudderless. She carried an extremely valuable cargo of silver in coin and bullion. A local smuggler, Anthony Watson, waded out with his gang, boarded the vessel undetected, smashed open a chest and stole £1,200 in silver ingots. Despite the lashing wind and rain, a crowd of a thousand was soon on the beach, some equipped with long, hooked poles. However, soldiers arrived, under proper discipline this time, and a salvage team took the cargo off to Hastings customs house, much to the wreckers' chagrin. (The *Amsterdam* sank so rapidly into the silt that the ship and part of her cargo are still there; there is a project to excavate her and bring her home to Holland for reconstruction.)

Some wreckers were not content with letting the elements do their work for them. The 'Shags' (or Seaford fishermen) placed lights on their cliffs, to lure ships on to the rocks below. On 7 December 1809, an eighteen gun sloop, HMS *Harlequin*, commander, Lieutenant Anstruther (whose wife and children were on board), together with six merchantmen which he was escorting, struck at Seaford Bay just after five o'clock in the morning; they thought they had rounded Beachy Head and may have been lured in by the Shags' lanterns. She broke up, attacked by greedy crowds who, says an eye-witness, 'regardless of the fate of the tempest-beaten seamen, untouched by the agonised shrieks of the exhausted and dying, were intent on plunder only; nor could the ghastly corps that, at intervals, the tide cast between them and the objects they were grasping at, for an instant suspend their horrible and infamous purpose.' In 1836 the same 'monsters of rapine' flocked to another wreck in Seaford Bay.

For many years the sea-poachers' instinct remained very strong among dwellers on the Sussex coast – if not for active wrecking, then at least with an unshakeable conviction that anything cast up by the sea was fair game. When in 1881 the SS *Simla* went down in a Channel storm, a number of barrels from her cargo of high proof spirits were washed ashore at Rottingdean. Just as in days gone by, the villagers smashed them open, drinking deep enough for some to tear their clothes off and dance naked on the beach. One thirsty old man swallowed so much of the delicious fluid that he dropped down dead. Luckily the local constable, immune to temptation, dragged inland the stupefied bodies of all the others who had fallen, before they could be drowned by the incoming tide.

If there were wreckers, there were also Sussex men who did their best to save lives from the sea. No doubt those watching the doomed *Harlequin* and her convoy from the cliffs were there for loot, drinking wine out of their hats from barrels washed ashore. Nevertheless, everyone on board the sloop was pulled to safety by a rope, just before she broke up. Many from the other ships were rescued as well, some by a human chain. The landlord of the Lifeboat Inn at Portobello cliff, Langridge, had his 'unsinkable' lifeboat hauled along the beach, presumably by oxen, but by the time it arrived the tide was too far out to launch it – in any case, it only held three.

Sussex had already begun to make a notable contribution to life-saving. Since the end of the eighteenth century there had been two cranes on the cliffs near Newhaven to rescue survivors from the rocks, winching them up by oxen. Langridge had built his lifeboat in 1804, though probably it was never used – like the lifeboat bought by Newhaven in 1807. However, many rescues were made on the Sussex coast with the 'Manby Apparatus'. Invented by Captain Manby in 1808, this was a mortar which fired a ball with a rope to vessels in distress; there were flares for its use at night. The apparatus was first tried in June 1817, when a dismasted brig had gone aground on the rocks at Rottingdean Gap. A rope fired from the cliff-top was got aboard the vessel, followed by others, and within a short time the entire crew was hoisted up the cliff; without it they would certainly have drowned. During a storm on 13 November 1840 the apparatus saved two crews on the same day. One had already been called ashore from a brig wrecked at Roedean, when news came that a schooner had gone aground west of Rottingdean, in shallow water but a long way out. For twelve hours the crew hung from the rigging, expecting the ship to break up beneath them at any moment, but at last, at 6.00 p.m., a rope reached her.

Even in this century there have been shipwrecks with an unhappy ending. One of the saddest was the loss of the Rye lifeboat on 15 November 1928. Just before dawn the *Mary Stanford* of 4½ tons, a sailing boat with a crew of seventeen, put out into a mountainous sea to rescue a Latvian steamer which had been rammed. Five minutes after launching her, news came that the Latvian crew had been rescued by the vessel which rammed their ship, but the lifeboat did not see the Very lights fired to call her back. Eventually she tried to return but was overwhelmed by a gigantic wave, capsizing within sight of harbour. All seventeen on board were drowned. The Rye lifeboat station was shut down, not to be re-opened until 1966.

The Sussex sea is unpredictable, frequently violent. Many beaches are subtly menacing on all save the quietest days. Kipling understood this very well:

> Here leaps ashore the full Sou'west
> All heavy winged with brine,
> Here lies above the folded crest
> The Channel's leaden line

I remember the gale which sank Sir Edward Heath's *Morning Cloud* off Bexhill in 1974. I also recall waking up on a winter's morning in 1980 to see the cargo vessel *Athena B* beached only a few yards away.

During a Susex storm those ashore know what it is to watch heavy benches six foot long flung across the road by a howling wind, to have their windows smashed by shingle hurled from the beach. No one at sea ever forgets it. Some Christians, especially fishermen, still say the prayer to be used in a storm: 'Look down, we beseech thee, and hear us, calling out of the depths of misery and out of the jaws of this death, which is now ready to swallow us up: Save, Lord, or else we perish.'

XVIII
Writers in Sussex

Although the tradition has been killed off by the sheer cost of a country cottage, Sussex has always attracted writers, especially during the first half of the present century. The Bloomsbury Group were not alone in seeing the county as an earthly paradise.

Literary men began to come down regularly from London in the 1780s when the roads had improved. Some were invited by William Hayley, the friend of Edward Gibbon, and of the painters Romney and George Morland. A forgotten poet – though his *Triumphs of Temper* was popular in its day – he lived at Eartham near Chichester. The only work of his which has stood the test of time is his life of another poet; on Hayley's monument in Felpham Church are the words 'The Friend and Biographer of Cowper'. William Cowper spent six weeks with him in his now vanished mansion. Poor Charlotte Smith also visted Eartham, dedicating her first book to Hailey, her *Elegiac Sonnets*. In 1789 he moved to Felpham near Bognor where in about 1800 he built a house not far from the church, 'The Turret'; it still stands, in a style which has been described as 'pasteboard stucco Tudor'.

In 1800, Hayley persuaded his friend William Blake to rent a thatched flint cottage near Felpham, from which in those days one could see the sea. 'The Country is Most Beautiful and the People are Genuine Saxons, handsomer than the people about London' wrote Blake. 'Sussex is certainly a happy place and Felpham in particular is the sweetest spot on earth.' He believed he had seen a fairy's funeral there. 'I saw the broad leaf of a flower move, and underneath I saw a procession of creatures, of the size and colour of green and grey grasshoppers, bearing a body laid out on a rose-leaf, which they buried with songs, and then disappeared.' However, another side of Blake appeared in 1804 when he was tried for sedition at Chichester. A soldier had accused him of shouting 'Damn the King, damn all his subjects, damn all his soldiers; when Bonaparte comes, it will be cut-throat for cut-throat, and the weakest must go to the wall; I will help him'. The court room cheered when Blake was acquitted. No one realised that once he had been a secret Jacobin and a friend of Tom Paine.

One of the first writers to settle in Sussex was Harrison Ainsworth whose now almost forgotten historical novels, such as *Rookwood* or *Old St Pauls*, were very fashionable during the 1830 and 1840s. Although a popular figure, the friend of Dickens and Thackeray, he suddenly opted out of literary life in London and moved to Brighton. Here he took a large white neo-Classical house facing the sea in Arundel Terrace, which in those days was on the very edge of the town. He often rode out over the Downs and one of his novels centres around what was then a lonely downland village, *Ovingdean Grange* – the mansion of the title being, I suspect, modelled on Glynde Place.

During the nineteenth century other 'men of letters' came to Sussex by the score, and above all to Brighton. Among them was Charles Dickens, who often stayed at Brighton which features in several of his novels, his first visit being to the Old Ship Hotel in 1837. In *Nicholas Nickleby*, after having killed Lord Frederick Verisopht in a duel, Sir Mulberry Hawk flees to Brighton *en route* for France. In *Bleak House*, Mr Turveydrop claims to have been noticed at Brighton by the Prince Regent when the latter was driving out from the Pavilion – 'Who is he? Who the Devil is he? Why don't I know him?' Dickens wrote part of *Dombey and Son* while staying at the Bedford Hotel and sent Paul Dombey to school at Dr Blimber's Brighton establishment in 'a mighty fine house, fronting the sea'. (Dr Blimber is said to have been a Dr Everard who ran a similar academy, Chichester House – known locally as 'The Young House of Lords.') The little boy also lodged with the awful old

Mrs Pipchin whose house 'was in a steep by-street at Brighton, where the soil was more than usually chalky, flinty and sterile, and the houses were more than usually brittle and thin'. Dickens knew his Brighton.

During a visit in 1849, when Dickens and his wife stayed in lodgings, their landlord and his daughter suddenly went raving mad in the most alarming fashion. He wrote afterwards:

> If you could have heard the cursing and crying of the two; could have seen the physician and the nurse quoited out into the passage by a madman at the hazard of their lives; could have seen Leech and me flying to the doctor's rescue; coud have seen our wives pulling us back, could have seen the M.D. faint with fear; could have seen three other M.D.s come to his aid; with an atmosphere of Mrs Gamps, straight-waistcoats, struggling friends and servants, surrounding the whole, you would have said it was quite worthy of me, and quite in keeping with my usual proceedings.

His last visit was in November 1868 – eighteen months before his death – when he gave a public reading of *A Christmas Carol* and of *Boots at the Holly Tree Inn* at the Grand Concert Hall in Western Road.

Clearly Brighton held insufficient charms for Anthony Trollope, though in *Phineas Finn* he sends the old Duke of Omnium to stay at the Bedford. However, if you go to South Harting church, after some searching you will see a glass case in which there is a little portrait of Trollope together with his pen and paperknife. He came to live at North End (now The Grange) nearby in 1880, two years before his death, hoping that the air on the Downs would cure his asthma. He was comfortable enough, North End being the first house in the neighbourhood to have a bathroom, but sadly Sussex failed to work its magic on him. He was by now too ill to hunt, while he missed his London clubs. Even so, he wrote his last four novels at South Harting, including *An Old Man's Love*, and began the unfinished *Landleaguers*.

No late Victorian or Edwardian library was complete without the guide books of Augustus Hare (1834–1903). Even today, the ones on Italy and on Sussex are well worth reading – full of useful information, and with acid comments reflecting the temperament of this fussy old bachelor. He spent his childhood at 'The Lime', a mile from Herstmonceux, with his aunt Maria whom he called 'The Mother'. His uncle was the parson, a brute who flogged the little boy with a horsewhip; on one occasion his cat was hanged to punish him. Surprisingly, Augustus had happy memories of Herstmonceux (which he recorded in *The Years with Mother*), of the old white gabled house which, so he claims, stood on the site of a medieval monastery:

> No description can give an idea of the complete seclusion of the life at Lime, of the silence which was only broken by the cackling of the poultry or the distant threshing in the barn, for the flail, as well as the sickle and the scythe, were then in constant use at Hurstmonceux, where oxen – for all agricultural purposes – occupied the position which horses hold now.

In 1861 'The Mother' purchased Holmhurst near St Leonards. He spent the rest of his life beautifying it, with such treasures as Francis Field's statue of Queen Anne which had once stood outside St Pauls. (Both houses survive, and Queen Anne still stands in the garden at Holmhurst.) He records how the crickets sang deafeningly as never before, on the June night when his adoptive mother died, keeping a sinister silence on subsequent nights. In 1894 Augustus published his splendid guide to Sussex. Clad in dark suit, stiff collar and bowler hat accompanied by valet and easel, he had explored the county by train, dog-cart or 'fly', staying at pubs, many of which are listed in the index; those at Haywards Heath were 'all indifferent, a better inn at Cuckfield' where the *King's Head* and the *Talbot* were 'both good and much frequented in summer' – the *Tiger* and the *Red Lion* at Lindfield nearby were 'very humble'. A gifted water-colourist who illustrated his own books, his advice to painters encapsulates the taste of the 'nineties:

> The *artist* will chiefly delight in deserted Winchelsea and the foreign elements of Rye, in many of the coombes of the South Downs, in the river scenery near Arundel, the wild scenery and ruins of Hurstmonceux, and the tamer beauties of Cowdray. At Chichester, Bosham, Boxgrove,

Pulborough, Scotney, Bodiam, Wilmington, and Michelham, other attractive 'subjects' are to be found.

The young Somerset Maugham visited Holmhurst frequently during Hare's last years. The routine never varied. He was woken by a maid in a print dress with cap and streamers, who brought him tea and bread and butter; this was at eight o'clock. Half an hour later, another maid brought a hip-bath and hot water. At nine, before breakfast, Hare read family prayers – there were no family, only staff – the subsequent meal including pheasant in season. There was a heavy luncheon, a heavy afternoon tea and a heavy dinner, all served by maids in black dresses and white caps and aprons, as in countless other Sussex houses.

Coventry Patmore was another Victorian who loved Sussex, famous in his day for 'The Angel in the House', a long poem eulogising marriage. At its best his verse resembles that of his friend Tennyson. The first Mrs Patmore died young, but a rich second marriage enabled him to buy a small estate near Uckfield in 1866, which he renamed Heron's Ghyll. (Today the house which he built there is a preparatory school called Templegrove.) Locals say that the former house's drive had been haunted by the ghost of its late owner's wife, killed by his ill treatment, and that seven clergymen were called in to exorcise her; there was a story of Patmore's daughter Emily dressing up as a ghost for a Christmas charade and then growing terrified lest she met the real ghost. Saxon place-names were not understood in those days; otherwise her father would have recognised the menace implicit in the house's original name, Pucksty or 'demon way'. He left Heron's Ghyll in 1875, to live at the Mansion House in Hastings, a Queen Anne House with a great magnolia tree outside.

Patmore's enthusiasm for the Sussex Levels between Newhaven and Lewes has already been quoted. He thought there were no hills in Sussex 'which look so much like real mountains as Mount Caburn and the eastern summit of the great down, the highest peak of which is Firle Beacon'. He also wrote of 'the extraordinary beauty of Lewes', how six weeks there and 'a long walk or drive every day would not bring you to the end of half the beauty within easy reach of it'.

The greatest novelist to live in Sussex was Henry James, who settled at Rye in 1897, at Lamb House in 'the little old, cobble-stoned, grass-grown, red-roofed town, on the summit of its mildly pyramidical hill and close to its noble old church – the chimes of which will sound sweetly in my goodly red-walled garden'. Till his death in 1916, he spent from May to November at Rye. Here he wrote *The Wings of a Dove*, *The Ambassadors* and *The Golden Bowl*, cycling to visit Steven Crane at Brede Place or Ford Madox Ford near Winchelsea. After a stay in Florida, James declared 'I prefer the far end of Sussex. In the heart of the orange groves I yearned for the shade of the old Lamb House mulberry tree'. Sadly, the garden room with a wisteria framed window, where he worked during the summer, was destroyed by a German bomb in 1940.

In his strange, mystical autobiography, *The Story of my Heart*, Richard Jefferies – in many ways the greatest English country writer of the entire nineteenth century – speaks passionately of the Sussex downland by the sea, whose hills had become part of his very personal religion. He was fond of the Weald too; and even of 'Sunny Brighton'. He spent his last years at Goring-by-Sea where he died in 1887, not yet forty. He is buried near the old Norman church at Broadwater. (His house at Goring may still be seen, re-named 'Jefferies House'.)

At the turn of the century, that inspired naturalist but very difficult human being, W. H. Hudson, wrote the first part of the most lyrical of all books on the Sussex landscape, *Nature in Downland*, in the same house at Goring where poor Jefferies had died. He venerated Jefferies' memory, almost convincing himself that he had seen his hero's reincarnation in a tramp whom he encountered one day near Goring churchyard. 'Those who know the downs are all agreed that it *is* a rare pleasure to be on them' he writes. 'I mean the prospect of the vast round green hills extending away on either hand to the horizon.' He was especially fond of Kingston Hill near Lewes yet, in certain moods and particularly during the winters, sometimes thought that the area to the west of Midhurst contained the most beautiful scenery in the whole county – 'that wild stream of the Rother; the small old world peaceful villages; the hills of so pure and fresh a green, their lower slopes and valleys purple and dark with beech and pine . . .' When he ended his sad, poverty stricken life in 1922 he was buried at his own request near Jefferies at Broadwater. Until recently, the dog roses that were planted next to the grave blossomed every year, and may still do so; an inscription, often quoted, reads: 'He loved birds and green places and the wind on the heath, and saw the brightness of the skirts of God.'

'Certainly Sussex, or any part of it, can hardly be said to exist in literature; or if it has any place there or in our hearts it is a mean one, far below that of most counties', Hudson lamented in 1900, adding that had Richard Jefferies lived he would eventually have produced a book about the Downs and the coast which would have been worthy of them. Nevertheless, Hudson himself had begun to repair the omission, and he was soon to be followed by Kipling and Belloc.

Some people sneer at Rudyard Kipling's recreation of 'Old England' in *Puck of Pook's Hill* or *Rewards and Fairies*, but most enjoy it. There is no need to doubt his claim that in Sussex he could feel history twelve men deep, his real hero being not the goblin Puck but Hobden the hedger whose ancestors had made the landscape which inspired him. Despite his admiration for the old Hobdens, he was unsentimental about Sussex folk. 'Of the little one-street villages up the hill we only know that, according to the guide books, they came of a smuggling, sheep-stealing stock, brought more or less into civilisation within the past three generations' he recalls, describing his arrival at Burwash in 1902. 'Those of whom worked for us, and who I presume would today be called "Labour", struck for higher pay than they had agreed on . . .' Yet Kipling could draw them out, like his friend the old poacher. 'Of poaching he talked in all its branches, and of pitched battles (guns barred) with heavy-handed keepers in the old days in Lord Ashburnham's woods where a man might pick up a fallow-deer . . . His wife, after she had known us for ten years, would range through a past that accepted magic, witchcraft and love-philtres, for which last there was a demand as late as the middle-sixties.'

Hilaire Belloc and Sussex were made for each other. He wrote:

> The Southern Hills and the South Sea
> They blow such gladness into me

For all his aggressive Catholicism, he had a spiritual devotion to such places as Halnaker Hill or the Rother and Arun valleys which verged on paganism:

> The valley of the River Rother;
> The sacred and fruitful river between
> The downs and the weald

The Arun valley, on whose river banks he lived, was 'a valley of sacred water'; Sussex soil was holy, 'knit in with our flesh'. His home from 1906 till his death in 1953 was King's Land at Shipley, a long fifteenth-century cottage which had once been a monastery tithe barn and stood beneath a smock-mill:

> If ever I become a rich man,
> Or if ever I grow to be old,
> I will build a house with deep thatch
> To shelter me from the cold
> And there shall the Sussex songs be sung
> And the story of Sussex told

Today the house is a Belloc museum, while the mill has been restored. The best known of his Sussex books is *The Four Men*.

I do not think that I would have liked the Bloomsbury Group, a mutual admiration society of bloodless men and anaemic women dabbling in art and literature, ineffably self-satisfied. In my view – one which I realise is not shared by everybody – their painting is forgettable and their writing has been overpraised, especially the surrealist, plotless novels of Virginia Woolf. They had one redeeming feature; they genuinely loved Sussex, where they lived the simple life on nice private incomes.

In his endless autobiography, amid all its turgid moralising, that humourless old prig, Leonard Woolf, writes with rare passion of the Sussex landscape, in a way which almost endears him. 'It was still the unending summer of that marvellous year [1911], and it seemed as if the clouds would never again darken the sky as we sat reading in Firle Park or walking over the downs' he recalls. 'This was the first time that I had seen the South Downs as it were from the inside and felt the beauty of the gentle white curves of the fields beneath the great green curves of their hollows; I have lived close to them ever since and have learnt that, in all seasons and circumstances, their physical loveliness and serenity can make one's happiness exquisite and assuage one's misery.'

When, in 1912, the Woolfs settled at Asham, in a green hollow beneath Itford Hill, the farms nearby still used oxen and threshed with flails. L-shaped and yellow-washed, built about 1820 in the 'Gothick' style, their house had a romantic, melancholy atmosphere; locals said it was haunted and, according to Leonard, its ghostly footsteps and whisperings gave Virginia the idea for *The Haunted House*. David Garnett, a frequent visitor, claimed that no-one could understand Virginia Woolf unless they had been to Asham. Many of her friends came here, including the young Dora Carrington, who wrote a lyrical description of running up Itford Hill at sunrise. The Woolfs left Asham in 1919, moving across the river to Rodmell two miles away. A few years later Asham became the site of a cement works, the house being turned into the manager's office. Leonard prophesied that it would soon go bankrupt but it out-lived him, closing only in the 'eighties. What was left of Asham House was bulldozed into the ground in 1994.

The Woolfs' new abode at Rodmell was Monks House, weather-boarded and painted pink, with a garden next to the church, looking across the Levels (Leonard's water-meadows), over the Ouse and up to the Downs. From here Virginia walked out on those nine mile tramps which almost saved her mind; from here she went out in 1941 to drown herself in the river.

When the Woolfs arrived at Rodmell, they cooked on an oil stove and read by the light of oil-lamps or candles, the sanitation consisting of an earth-closet in the garden. Coming down from London, they occasionally took a single horse hackney carriage from Lewes Station, but usually they walked the four miles along the Ouse, a walk which remains much the same today. Leonard says that going into the rectory at Southease, the next village, during the 1920s was like walking into the sixteenth century and talking to someone unaware of the twentieth. He adds that in those days village folk were nearer to Chaucer's England than to when he was writing in 1963. 'In many ways it was a terribly hard life and an uncivilised society. It was full of unhappy . . . village women, worn out by childbearing and domestic slavery, men of considerable brutality.'

The other Bloomsbury shrine besides Monks House, also open to the public, is Charleston Farmhouse not far away, the home of Clive and Vanessa Bell (Virginia's sister) and Duncan Grant. When they came here in 1916, life was just as primitive as it was for the Woolfs. There were no buses and in the days before cheap motor cars it seemed very remote; a first glimpse of it on a wet and misty day, after walking through the fields from Glynde Station, put Desmond MacCarthy's wife in mind of *Wuthering Heights*. It, too, saw many Bloomsbury visitors: the Woolfs, Lytton Strachey, Roger Fry and Maynard Keynes. It has been lovingly restored, preserving the painted walls and furniture of Vanessa Bell and Duncan Grant. A pleasant book has been published about the house, *Charleston Past and Present* by Quentin Bell, Angelica Bell, Henrietta Garnett and Richard Stone; the chapter in which Angelica Garnett – Vanessa's daughter – remembers her childhood here is headed 'The Earthly Paradise'.

Between the World Wars, countless writers and would-be writers settled in Sussex. Many people, and not just 'men of

letters', romanticised the county during the 1920s. They saw it
as a pastoral dreamland, a place in which to recover from the
traumas of the trenches or where they could live the ideals of
the Arts and Crafts movement. They more or less ignored the
agricultural depression, although farmers all around them
were constantly going bankrupt – some even committing
suicide. Even before 1914, the advent of machinery had begun
to force farm workers off the land. Now, thousands more lost
jobs which had given their ancestors a living since time
immemorial; there was no longer any demand for ox-men or
sheep shearing gangs, nor even for cowmen and shepherds.
They became builders, railwaymen or mechanics instead, if
they were young enough, taking whatever employment they
could find. In many ways the Sussex countryside remained a
depressed area until 1939.

In consequence, the farmers had plenty of surplus
labourers's cottages, tumbledown and often ruinous, which
they were only too glad to let for a few shillings a week. Such
accommodation, uncomfortable but cheap and in beautiful
surroundings, beckoned novelists and poets alike. If there
were no modern conveniences, skivvy power was always
available, at pitifully small cost. A friend tells me that during
his childhood here in the 1930s there was a typewriter
whirring behind every hedge, and that he can never forget the
smell of damp books.

The experience of Ford Madox Ford (a far better if less
appreciated novelist than Virginia Woolf) typifies the life led
by writers all over Sussex at this period. The Great War had
made him tolerant of discomfort. In April 1919 he rented Red
Roof near Pulborough, which he described as a 'leaky-roofed,
tile-headed, rat-ridden, seventeenth-century, five-shilling-a-
week, moribund labourer's cottage'. Here he slept on a
camp-bed, brought water from a well in the garden and cooked
on an oil-stove under a lean-to, keeping goats, pigs and poultry
– and wrote by the light of an oil lamp. He moved to
Scammell's Farm at Bedham near Fittleworth and then bought
a cottage at Bedham called Cooper's for £400, both of which
were just as primitive as Red Roof.

Ford had had an earlier Sussex period, at Winchelsea, from 1901–4, where he had lived in Friars Road and published a *History of the Cinque Ports*. A man of the Levels rather than the Downs, he loved the marshes, writing that to wander through them was to be caught by them. 'You will catch a malady of tranquillity – a kind of idle fever that will fall on you in distant places for years after. And one must needs be the better, in times of storm and stress, for that restful remembrance.'

If the 'Bloomsburies' had no time for Ford's company, or he for theirs, it is unlikely that either even knew of Barclay Wills' existence. The author of *Bypaths in Downland* (1927), *Downland Treasure* (1929) and *Shepherds of Sussex* (1938) was born in Islington in 1877. After working as a clerk in the City, he moved to Brighton in 1922 and then to Worthing, running a small general shop, a café and, finally, a little grocery, all without much success.

Somehow this mild, self-effacing townee with a Cockney accent made friends with the hill shepherds, whose ancient way of life was already being destroyed by modern farming, housing estates and the motor car. Wills preserved the memory of it, taking notes and photographs, collecting sheep bells, horn lanterns and crooks; he visited the smithies where the crooks were forged, and the clearings in the woods where hurdles for sheep-folds were woven from cleft hazel rods. An excellent field naturalist, he was also interested in archaeology with a keen eye for flint axes and arrowheads. (Some shepherds called him 'The archipelago bloke'.) In his gentle, sensitively observed and often moving accounts he recaptures both the bleakness and the poetry of a Sussex shepherd's lonely existence; the cold and sometimes snowbound lambing days of February, or sheltering from drenching rain in holes or under thorn bushes, as well as the uncanny understanding between sheep and shepherd, the gaiety of Findon Fair and the shearing songs. He also recalls the last oxen teams, a time when there were still corncrakes on the Downs. No other writer recreates so vividly the final days of that old, old Sussex which had existed since the Stone Age but had vanished by the time he died in 1963.

Graham Greene wrote about a very different sort of Sussex in *Brighton Rock*, that of the increasingly seedy Brighton of the 'thirties with its vicious gang warfare in which the cut-throat razor was a favourite weapon. Its central character is a twisted young murderer. (Thirty years ago, in a Brighton pub I met an unpleasant man, small and bald, who proudly claimed to be the original Pinkie, but he looked much too old.) The book is worth reading for the vignettes of the town alone – no one has described it more vividly.

A less distinguished novelist, equally obsessed with the sordid, who wrote about Brighton was Patrick Hamilton. He was born in 1904 in Hove, in a house of suffocating respectability which is still there. J. B. Priestley admired his flair for conjuring up 'a kind of No-Man's-Land of shabby hotels, dingy boarding-houses and all those saloon bars where the homeless can meet'. Many of the scenes in his under-appreciated books are set in Brighton e.g. *Hangover Square*.

Arundel was the inspiration of the monstrous Gothic castle in Mervyn Peake's *Gormenghast*, if an Arundel seen in the far distance from across the Arun. (Although the 77th Earl of Groan could never have been inspired by the 16th Duke of Norfolk.) Peake's parents had retired to Burpham, so early in 1940 he and his wife Maeve rented a tiny thatched cottage there, with a single cold-water tap; it was unpleasantly damp and they had to read by candle-light but it possessed a precious amenity which appealed deeply to Peake – a ghost. They moved into rooms in Upper Warningcamp, then into another cottage at Burpham, at a rent of three shillings a week, where Mervyn worked on *Titus Groan*. He left Sussex in 1944 and never lived there again. However, when he died in 1968 he came back to Burpham, to be buried in the churchyard beside his father and mother. The little cottage where *Titus Groan* was created is still there, though very much smartened up, with tiles instead of thatch.

*

The tradition of the writer's cottage in Sussex more or less died out after the Second World War, when all the cottages were bought up and beautified by commuters or weekenders. There were some writers, however, who still chose to live in the county for a time, such as Anthony Burgess at Etchingham. He thought the locals so suspicious of strangers as to be 'xenophobic', and fearful of leaving their villages – he tells how a Burwash butcher, forced to move to Etchingham, cried sadly 'Goodbye Burwash moon'. One or two novelists went on living at Brighton, though Francis King departed at the end of the 1960s. As late as the 1970s Graham Greene would spend a few days at the Albion Hotel on the Old Steyne whenever he was suffering from a particularly bad case of 'writer's block'.

If Sussex cottages or Brighton flats no longer seem to attract literary talent from outside the county in such profusion as they did in the old days, the home grown sort survives very well. In 1994, after a silence of nearly twenty years, Bob Copper published a magnificent book with a self-explanatory title – *Across Sussex with Belloc: in the footsteps of the Four Men*. Not only is this a wonderfully sensitive evocation of both landscape and people, but it has a heartening message for anyone who genuinely loves the county. 'Sussex has changed, of course, but it has changed far less than might be imagined by anyone not looking close enough', he concludes after his long, colourful exploration. 'I had discovered that the true Sussex still lives and speaks with a thousand voices, and even sings for those that have ears to hear.'

XIX
Brighton

Brighton is an odd town with an odder history. Once the most fashionable watering place in Europe, then 'London by the sea', until recently it had colonies of writers and actors. Nowadays it depends on conferences, even the best hotels taking coach parties, while many of the old boarding houses have been converted into flats. Faded elegance, somewhat marred by high-rise blocks, is enlivened by sleazy vitality. Anonymity is perhaps its greatest charm. A place of secret gardens, it is ideal for living alone without realizing you are lonely.

Until the eighteenth century it was a big fishing village, known as Brighthelmstone. Its fishermen depended on sole, mackerel and herring, 'landmen' farming the Downs. The former dominated the Society of Twelve who governed it and appointed the all powerful Constable. Its main handicap was a lack of fresh water, what there was being drawn from the muddy River Wellsbourne (now underground) which ran through the Steine – where the fishermen dried their nets – or from inadequate wells. The town was bounded by East Street, West Street and North Street. Once there was a South Street, too, but it has vanished beneath the sea with the rest of the Lower Town. This went down roughly to where the end of the Palace Pier now stands amid the waves, and was inhabited by fishermen together with boat builders, rope makers, net makers, tar makers and all the other workers needed for their trade. Partly underground, the thatched houses of flint and clunch were never more than fourteen feet high to avoid the attentions of French privateers. Before the Reformation, there was also a small Benedictine priory, a cell of the monastery at Lewes. The parish church of St Nicholas stood outside, on the open Downs.

We know that Brighthelmstone existed in Saxon times. Domesday Book tells us that it paid 400 herrings a year to its lord of the manor at Lewes. Apart from storm and famine, little of note happened here. There must have been several raids by the French, though the only one recorded is that in 1514 by a 'Prior John' who burnt the poor little houses. It recovered, and in 1580 had eighty deep sea boats crewed by 400 fishermen. However, during the seventeenth century, restrictions on the Yarmouth herring catch reduced many of the community to beggary.

The first event of national importance in Brighton's history was the furtive visit by Charles II, *en route* to Shoreham to find a ship to take him to France after his defeat by Cromwell. At an inn here, probably the long vanished George in Middle Street, he bargained with Nicholas Tettersell, who was master of a small coaling brig, to smuggle him across the Channel. They sailed at 7.00 a.m. the next day. That evening a troop of Ironsides rode in, searching for 'a tall black man, six feet four inches high'. The skipper was rewarded at the Restoration, becoming Constable of Brighton. A tombstone in St Nicholas's churchyard commemorates 'Captain Nicholas Tettersell, through whose prudence, ualor and loyalty, Charles II King of England, after he had escaped the sword of his merciless rebels, and his forces received a fatal ouerthrow at Worcester, September 3rd, 1651, was faithfully preserued and conveyed to France . . .' No one would think that 'This ualiant soul' had haggled with Charles about the price.

When Mr Whaley, a Fellow of King's College, Cambridge came here in 1736 he wrote in his journal of 'Brighthelmston, which is the Ruins of a large Fishing Town.' It had never recovered from the Great Storm of 1703 when most of the Lower Town fell into the sea with the cliffs.

Fortunately Dr Richard Russell's promotion of the medicinal virtues of seawater (in a book published in Latin in 1749), and his choice of Brighton as the best place for bathing, transformed it into a watering-place. Visitors came to be 'dipped' by 'bathers', the ladies wearing long flannel night shirts as they descended from bathing machines into the sea.

Assembly rooms and circulating libraries appeared. The Duke of Marlborough built a house on the Steine in 1769, later transformed by Robert Adam into the finest mansion in Brighton. Dr Johnson came to stay with the Thrales and, unexpectedly, enjoyed riding with the local hounds who hunted a carted buck over the Downs; it is said that he put his wigless head under the pump every morning to dispel the fumes of the previous night's potations. From 1779 George III's youngest brother, the Duke of Cumberland, rented Russell's House (on the site of the Albion Hotel) in order to follow the buck hounds.

On the evening of 7 September 1783, the twenty-one-year-old Prince rode into Brighton to be greeted by a salvo from the battery on East Cliff – one of the gunners being blown up when a cannon misfired. Prince George had come down to stay with the Duke of Cumberland, despite his uncle's irritating habit of calling him 'Taffy'. Soon he bought a house for himself, a single story farmhouse in the Steine, and in 1786 Henry Holland built a single story range to balance it, joining them by a tall, domed rotunda. He gave the house the first bow windows in Brighton, which were widely copied. The first 'oriental' touches were the work of a little known architect, P. F. Robinson; it was he who in 1804 created the onion shaped cupolas which are the building's most distinctive feature. The Prince went on adding to his villa – including a riding school, now the Dome – besides decorating it in Chinese taste. In 1815, Nash began work on the Royal Pavilion (as we now know it) in 'Hindoo-Gothic' style. The Comtesse de Boigne called it 'a master-piece of bad taste' and many agree with her. Others have thought it a triumph, including the Prince – by then King George IV – who was moved to tears when it was completed in 1821.

'It is scarcely in the power of words to convey an accurate idea of its rich and glowing magnificence' the *Brighton Herald* reported on 27 January 1821, when describing the Royal Music Room. 'The aerial imagery of fancy, and the embellishments of fertile invention, profusely described in "The Thousand and One Nights", and the popular tales of magic, involving the enchanted palaces of *the Genii*, fall short, in splendour of detail, to the scene of imposing grandeur . . .' It was 62 feet long and 41 feet high, surmounted by a dome 30 feet in diameter which was 'gilt with green gold'; the organ was the largest in the kingdom, distinguished for its peculiar delicacy of tone. The Banqueting Room, 'this most beautiful and splendid apartment', had the same dimensions and was decorated in the same 'Chinese' taste; its windows had curtains of deep crimson and sky blue silk. 'To speak of THE PALACE as a whole, it involves the perfection of *British Art*' the article concludes.

Elsewhere the king was abused right and left, even for his love of Brighton. 'It was neither the maritime views, the benefit of the change of air, nor the salubrity of the place, which possessed in the eyes of His Royal Highness at any time any great attractions, but that he was drawn thither by the angelic figure of a sea-nymph whom he one day encountered reclining on one of the groins on the beach' wrote Robert Huish, his first and most hostile biographer, in 1832. This is unfair. 'His natural companions were dandies and parasites' sneered Thackeray, no less unjustly, 'a creature, lazy, weak, indolent, besotted, of monstrous vanity, and levity incurable.' If at times ridiculous, George IV was undeniably fun, the most imaginative patron of decorative art in English history. He genuinely loved Brighton and the world he created there, giving the town a name for pleasure which it has never lost. After he became Prince Regent, he entertained statesmen from all over Europe at the Pavilion. He was able to do so because of the Brighton Packet Boat, which sailed to and from Dieppe and was for many years England's main Channel ferry.

From the 1780s onward the fashionable world flocked to Brighton and required accommodation. Mrs Fitzherbert, secretly married to the Prince, built Steine House next to the Pavilion. (Now the YMCA, it was mutilated beyond recognition during the 1930s.) However, most people stayed in lodging houses, the ground floors being occupied by the proprietors, who let the rooms above. Generally retired servants, they gave their guests good food.

'The best mutton-broth, the best veal cutlets, the best necks of mutton and French beans, the best fried fish and plumpest partridges' says Thackeray, writing in the 1850s, but even in the Prince's time food here had an excellent name. Inevitably, there was a less decorous side to life. John Byng, visiting Brighton in August 1788, saw 'such a harpy set of painted harlots, as to appear to me as bad as Bond St. in the spring'.

During the 1780s, the old town began to expand inexorably over the neighbouring arable land, which was still grouped in five huge medieval 'laines' or open fields for strip-farming. Then new squares and terraces started to go up, a good example being the beautiful Regency Square of 1818–28. Its architects were almost certainly Amon Wilds and Charles Busby who, with Wilds' son Amon Henry Wilds, designed most of the Brighton buildings of those years. Bow-fronted and bow-windowed, some with poke-bonnets over the bows, many of the houses in Regency Square have floors made from shipwreck timber off the beach and are linked by secret doors. General Sir Hudson Lowe (Napoleon's gaoler on St Helena) spent the winter of 1823–24 at No. 53, while Landseer spent most of 1841 at No. 65. The big house at the bottom right corner, St Albans, was erected by the Duke of St Albans and his duchess, Harriott Mellon. (Twenty-four years older than the duke, she had been an actress and had first married the immensely rich Mr Coutts, who was forty-two years her senior.) Brighton is a very haunted place and the square has at least three resident ghosts. The saddest is that of a crippled girl who, during a fire alarm during the last century, threw herself from the window of the house where she lodged – now the Regency Tavern, just round the corner.

Development spread westward until the adjoining village of Hove became a town in its own right. Hove's glory is Brunswick Square, and its flanking terraces along the seafront. It was built by Charles Busby in 1825–28, very much under the influence of Nash's Regent Street in London.

The stucco 'Regency' squares, crescents and terraces of Brighton and Hove are their most striking feature. Some date from long after George IV's reign, let alone from the Regency. Among the very best are Sussex Square, Lewes Crescent and Arundel Terrace, in Kemp Town at the eastern end of Brighton. Cream or white, nearly all of them are generally well maintained and retain an air of cheerful elegance.

When George IV died in 1830 Brighton was a large and thriving town. No doubt, as Ian Nairn points out, the Pavilion was splendid as entertainment but failed as a habitation; the king visited it only once during the last eight years of his reign. Even so, he had spent enough time in the town to ensure its popularity. 'The presence of HIS MAJESTY at the Pavilion enlivens Brighton and its vicinity' Dr Evans claimed with justice. During the Second World War Rex Whistler painted 'The Prince Regent awakening the Spirit of Brighthelmstone', a fresco in which the Prince wears only the Garter and the Spirit nothing at all. No English town owes more to a monarch.

What it was like to stay here in Regency times is described in a little book published in 1821, *An Excursion to Brighton* by Dr John Evans. The author, a Welsh schoolmaster and Nonconformist clergyman who ran a school at Islington, had spent the summer of 1818 in the town, accompanied by his family. When he had first visited it, twenty-five years before, the road into Brighton had gone over a steep hill, past the church and then down into the town. 'On this eminence, at that period, the bodies of *two mail robbers* were seen suspended on the ignominious gibbet – buffeted about by the four winds of Heaven.' But now the coach went in along the New Road, avoiding the hill and 'winding through the romantic valley of Preston' to deposit the family at the Old Ship Inn where they spent a comfortable night. Next day they took apartments for five weeks in a house in 'Pavilion Parade, one of the most lively situations in the town'. They would have asked for full board since in those days there were no Brighton restaurants.

'Full fronting THE PAVILION, we had in view the chief attraction of Brighton,' to which the public were admitted when the king was away. (By then George only used it as a winter residence.) 'The embellishments, wholly Chinese, remind the spectator of oriental splendour', Dr Evans enthuses. 'The eye is fascinated by decorations appertaining to royalty . . . It is said to be an imitation of the *Kremlin*, at Moscow'.

Every evening a military band played in the Steine, along which 'are seen parading fashion and beauty' at that time of day and especially on Sundays, although fishermen still dried their nets there. The town, whose population had doubled in a decade to over 22,000, possessed some excellent shops, especially in St James's street and North Street, besides banks, hotels and boarding houses. 'The visitant to Brighton experiences due attention and his wants of every kind are gratified.' There were schools. 'Among others are Dr Morell's classical seminary, Hove; Mr Alexander Tate's academy, Dorset-gardens; and the Rev. Mr Tilt's, author of *The Greek Verb delineated*. There are also the Miss Powell's and the Miss Shelley's seminaries for young ladies.' The principal amusements were the theatre, the promenade concerts in the assembly room at the Castle Tavern, and the libraries. 'Donaldson's fronts the cheerful Steyne, Tuppen's has a fine view of the ocean' he tells us. 'Loder's establishment has a very valuable collection of books, and Wright's, in its musical department, is entitled to commendation.' Such libraries did more than lend books or sell stationery; in the evenings they became places of entertainment, with music parties, poetry readings and games of chance.

Dr Evans hints at less decorous Brighton amusements, when describing Hastings in an appendix: 'The society here has the character of being gay without profligacy.' Passing the cricket ground on the Brighton Levels, while recalling that 'In this exercise the Prince Regent excelled' he warns: 'Dislocations of the hip joint are not uncommon, from the awkward posture occasioned by employing *both* arms at the same time in striking a distant object. Dr Willich trusts that the time is not remote when this *game of Cricket*, like that of *Pugilism* (a most barbarous practice), will be exploded.'

Thirty or forty coaches ply daily, some 'conveying the passengers in *six hours*, either up to London, or down to Brighton. This is a convenience to the *mercantile* class of visitor, especially to those birds of passage who, going down on Saturday afternoon, return on Monday morning.' Eventually balloons will do the journey in a mere two hours. 'Our gracious Monarch, taken up in an ethereal vehicle at Carlton House, might, in *half an hour*, alight at his beloved Pavilion.'

He recommends walking along the seashore and examining the seaweed, 'an entertaining portion of natural history', or visiting the Mineral Well a mile west of the town, in front of a wood of 'Druidical appearance'. Here 'A glass of water is brought to you by a female, for which you pay *sixpence*'; it tastes like the chalybeate spring at Tunbridge Wells. (Today the well spring flows into a pond in St Anne's Well Gardens at Hove, its healing powers long forgotten.) Or a walk to 'the rural village of Preston . . . along a road overshadowed by the foliage of large and lofty trees, which imparts the sensation of your being immersed in the depths of the country'. It contains 'near 40 houses, and about 200 inhabitants'. Here, at the Crown and Anchor, 'we rested one fine summer's evening, cider and biscuit constituting our refreshment'. Or going up to the Race Ground 'through corn fields, where the harvest smiled upon us with bounteous profusion'.

Although a cripple and unable to walk, clearly Dr Evans had no difficulty in getting about Brighton. He must have used those 'barouches in miniature' which he describes so admiringly, each drawn by two donkeys, with a postillion in a velvet cap and scarlet jacket running alongside – 'Ladies are seated in them and receive no inconsiderable enjoyment.' Or the 'fly-by-night', a sedan-chair on wheels pulled by one man and pushed by another which was a Brighton speciality.

Accompanied by his family, he explored the surrounding country in a carriage. Sampling the view from Devil's Dyke, they had a cup of tea at a booth kept by 'an old British tar' who boasted 'that among other nobility, the *Duke of York* had partook of his entertainment'. They were alarmed by the perilous lane over the cliffs to Rottingdean, surprised to find 'machines for sea bathing' at so remote a village. They drove through Hove, 'a pretty hamlet', on their way to Worthing, 'a small place, but increasing rapidly and rising into eminence' or to Bognor, 'genteelly frequented, and well filled most seasons . . . It was once called *Hothampton*, from Sir John Hotham, who first visited the spot, and brought it into notice.'

Then it was time to go home to London. Instead of taking one of the fast coaches – 'There are many who would not like to risk their necks' – they chose a more sedate vehicle. 'Well stowed, we drove off between nine and ten, reaching Islington by seven in the evening.'

Then as now, there were plenty of drop-outs, though a different term was used. On 22 February 1821 the *Brighton Gazette* reported how 'seven vagrants, taken from the streets by the Beadles, were committed to the House of Correction . . . to be passed to their several parishes'. The Bench also ordered two of them to be whipped. A dungeon in the old workhouse on Market Street (demolished two years later), the 'House' was not a nice place. 'Can't you send us to Lewes instead of to that lousy hole?' complained a youth accused of burgling a shop in East Street and sent there on remand, according to the same issue of the *Gazette*. When told that he and his accomplices must stay there till Thursday, he rejoined 'Why then, we shall all be lousy as pigs by that time'.

George's successor, the 'Sailor King' William IV, was just as fond of Brighton as his brother, partly because strolling along the Chain Pier reminded him of pacing the deck of a man o'war. (The pier, built in 1823 as a landing stage for cross-Channel packets, was the first in England and survived until 1896 when it was destroyed by a terrible storm.) King William added 'Royal' to the Pavilion's official name, giving it a North Gate which still bears the cipher 'WR IIII'.

Western Terrace, a leafy cul-de-sac off Western Road, is a neat corner from this period. It contains the delightful Western Pavilion, a little house with a Moorish dome which was built by Amon Henry Wilds as his own residence in about 1833. Opposite is what is left of the 'Gothick House', designed by his father and Busby a few years earlier; only the back survives, the front (which faces onto Western Road) having been turned into a department store. Next door is the majestic facade of Sillwood House, one of Amon Henry's finest, which he began to build for an East India Company nabob in 1827. Restored only recently, as a small white stucco terrace, it has columns whose tops are decorated with fossil ammonites; the architect's trademark, they had been suggested as a pun on his name by his friend Gideon Mantell, the Lewes geologist.

Unfortunately, Queen Victoria disliked being stared at through the Pavilion windows by a crowd in the Steine and paid her last visit in 1845. Three years later, Prince Metternich, staying at Hove in exile, wrote that the Royal Pavilion 'has now been abandoned, leaving it to fall into ruin. The Court wants to sell the buildings, which are quite empty, but can't find a purchaser because nothing could be done with it.' At last the town bought it, in 1850, for use as Assembly Rooms.

Day excursions from London to Brighton had begun early in the century, allowing two and a half hours by the sea, the return fare being six shillings. 'Great parcels of stockjobbers stay at Brighton with the women and children' snorted William Cobbet in 1823. 'They skip backward and forward in the coaches and actually carry on stockjobbing in Change Alley though they reside in Brighton.' The London, Brighton and South Coast Railway arrived in 1841; three years later, day excursions by rail began; the trains took only half an hour less than the coaches but soon grew faster and faster – bringing Londoners who wanted to see the waves and to paddle. Meanwhile the town became 'London by the Sea', with bed-and-breakfast as its main industry.

In 1895, George Augustus Sala reported: 'In July the more affluent members of the Hebrew community come down in vast numbers; in August and September there is a tradesmen's season.' The first synagogue, erected during the 1790s in Jew Street, had been superseded in 1826 by an elegant neo-

Classical building in Devonshire Place – now a 'health studio'.

For many years there were fewer Catholics than Jews in Brighton, only 400 in 1851. The first were refugees from the French Revolution, but they had the support of Mrs Fitzherbert, who lived in the Old Steine from 1804 until her death in 1837. A humble Catholic chapel was built in High Street, to be superseded by St John the Baptist in Bristol Street in 1835. Designed by William Hallet, although enlarged in 1890 and turned into a noble room which has irreverently been described as 'suitable for a hunt ball', this retains the atmosphere of the recusant chapels familiar to Maria Fitzherbert. Her monument, a relief by John Edward Carew, shows her with three wedding rings – the last signifying her marriage to George IV. Cardinal Newman preached here while the church had the questionable honour of providing the confession scene in *Brighton Rock*.

Brighton contains nearly forty churches and chapels which date from the nineteenth century. Even the old parish church of St Nicholas belongs to the Victorian era rather than the Middle Ages because of the over enthusiastic restoration which it suffered in 1853. (Though it preserves a Romanesque font which has been described justly as the finest piece of Norman carving in all Sussex, with scenes of St Nicholas and the ship, and of the Last Supper – attributed by some experts to the monks of Lewes Priory.) Two of the town's most attractive churches are by Sir Charles Barry, architect of the Houses of Parliament. One, St Peter in Victoria Gardens, is a magnificent piece of Gothic revival, which dates from the 1820s when Barry was a young man. The other, from about the same time, is St Andrew in Waterloo Street, which, as if to demonstrate his versatility, is not Gothic but early Italian Renaissance.

However, the best church here is undoubtedly the superb St Bartholomew of 1872–74, one of many churches built by a famous Brighton priest, Fr Wagner. Enormously tall, with a nave higher than that of Westminster Abbey, it is constructed of a dingy brick which does not prepare one for the glory within. Although its overall design is vaguely Gothic – if aisleless – the green marble ciborium or canopy over its glittering altar and the mosaic of Christos Pantocrator (Christ the World Ruler) behind are unequivocally Byzantine, despite their Arts and Crafts metal ornament. Few lovers of truly great architecture can remain unmoved by so noble a house of God. It is a temple of the Anglo-Catholic religion, of which Brighton has long been a centre.

Even though the Pavilion ceased to be a royal palace, the smart world did not desert Brighton just yet. As late as the 1870s, during their season (which lasted from November to the New Year) the town was still full of peers and peeresses. 'It is a Piccadilly crowd by the sea – exactly the same style of people you meet in Piccadilly, but freer in dress, and particularly in hats' observed Richard Jefferies in 1884. 'All fashionable Brighton parades the King's Road, twice a day, morning and afternoon, always on the side of the shops.' He adds that there was more talk of horses than boats. A. E. Coppard recalled 'goat-chaises with aristocratic children attached to spades and shrimping nets'.

'There are more handsome women in Brighton than anywhere else in the world' was the delighted Jefferies' considered opinion. 'The only antidote known is to get married before you visit the place, and doubts have been expressed as to its efficacy.' He added coyly that 'no one can be altogether good in Brighton', though as an invalid who was slowly dying, he himself had little hope of being bad.

He was especially fond of the West Pier which, when he lived at 'Sunny Brighton' (87 Lorna Road, Hove, to be precise), had then been open for not quite twenty years. From the far end of the pier, where the heaviest waves roll in, he loved to watch the bathing beauties – 'a gallant band in gay uniforms, facing the water'. He also liked the fair held next to it every morning, while detesting the sellers of 'singular baskets coated with shells [which] date from George IV. The gingerbeer men and the newsboys never cease from troubling.' He was horrified by reports of a scheme for planking over the sea at the bottom of West Street, and building an immense central pier which would fill the only site available for beaching the fishing fleet's hog-boats. The fishermen in their blue jerseys, always waiting on the tide, he regarded as an indispensable part of the Brighton scene. They told him there had been no herring for two years, that sole was very scarce, yet he also heard that from £50 to £80 was a common enough sum for a night's catch (a vast amount in the period's money) which was often sold in France. 'The poor who live in the old part of Brighton, near the markets, use great quantities of the smaller and cheaper fish, and their children weary of the taste to such a degree that when the girls go out to service they ask to be excused from eating it.'

During his very short reign King Edward VII was to visit Brighton no less than three times. His daughter, Princess Louise Victoria, Duchess of Fife, had a house in Lewes Crescent, but the king preferred to stay at Hove with his friend Arthur Sassoon whose mansion was staffed by forty servants.

There was a bleak contrast between the areas occupied by visitors and by those who looked after them. The narrow back streets were as bad as in any industrial town, with shoddy little houses which stank because of inadequate drains; some had open cesspits. The worst area was in and around Edward Street, where fishermen, washerwomen, costermongers and shop-assistants were crammed into airless, ill-lit, vermin-infested dens. More people died from consumption than in Liverpool while there were outbreaks of typhus and even smallpox. Their inhabitants turned to the bottle; by 1860 there were nearly 500 'drink shops' and Saturday nights saw scenes of indescribable degradation, young and old reeling through filthy streets down which the police dared not go alone. The gin palaces and music halls were full of prostitutes of whom there were said to be more than 600 in 1859. (Many had been maids.) They served their customers on the Level or the beach as well as in a hundred brothels. Drunkenness and prostitution were no less rife in 1900.

The respectable 'lower orders' led lives of grinding poverty. In *It's Me, O Lord!*, that writer of enchanting short stories, Alfred Edgar Coppard, remembered Brighton in the 'nineties, where his mother worked in a laundry just off the Steine, earning 2s 3d for a twelve-hour day. Frequently, the family was near starvation. And yet, looking back, Coppard could write, 'Ah it was a beautiful world, where the shops kept open late and soldiers arrayed like gorgeous gods passed to and fro all day, and men on penny-farthing bicycles toured on roads always coated with dust or thick with lovely mud'.

Suburbanisation continued inexorably as the population grew to over 120,000 by the time Edward VII came to the throne. Hove swelled to nearly 40,000. More and more trippers arrived every weekend. Despite royal visits it had ceased to be smart. Harry Preston, who bought the Royal York Hotel in 1902 and the Albion in 1913, did his best to restore past glories, launching vigorous campaigns in the press and founding a tradition of motor rallies – ancestors of today's vintage and veteran car runs. He succeeded up to a point, his hotels being keenly patronised by the stage and by boxing promoters. Until 1929, Sir Harry was a familiar figure cycling along the front for exercise, in bowler hat and spats, accompanied by his bull-terrier Sambo.

During the Great War, Brighton became a hospital town for casualties from the Front, and still more popular with Londoners as a refuge from Zeppelin raids. 'No signs of wars, save for the poor legless men whom Michael [her young son] tries to encourage by saying, "Poor wounded soldiers – soon be better" ' wrote Lady Cynthia Asquith in her diary for 29 July 1916. She goes on, 'There is no doubt that Brighton has a charm of its own, almost amounting to glamour. I am beginning to be quite patriotic about this end of the town – Kemp Town as it is called – in opposition to the parvenu Hove, which has less character and is to this rather what the Lido is to Venice.' If she laughed at it a good deal, she was plainly sincere in calling the town 'Dear Brighton'.

A tired elegance persisted between the wars, mainly centred around the Theatre Royal. There was a fine repertory tradition. Founded in 1807, though rebuilt and much altered, the theatre has a long and august history, with managers who sported such splendid names as Nye Chart, Lawson Lambert and Baxter Somerville.

During the 1920s, one or two lurid murders earned Brighton the name 'Queen of the Slaughtering Places', while it was much used for providing private detectives with the evidence of adultery then needed for divorce. It had an unenviable reputation for gang warfare, rival gangs operating protection rackets on the Brighton and Lewes race courses; their favourite weapon was a cut-throat razor which inflicted ghastly wounds. The gangs were finally broken by the heavy sentences passed on their leaders after a pitched battle on the course at Lewes in June 1936.

Graham Greene's novel of 1938, *Brighton Rock*, is a true picture but at that time it caused great anger in the town, where tradesmen feared that the book might deter holiday makers. It is a marvellous evocation – 'the new silver paint sparkled on the piers, the cream houses ran into the west like a pale Victorian water-colour'. He captures 'the grain of pleasure' extracted by the day trippers, together with the gaudiness and the seediness, the occasional violence.

After the fall of France in 1940, Brighton was in greater danger than at any time since the sixteenth century. 'Operation Sea-Lion', prepared by the German General Staff, envisaged an invasion ground stretching from Ramsgate to the west of the Isle of Wight; 5,000 troops were to be landed at Brighton from motorboats. The threat was taken very seriously indeed, Churchill warning the House of Commons that Hitler had enough shipping to send over 'half a million men in a single night'. There was barbed wire along the entire front, the beaches were mined, and there were tank parks in the avenues of Hove.

Some damage was done by German bombs but it was as nothing to the self-inflicted wounds during the decades after the War. In 1945, Hove Council seriously considered a proposal to demolish Brunswick Square (Busby's masterpiece) and the beautiful Adelaide Crescent (by Decimus Burton), and to replace them by blocks of flats. The nadir was the erection of Churchill Square, a 'shopping precinct' in the town centre; a spokesman called it the most important development since the

Pavilion – which was like saying that the Bomb was a significant event in Hiroshima's architectural history. High rise flats and tall office blocks sprouted; the Bedford Hotel was burnt down, being replaced by a concrete ziggurat. As late as the '70s, the Gothick Central School was torn down to make way for a car-park. It seemed as though Brighton would become Croydon-on-Sea.

Outside the town, Sir Basil Spence's red brick University of Sussex went up at Falmer during the 1960s. The architect claimed to have been inspired by the Colosseum but the overall effect is that of an unusually handsome airport; one is constantly searching for the right terminal. No doubt Brighton is very well suited to be a university town, but if only it had happened a century earlier, and the university was in stucco instead of bright red brick.

Light industry, suburbs, motor-ways and traffic, together with settlers from all over Britain – from all over the world – have seemingly transformed Brighton's character. Bathing machines and fishermen have gone. The slow Sussex speech has been replaced, not just by the tones of South London, the Midlands or the North, but by accents from all over the world. No longer is it, in Lucas's words, 'a suburb, a lung, of London; the rapid recuperation of Londoners with whom the pace has been too severe; the Mecca of day-excursionists, the steady friend of invalids and half-pay officers'. Dr Brighton is dead, while day trippers have lessened to a trickle. The hotels which remain cannot compete with the lure of continental package tours and rely on the uncertain conference trade. The passing of the Brighton Belle trains in 1972 was a very ill omen indeed.

Some point to the Marina beneath Black Rock as evidence of vitality, others cite the West Pier (opposite Regency Square) as a symbol of decay. The latter, a once gleaming object which was built in 1866, has been abandoned since a barge ran against it during a storm in 1973 and knocked part into the sea. It stands forlornly, like a long line of shipwrecks with a gap in the middle, mouldering iron and rusty timber; a dozen or so cormorants perch at the far end, some 2,000 pigeons nest on it and every evening its great flock of roosting starlings darkens the sky with aerobatic displays. Over the years there have been many schemes to restore the pier, besides proposals to demolish it, but all have come to nothing.

There is an old joke that Brighton looks like a town helping the police with their enquiries. As Richard Jefferies said, no one can be altogether good here. Undoubtedly the inhabitants drowned Mrs Grundy long ago and display a quite extraordinary degree of tolerance. There is no censure, all save the most outrageous behaviour being regarded with indulgence. This may derive from a constant flow of foreign sailors, from the time of the old fishing port down to the present day, and the need to cater for their tastes. Such broadmindedness tends to disappear as soon as one reaches Hove or Rottingdean.

A less agreeable feature is the number of bankruptcies, which is said to be proportionately higher than anywhere else in Britain. The main casualties are cafés and restaurants, but since the recession boutiques have joined them. One street seems to be a species of death row for shops, so frequent are the closures. Neighbours watch with gloomy fascination. I remember two victims in particular, a chemist and a toy-shop owner, and their bewilderment and bitterness.

You see plenty of poverty here. The least distressing among the human flotsam are the buskers. 'Only a few years since, Brighton was greatly infested with street music from organs, hurdy-gurdies, and pianettes' J. A. Erredge wrote primly in 1862. 'A crusade, however, of the peace authorities drove them from the town, to which they have not since been allowed to return.' This sort of attitude is far from extinct today. One old man used to play a mouth-organ in the street, sleeping in a cellar; he gave in to drink, was thrown out of his cellar and now sleeps under the Palace Pier, trying to warm himself by sitting in the public library. Shopkeepers would like to have the pier put out of bounds for dossers like him, dossers who cannot find squats, since they are bad for trade. Many down-and-outs come from the North, especially the younger; it is marginally better perhaps to be jobless in Brighton than in Runcorn or Sheffield. A number have acquired dogs or puppies, possibly for companionship, more probably to arouse sympathy, though sometimes one feels sorrier for the dogs than their owners. The drug addicts, of whom the town has hundreds, are genuinely harrowing – nothing is more pitiful than a heroin baby.

Nevertheless, there is continuity. If Brightonians no longer speak in the old way, those born and bred in the town keep an 'r' with the ghost of a burr, while alleys are still 'twittens' and dogfish is still 'huss'. Above all, the squares and terraces are in good condition. What Osbert Sitwell wrote in 1934 applies just as much sixty years on. 'Brighton today, in spite of lovely old houses destroyed, in spite of the ugly new blocks erected in their stead, still retains much of the character it manifested under the Regent.' It remains a town of stucco and bow windows; from the Palace Pier the cream coloured houses still run away into the west like a pale Victorian water-colour. The Lanes, the narrow streets of the old fishing town, flourish; they have been pedestrianised, acquiring a continental air with their open air cafés and restaurants. Nowadays, whenever there is redevelopment it is generally (if not always) sympathetic, while almost every Regency building is safe from demolition.

Recently a heroic attempt has been made to restore the Pavilion Gardens to what they were in the Regent's time, with serpentine paths, herbaceous plants and rare shrubs, although the scores of gardeners needed to maintain them properly are beyond the resources of local government. Nearby, the Dome (the Regent's old riding school turned into a concert hall), the library and the museum form a cultural complex which deserves wider recognition – the museum contains a superb collection of art nouveau and art deco. A fishing museum has just been established on the front, near the Palace Pier; minute but excellent, it shelters a Sussex sailing lugger which was built as late as the 1950s. The twittens, alleys with pretty little houses and even prettier little gardens such as St James's Passage or Crown Passage are among many other pleasing surprises. The antiquarian bookshops are magnificent –

Holleyman & Treacher in Duke Street has no rival at Oxford
or at Cambridge.

The town is still exhilarating for those who know how to
appreciate it, a British Naples in miniature. Dr Brighton may
have passed away but his reviving breezes blow on briskly.
Despite all the daunting onslaughts of the modern world, you
can be quite sure that the old exuberance and vitality will
somehow survive here until well into the twenty-first century.

XX

Sussex Pigs –
'We Won't be Druv'

Victorians, Edwardians and to some extent the English between the Wars had a stereotyped image of Sussex men and women – yellow haired, ruddy faced and blue-eyed, the true South Saxon breed. In temperament they were stubborn, slow to anger and incapable of panic. These were the people Kipling had in mind so often:

> When he stands like an ox in the furrow with his sullen
> set eyes on your own,
> And grumbles, 'This isn't fair dealing', my son, leave
> the Saxon alone.

Sussex folk put it less gracefully: 'You may push and you may shove but I'm damned if I'll be druv.'

The way they behaved during the Captain Swing riots of the 1830s tells us a good deal about the old Sussex temperament. Although Cobbet might write 'I have seen no wretchedness in Sussex', in reality the years after the Napoleonic Wars were increasingly miserable because of an agricultural depression. A fifth of the labour force was unemployed, only saved from starvation by the demoralising Speenhamland System – receiving handouts from the parish in return for which it slaved in labour gangs. Struggling smallholders were crippled by the parsons' tithes while enclosures took away common land, the cottagers being compensated with worthless, undrained plots on which they could not grow vegetables. A bad harvest in 1829 sent the price of bread soaring, with the prospect of another bad harvest ahead. Threshing machines threatened to deprive men of the seasonal work on which they depended to see them through the winter.

Early in November 1830, Mr Thomas Abel, the heavy handed assistant overseer of Brede workhouse, was run out of Brede by 300 men in a mock ceremony during which they shouted for higher wages. Much beer was drunk and it was all very good humoured, no one being hurt. However, a hundred more serious incidents soon followed, mostly in East Sussex; machine breaking, window smashing, rioting and rick burning. (Arson was a capital offence.) Frequently they were accompanied by letters signed 'Captain Swing', with messages such as that to Sir Thomas Shelley – 'Beware of the Fatel daggar'. But there was never any killing. On the whole, working men were reluctant to become involved: one labourer at Warnham had to be dragged at the cart's tail before he would join an illegal union. The lunatic Sir Godfrey Webster of Battle raised a mounted squad of what would nowadays be called 'vigilantes', though most landowners simply put a guard on their ricks and machinery at night. (A young man who served as a special constable was William Borrer, the great bird-watcher.) Lord Gage defused the situation on his own estates merely by raising wages. That winter fifty-two luckless men and women were tried at Lewes Assizes, of whom sixteen were transported and seventeen given prison sentences, while one was hanged outside Horsham gaol for setting a torch to a haystack. Isolated outbreaks of rick burning, together with more sheep stealing than usual, continued for some years. By 1834, another three men had been hanged at Horsham for firing ricks, while during the following year troops had to be sent from Brighton to quell a riot at Steyning. Eventually calm was restored, largely because the landowners had provided allotments or money for emigration.

The Sussex Swing riots were never so violent as in neighbouring counties. There had been comparatively little resentment of landlords who behaved decently. 'I suppose that every inch of land, that I came through this morning, belongs either to the Duke of Richmond, or to Lord Egremont', that blunt spoken radical William Cobbett had written in 1823. 'No *harm* in that, mind, if those who till the land have *fair play*; and I should act unjustly towards these noblemen, if I insinuated that the husbandmen have not fair play, as far as the landlords are concerned; for everybody speaks well of them.' Admittedly, not all landowners were like the Duke of Richmond or Lord Egremont, and among the classes in between there was a good deal of sympathy for Captain Swing's men; at the height of the riots the Home Office was informed of the difficulty in finding special constables, 'most of the tradespeople and many of the farmers consider the demands of the people but just and fair'. What emerges from the whole pathetic saga is the comparative moderation of Sussex workers, farmers and gentry, a distaste for brute violence and an ingrained sense of 'fair dealing'.

The Sussex character, as it used to be, has its truest monument in the sensitive, elegiac prose of the folk-singer Bob Copper, surely the best of all home grown Sussex writers. His enchanting books, which appeared in the 1970s, ought always to be in print. A son of the Downs, born during the Great War into a farming family settled at Rottingdean since at least the sixteenth century, he left the land to become a Life Guards' trooper and then a policeman, after which he kept a pub, before settling down to write. No one has done more to hand on the songs of his forebears – or to preserve the memory of an ancient way of life which has disappeared for ever. Countless generations of farm workers and shepherds must thank him from the grave for giving their hard, seemingly bleak existence such dignity and even magic. His books (and his songs) are the key to any understanding of the Sussex folk as they were in the past.

'The back-breaking, shirt-soaking nature of farm work in those days, when muscle-power from man and horse was the only motive power, demanded practically all the energy a man could muster to carry him through his working day' he recalls in *Early to Rise*. 'In return, he had the use of a cottage, a garden in which he could grow a great deal of his food and keep half-a-dozen hens and a few, a very few shillings each week to purchase for his family those further bare necessities of life that could be bought from the butcher, baker or general stores.' However, Bob Copper – a resilient soul, if ever there was one – insists that despite pinching poverty, the heavy grind of repetitive work and exposure to all winds and weathers, 'there were a good number of fulfilled and well-adjusted people'.

Undeniably, there was always a melancholy streak, a sense of mortality, in the Sussex character. Old countrymen used to sing a song, 'What's the Life of a Man?' No doubt they sometimes sang it jovially (like Bob Copper's father in his bath) yet its words are gloomy enough:

> Down in yonder churchyard many names you will see.
> They have fallen from this world as the leaves from the tree;
> Old age and affliction upon them did fall,
> And death and disease came and blighted them all.

The chorus goes:

> What's the life of a man any more than a leaf?
> A man has his seasons, so why should he grieve?
> Although in this world he appears fine and gay,
> Like a leaf he shall wither and soon fade away.

The sundial which you find on certain church towers was put there not so much to tell the time as to remind people how quickly it passes. Sometimes the sundial is accompanied by the wistful inscription *Umbra sumus* – 'We are but shadows'.

Besides stubbornness and phlegm, the Sussex character was marked by dogged independence and self-reliance together with a sturdy refusal to be impressed or overawed by anybody or anything. The last trait may have come from there being so many small-holders and yeomen farmers, since Sussex was one of the few English counties where there really were peasants in the true sense of the word. Deep, ingrained, reserve was accompanied by taciturnity and a dry, ironical and occasionally savage sense of humour.

Yet gratitude was a quality much in evidence. Doctors who patched up wounded smugglers without asking too many questions would, for long after, find that tubs of fine brandy or oilskin bags of choice tea had been left on their doorsteps during the night.

In the reign of George IV, William Cobbett – a ferociously critical observer, who sneered at Brighton as a resort of the 'whiskered' or smart – was much taken by the clean, well set up look of country people here. 'The Sussex women are very nice in their dress and in their houses' he commented. Oddly enough, Arthur Beckett, perhaps the most besotted of the county's Edwardian admirers, claimed insultingly that the 'Sussex hind' had many of the qualities of his favourite animal, the pig – notably rudeness, together with a weakness for gorging on pickled cabbage and swilling beer. But this was the contempt of a 'have' for the 'have-nots', in an age when farm-workers lived lives of grinding privation. Kipling may have glamorised his 'Hob' a little too much, yet his was a fairer assessment.

Formerly, most people in the county spoke with a broad, slow, drawl, using many words which are now forgotten. In 1875, Mr William Douglas Parish, vicar of Selmeston, published a *Dictionary of the Sussex Dialect*, which has been reprinted several times. In his introduction he observed 'The fact that I have lived for several years in a village spelt Selmeston and pronounced Simpson; within reach of Brighthelmston, pronounced Brighton, and next to the village of Chalvington called Charnton will, I think, be considered sufficient excuse [for my book]'. Some of the dialect is conveyed by a rhyme:

> If true Sussex you would be,
> Say sure*lye*, not surely.
> In names of places stress should dwell
> Upon the final syllable.
> Thus, Arding*lye* doth well accord
> With South*wick*, Ber*wick* and Sea*ford*.

Chiddingly was 'Chidding*lye*', Pevensey was 'Pemsey' and Firle 'Furrel'. A gate was a 'gëat' and a ladder was a 'läader'.

'Jim Cladpole' (James Richards), who lived from 1866 to 1944, translated 'The Song of Songs' and several books of the Bible into Sussex besides writing a good deal of verse in it. He has even been described as 'a minor William Barnes' though he is not in the same league as the great Dorset poet.

Sadly, the old speech is nowadays very much on the retreat. Most of late twentieth-century Sussex talks with the flat, nasal vowels of the new, supposedly classless, BBC English. Yet sometimes you meet men and women – young ones too – who speak South Country as opposed to South London, even if it does not have quite so strong a burr and if much of the vocabulary has gone. Anybody who loves the old Sussex must feel a powerful nostalgia whenever he hears it.

How far has the old Sussex character survived?

A hundred years ago most Sussex people worked on the land, leaving school at twelve to toil for fourteen hours a day for the rest of their lives. In the 1990s many of their descendants have been to universities or polytechnics. Executives, engineers or salesmen, who take central heating and washing-machines for granted, they can have very little in common with great-grandfathers who were ploughboys, shepherds or woodmen. The only Sussex men genuinely at home in their forebears' houses are a handful of farmers and landowners.

Moreover, 'furriners' have been swamping native born Sussex folk for a very long time. (Tennyson was a Lincolnshire man, Belloc half-French.) Today, the inhabitants come from all over Britain, while some villages boast a Tandoori restaurant or a Chinese take-away. The blond Saxon stock has been diluted to the point of extinction.

And yet, and yet . . . I for one would like to think that the old Sussex spirit somehow lives on, instilled by chalk, wealden clay, woodland and the sea. It is well worth preserving. 'Sussex pigs' was what people used to call themselves, meaning pigs of iron, and they were a very tough race indeed -- almost every man and woman in the county seemed to possess a slow, stubborn, unflinching streak which was truly indomitable. Some still do:

> For Sussex will be Sussex,
> And Sussex won't be druv.

Bibliography

Albery, W., *A Parliamentary History of Horsham 1295–1855*, London 1928

Aldsworth, F. and Freke, D., *Historic Towns in Sussex*, London 1976

Allcroft, A. H., *Earthworks of England*, London 1908

——, *Downland Pathways*, London 1924

Anglo-Saxon Chronicle (ed. D. Whitlock), London 1924

Armstrong, J. R., *A History of Sussex*, Chichester 1974

Arnold, Rev. F. H., *Petworth*, Petworth 1864

Ballard, *A History of Chichester*, Chichester 1898

Banks, W. and Webb Turner, W., *Seaford Past and Present*, Seaford 1892

Barr Hamilton, A., *Saxon Sussex*, Bognor Regis N.D.

Beckett, A., *The Spirit of the Downs*, London 1909

——, *The Wonderful Weald*, London 1911

Bede, *History of the English Church and People*, London 1955

Beevers, D., Marks, R., and Roles, J., *Sussex Churches and Chapels*, Brighton 1989

Belloc, H., *The Four Men*, London 1912

——, *The County of Sussex*, London 1936

——, *Verse*, London 1954

Blunt, W., *John Christie of Glyndebourne*, London 1968

Borrer, W., *The Birds of Sussex*, London 1891

Brandon, P., *The Sussex Landscape*, London 1974

—— ed., *The South Saxons*, Chichester 1978

Brandon, P. and Short, S., *The South East from AD 1000*, London 1988

Brent, C., *Georgian Lewes 1714–1830*, Lewes 1993

Brunnarius, M., *The Windmills of Sussex*, London and Chichester

Burrows, M., *The Cinque Ports*, London 1988

Byng, J., *The Torrington Diaries*, London 1939
Candole, H. de, *The Story of Henfield*, Hove 1947
Cary Elwes, P. G. and Robinson, C. J., *A History of the Castles, Mansions and Manors of Western Sussex*, London 1879
Garden, T., *The Encyclopaedia of Brighton*, Lewes 1990
Cheal, H., *The Story of Shoreham*, Hove 1921
——, *The Ships and Mariners of Shoreham*, Shoreham 1909
Clark, K., *Winchelsea*, St Leonards-on-Sea 1988
Cobbet, W., *Rural Rides*, London 1830
Cook, C. F., *The Book of Sussex Verse*, Hove 1914
——, *Another Book of Sussex Verse*, Hove 1928
Coppard, A. E., *'It's Me, O Lord'*, London 1957
Copper, B., *Across Sussex with Belloc*, London 1994
——, *Early to Rise: A Sussex Boyhood*, London 1976
——, *A Song for Every Season: A Hundred Years of a Sussex Farming Family*, London 1971
Cunliffe, B., *Fishbourne*, London 1971
Curwen, E. C., *The Archaeology of Sussex*, London 1954
Curzon, Marquess, *Bodiam Castle*, London 1926
Dale, A., *History and Architecture of Brighton*, London 1950
——, *Fashionable Brighton, 1820–1860*, London 1947
Dallaway, J., *History of the Western Division of Sussex*, 2 vols, London 1815–32
Defoe, D., *A Tour through England and Wales*, London 1727
Dell, R. F., *The Glynde Place Archives*, Haywards Heath 1964
Domesday Book, Sussex, ed. J. Morris, Chichester 1971
Done, W. E. P, *Looking Back in Sussex*, London 1953
Drewett, P., Rudling, D. and Gardiner, M., *The South East to AD 1000*, London 1988
Durrant Cooper, W., *History of Winchelsea*, Hastings 1850
Egerton, J. C., *Sussex Folk and Sussex Ways*, London 1924
Ellman, E. B., *Recollections of a Sussex Parson*, Hove 1912
Erredge, J. A., *History of Brighthelmston*, Brighton 1862
Evans, A., *On Foot in Sussex*, London 1935
Evans, J., *An Excursion to Brighton*, London 1821
——, *Picture of Worthing*, London 1805

Farrant, J. and S., *Brighton before Dr Russell*, Brighton 1976

Fisher, E. A., *The Saxon Churches of Sussex*, Newton Abbot 1976

Fletcher, A., *A County Community in Peace and War: Sussex 1600–1660*, London 1975

Freeman, E. A., *The History of the Norman Conquest*, Oxford 1870–75.

Gilbert, E. W., *Brighton: Old Ocean's Bauble*, London 1974

Godfrey, J., *Sussex*, London 1990

Godfrey, W. H., *A History of Lewes*, Lewes 1974

Greene, G., *Brighton Rock*, London 1938

Haes, E. C. M., *Natural History of Sussex*, Hassocks 1977

Hampden, A., *Henry and Eliza*, Haywards Heath 1981

Hare, A., *Sussex*, London 1894

Harrison, F., *Notes on Sussex Churches*, Hove 1911

Hay, A., *A History of Chichester*, Chichester 1804

Hernamon, H., *West Grinstead and our Sussex Forefathers*, London 1924

Hill, R., *Underdog Brighton*, Brighton 1991

Horsfield, T. W., *History and Antiquities of Lewes*, 2 vols, Lewes 1824–7

——, *History, Topography and Antiquities of Sussex*, 2 vols, Lewes 1835

Hudson, W.H., *Nature in Downland*, London 1900

Hufton, G. and Baird, E., *Scarecrows' Legion: smuggling in Kent and Sussex*, Sittingbourne 1982

Huxford, J. F., *Arms of Sussex Families*, Chichester 1982

Jefferies, R., *Nature near London*, London 1883

——, *The Open Air*, London 1885

Jessup, E. F., *The Cinque Ports*, London 1952

Kaye-Smith, S., *Weald of Kent and Sussex*, London 1953

Kent, J., *Records and Reminiscences*, Chichester 1896

Kenyon, H., *The Glass Industry in the Weald*, 1967

Kipling, R., *Puck of Pook's Hill*, London 1908

——, *Rewards and Fairies*, London 1910

Kitch, M. J., *Studies in Sussex Church History*, London 1979

Knowles, D. and Hadcock, R. N., *Mediaeval Religious Houses—England and Wales*, London 1953

Knox, A. E., *Ornithological Rambles in Sussex, with a Systematic Catalogue of the Birds of the County*, London 1849

Latham, C., some West Sussex supersititions lingering in 1868, in *Folk Lore Record* I, London 1878

Leconfield, Lord, *Petworth Manor in the Seventeenth Century*, London 1954

Lloyd, D. W., *Historic Towns of Kent and Sussex*, London 1991

Loder, G. W. E., *Wakehurst Place*, London 1907

Lower, M. A., *The Worthies of Sussex*, Lewes 1865

——, *History of Sussex*, Lewes 1870

——, *Chronicles of Pevensey*, Lewes 1863

Lowerson, J, *A Short History of Sussex*, Folkstone 1980

Lucas, E. V., *Highways and Byways in Sussex*, London 1935

Madox Ford, F., (Hueffer), *The Cinque Ports*, Edinburgh 1900

Mainwaring Barnes, J., *Outline of Hastings History*, St Leonards-on-Sea 1989

Mais, S. B. P., *Sussex*, London 1937

Manning, R. B., *Religion and Society in Elizabethan Sussex*, Leicester 1972

Margary, I. D., *Roman Ways in the Weald*, London 1940

Mason, R. T., *Framed Buildings of the Weald*, Handcross 1964

Massingham, J. H., *English Downland*, London 1936

Mawer, A and Stenton, F. M., *The Place Names of Sussex*, 2 vols, London 1924

Maxse, C., *The Story of Fittleworth*, London 1935

Maxwell, D., *Unknown Sussex*, London 1923

Mayhew, G., *Tudor Rye*, Falmer 1987

Meade-Featherstonhaugh and Warner, O., *Uppark and its People*, London 1964

Meynell, E., *Sussex*, London 1947

——, *Sussex Cottage*, London 1936

Morton, H. V., *I saw two Englands*, London 1942

Mosse, H. A., *The Monumental Effigies of Sussex*, Hove 1931

Mundy, P. D., (ed.), *Memorials of Old Sussex*, London 1909

Murray's Handbook: Sussex, London 1858

Musgrave, C., *Life in Brighton*, London 1970

——, *The Royal Pavilion*, London 1951

Nairn, I. and Pevsner, N., *The Buildings of England: Sussex*, London 1965

Parish, W. D., *Dictionary of the Sussex Dialect . . .*, Lewes 1875

Parry, J. D., *An Historical and Descriptive Account of the Coast of Sussex*, London 1833

Petworth House, Sussex: National Trust 1973

Piper, A. C., *Alfriston: The Story of a Sussex Downland Village*, London, 1970

Rees, A., *Old Sussex and her Diarists*, London 1929

Robinson, J. M., *The Dukes of Norfolk*, Oxford 1983

Robinson, M., *A South Downs Farm in the Sixties*, London 1938

Roundell, R. A. E., *Cowdray: The History of a Great English House*, London 1884

Sala, G. A., *Brighton as I Knew it*, London 1898

Salzman, L. F., *Hastings*, London 1921

Savidge, A. and Mason, V., *Wadhurst*, Rainham 1988

Shore, H. N., *Smuggling Days and Smuggling Ways*, London 1892

Sitwell, Sir O., *Brighton*, London 1935

Smart, P. M. H., *Jevington through the Ages*, Kendal 1971

Smith, B. and Haas, P., *Writers in Sussex*, Bristol 1985

Staines, Rev. E. N., *Dear Amberley*, Bognor 1977

Steer, F. W., *The Ashburnham Archives*, Lewes 1958

Steer, F. W. and Osborne, N. H., *The Petworth House Archives*, Chichester 1968

Stephens, W. R. W., *Memorials of the South Saxon See and Cathedral Church of Chichester*, London 1876

Straker, E., *Wealden Iron*, London 1931

Sussex Archaeological Collections passim

Sussex County Advertiser

Sussex County Magazine

Thomas, E., *The South Country*, London 1932

Thomas-Stanford, Sir C., *Sussex in the Great Civil War*, London 1910

Thurston Hopkins, R., *Kipling's Sussex*, London 1921

Turner, T., *The Diary of Thomas Turner of East Hoathly*, London 1925

Tudor, A., *Fernhurst: the Story of a Sussex Village*, Guildford 1934

Victoria County History

Vidler, L. A., *A New History of Rye*, Rye 1971

Walker, T., *The High Path*, London 1982

Walpole, G., 'An Historical, Descriptive and Biographical Survey of Sussex' in *The New and Complete British Traveller*, London 1784

Walpole, H., *Letters*, London 1891

Walpole-Bond, J., *A History of Sussex Birds*, London 1938

Waugh, M., *Smuggling in Kent and Sussex 1700–1840*, Newbury 1988

White, J. J., *The South East*, London 1977

Willard, B. M., *Sussex*, London 1965

——, *Ashdown: the Forest in East Sussex*, London 1989

Williams, N., *Contraband Cargoes*, London 1927

Wills, Barclay, *Bypaths in Downland*, London 1927

——, *Downland Treasure*, London 1929

——, *Shepherds of Sussex*, London 1938

Winbolt, S. E., *Wealden Glass*, Hove 1933

Wolley-Dod, A. H., *Flora of Sussex*, Bristol 1970

Wolseley, Viscountess, *Some Sussex Byways*, London

——, *Some of the Smaller Manor Houses of Sussex*, London 1925

——, *Sussex in the Past*, London 1928

Woodford, C., *Portrait of Sussex*, London 1972

Wooldridge, S. A. and Golding, F., *The Weald*, London 1953

Wright, P., *Frant: The Story of a Wealden Parish*, Southborough 1982

Young, A., *General View of the Agriculture of the County of Sussex*, London 1813

Index